Careers from the Kitchen Table 2010 National Home Business Directory

This publication is designed to provide accurate and authoritative information in regard to the subject matter covered. It is a compilation of ideas from numerous experts who have each contributed stories and information. As such, the views expressed in each section are of those who were interviewed or submitted information and not necessarily of the author/publisher. It is sold with the understanding that the author/publisher is not engaged in rendering professional services. If legal, accounting, medical, psychological, or any other expert assistance is required, the services of a competent professional person should be sought. Author/Publisher specifically disclaims any liability for the reader's use of any forms or advice provided in this book. It is not warranted as fit for any specific use or purpose, but is intended to give general information that is as current as possible as of the date of publication.

Interior formatting and design: Peggy Knudson
Editing: Arika Lewis
Cover Graphic Design: Darnell Brown

Dedication

I dedicate this book to all those who purchased this book having lost their jobs but not their hope or desire for a better tomorrow. Those who still believe in their dreams and are determined to create a better lifestyle for them and their family despite setbacks or challenges they face. For the entrepreneurs and business professionals who are choosing to not settle for survival during these difficult economic times but instead are determined to "thrive."

I also want to dedicate this book to the many contributing authors who helped make this book possible with their amazing stories they shared from their hearts. I especially want to thank the incredible featured experts I was blessed to interview on my show that gave up time from their busy schedule to come on *Careers From The Kitchen Table* radio show and share their insider secrets, strategies and formulas for success freely with the listeners. Their selflessness has assisted hundreds of thousands worldwide who have tuned into the show the past three years. Thank you so much for being a blessing to us all. Lastly but definitely not least, I dedicate this book to those that have supported me every step of the way which include my dear friends and mentors Regina Baker and Greg Norman. Peter Mingils owner of – PM Marketing Network Leads, Bonnie Bruderer founder of The One Coaching Vision Board training who are corporate sponsors as well as the many other sponsors who supported this book and the Careers show, both book and radio show.

Thanks to my family and close friends who always encouraged me along the way and especially to my DYNAMIC and Talented team Peggy, Arika, Joelle, Dr. Taffy, Jaemi and Darnell. Thank you for all the support, long hours and hard work you contributed to the creation and success of this book. I am very proud of the outcome and have no doubt *Careers From The Kitchen Table Home Business Directory* will be responsible for changing many lives, giving those who lost hope the will and desire to hope again; and assist those struggling in their business with tips and strategies to grow their business more effectively from the stories and insider secrets they read along the way. Thank you all so much. This book could not have been possible without you.

Sincerely,

Raven

Table of Contents

Introduction

What Started as an Idea Turned Into a Dream Come True with Only the Sky as the Limit:

The Life & Future of Careers from the Kitchen Table

First and foremost, congratulations on taking a step to make a difference in your life by starting your own home business. By purchasing *Careers from the Kitchen Table 2010 Home Business Directory*, you've just proven to yourself that you can do exactly what this book was written to help people do, which is to take action on creating the lifestyle you want and more importantly deserve! So, thank you for investing in yourself and taking that first step to becoming a successful home based business owner.

Don't mistake me however. Just because you've purchased this book, doesn't mean you're off the hook. In reality, the work has just begun. Being an entrepreneur requires much more than buying a book and reading it. You must apply what you read otherwise you've just wasted your time and you might as well have thrown that money in the garbage can. So, let's get things moving right along so you can start reading and taking action on the goodness inside these pages.

How Careers from the Kitchen Table was Born

I'm often asked how I got the idea for Careers from the Kitchen Table (CFKT). While you may know CFKT as a CBS (formerly CNN) Talk 650 Radio Show and the name of this book, I didn't just wake up one morning and start a radio show or write this book. In reality, like everything else, it started as an idea and progressed into action.

In 2007, I was hosting an Internet radio show called Women Power (http://www.WomenPower-Radio.com) and Greg Norman, Founder of Universe 7 Media, happened to hear one of the interviews I conducted, contacted me and asked me to bring Women Power Radio to WARL AM Radio. While the show was doing great online, I knew there were people I wanted to reach that didn't have access to it and this would give me a way to do so. With the station broadcasting to parts of Rhode Island, Massachusetts and Connecticut, I knew I could do just that. However, Women Power would not be the show I took to WARL.

It was at about this time we started to see the signs of a declining economy. More and more people were realizing they may not have the job security they once thought they had. They were getting smart and looking for a Plan B. I had a better idea for a radio show. I wanted to help those people. I wanted to do something that would address people worrying about that very thing. I wanted to give them ideas for creating their Plan B by working from home. I envisioned a show that would give listeners secrets, golden nuggets if you will, from people who had created their own home business, who had been through the struggles of doing so and were now successfully running what was once their own Plan B, but had now become their Plan A! In other words, they had been there, done that and didn't need the T-shirt to remind them because they made it through and are now living the lifestyle they've always wanted to.

In other words, I wanted to help listeners leave what I like to call the 'Hectic Highway' and show them how to live the same or better lifestyle on the 'Smooth Sailing Hallway' by starting their own home based business. The sole reason for starting Careers from the Kitchen Table was to help people. To help people gain control over their income instead of depending on a job that might not always be there. I knew if I could share the information and the successful business owners I'd had the privilege to learn from with others, listeners of the show could do the same things with their own home based business. From that vision and the connection with Greg, Careers from the Kitchen Table was born and began broadcasting on terrestrial radio in 2007.

Unbeknownst to me at the time, this was just the beginning of good things to come for CFKT. In less than 2 years, I would meet the person who would take us to the next level.

Those who know me know I'm a phone person, so live, in-person networking events are not one of my strong suits. Because of this I shied away from them for a long time, but in November, 2009 I attended an event with the goal of meeting and networking with new people, passing out my card and promoting the show, which at this time was broadcast on Las Vegas' KLAV and I was contemplating taking it to a Christian station out of Houston, Texas. Here I thought I was growing and growing big. Little did I know, by moving from my comfort zone and attending the event, my show would grow to something bigger and better than what even I had in mind at the time.

During this event, I met a gentleman who just so happened to be a producer at CBS (formerly CNN) Talk 650 Radio. We talked a bit about my show and exchanged cards. I still had no idea where (if anywhere) this meeting might take me. A few days after the event, this same gentleman called and invited me to lunch where we talked about bringing the show to CNN Radio to follow behind a cooking show, which was perfect. This show was about cooking in the kitchen and we were going to follow it up and teach people how to cook in their business by giving them recipes to success.

I'd like to say the rest was history, but baby, we've only just begun here at Careers from the Kitchen Table!

Like most business endeavors, another idea was born and from the radio show was born the idea for this book.

On the show I interview guests who have a story to tell. It's about more than just advertising your business when guests come on our show. Sure, the marketing side of things is a plus, but it's not the core reason for the show's existence, nor is it the number one reason our guests choose to be on the show.

Careers from the Kitchen Table is a show that lets listeners know even the biggest names and businesses started out the same exact way – as a person with an idea and a dream of creating their own business and lifestyle – on their own terms.

Every business owner faces challenges and hardships and our guests are no different. They come to the show to talk about those challenges, but more importantly how they overcame them to reach the level of success they presently enjoy. They also share their "recipes for success" in the form of tips, ideas, advice, suggestions, and the things that worked for them and helped them become successful with the hope that even just one of our listeners will gain some help or guidance from their story.

Everybody has a story to share and each person's story is different, just like their idea of success is different. By bringing so many thought leaders to the show – people like – Jack Canfield, Russell Simmons, Lisa Nichols, Wally Amos, Alex Mandossian and more – we are giving our listeners access to ideas, gurus and helpful tips so they too can create their own successful business.

For those who don't already have their own home based business, they'll read and hear about a collection of different people with different situations, challenges and adversities who overcame their circumstances and still did it. My hope is that this book will open your mind as well as inspire and empower you to think about what it is you can do to start or expand your own business.

Just as I did back in 2007, I wanted to help as many people as I possibly can to see their ideas and dreams of living a life they have control over come to fruition. Instead of someone else holding the reins on your income and ultimately your future, now it's up to you how you live your future. That's when it dawned on me that I can extend that helping hand beyond a radio or Internet show and one way to do so was to create this book and share the stories of some of our guests as well as other business owners we've had the pleasure of getting to know over the years.

The mission of Careers from the Kitchen Table Radio Show and this Home Business Directory has and will always be to let people just like you know:

- Whatever you do now in your job, or have a passion to do – it can be turned into a profitable and fulfilling business and you can do it without hype and empty promises.

- There is a ton of information out there to motivate and inspire you, and while we do that too we don't just stop there. Careers from the Kitchen Table offers you the missing link by also telling you what you NEED to be successful and giving you the opportunity to shine just like the big dogs do.

- We only put authentic people in front of you who can keep it fresh, have a customer service oriented business and base not only their business, but their lives on ethical choices. This is something that will never change at Careers from the Kitchen Table – not even when the economy has bounced back and is up and running again (and it will be).

- We are here to help you WAKE UP and create your own Plan B, instead of hoping, praying and relying on someone else to create it for you. As much as we may not want to think about it, the reality is thousands of people's Plan A, which they were certain, would always be there for them, and has been taken away in this downturned economy. So, let's get proactive and create a Plan B that can easily be turned into your first choice should it become necessary.

The truth of the matter is, owning your own business isn't a free or easy ride full of roses and sunny skies all the time. It takes hard work, determination and dedication among other things, but hopefully with the help of the excerpts of guru interviews and stories included in this book, you'll see that not only is it possible to create the life and business you've always dreamed of, but others have been there before you and are willing to help you along the way and make your journey a little bit easier. The key is not just reading this book – you must TAKE ACTION and APPLY the things you learn to your own business, which is why we've included sections throughout the book for notes. Jot down the steps you want to take as you're reading through the interview excerpts and stories.

Because I didn't want you to miss out on anything, I've also included a way for you to access the full audio recordings of each of the guru interviews. Be sure you take advantage of them downloading them to your computer, iPod, or other player so you can listen to them anytime you need a burst of inspiration or a reminder of the tips, advice or recipes for success included in them.

Remember, reading this book, listening to the audios, and even taking notes are important steps to reaching success as a home based business owner, but the most important part is taking ACTION! You have to put things into immediate action or they'll never work. Only when you APPLY the steps you read, hear or take notes on, will they actually work and take you to where you want to be.

Once you've started your business, you'll find CFKT is still there for you, giving you marketing information and opportunities, guidance on how to take your business to the next level and so much more.

Careers from the Kitchen Table Continues to Move Forward & Help Even More People

I've got a ton of different ideas and plans in the works for expanding Careers from the Kitchen Table in the future. As long as the ideas keep coming, I'll keep finding a way to make them happen so that I can help more people throughout the world.

I'm very excited about our current plans to take CFKT to the streets – to you! We're working on lots of ways to do this right now including creating a reality TV show, live workshops, a print magazine and future volumes of the book which will include even bigger and better guests, including celebrities, financial gurus, public figures and more. We also have plans to grow our radio show listenership by expanding to more cities, states and even countries.

Even with this continued growth everyone at Careers from the Kitchen Table promises you that we'll ALWAYS give you our best and do it in an authentic and ethical way without any hype! As much as we like celebrities we'll ALWAYS have normal, everyday folks on the show as well because that's where we all started and that's where we truly believe we can give the most. We want you to see for yourself just what it feels like knowing YOU are in control of your future.

My Hope for You

As I finish this introduction (I know you're in a hurry to get to the good stuff, right?) I want you to know deep in your heart that if anything is meant to be it's up to YOU. Realize that YOU are the architect of your life and you can design it anyway you want. You CAN change your lifestyle and your dreams really CAN become a reality.

Change starts within YOU. You must be the one to decide to make a change in your life and then take the actions necessary to make those changes. Search your soul, your true passion, your purpose and figure out the '*what*' part of the equation. What were you put on this Earth to do? Where does your passion lay? Once you figure out your '*what*', step away from worrying about the '*how*'. Figure out '*where*' to begin and the how will come on its own.

I'll leave you with this quote to think about before you dig into the interviews, stories, success tips, recipes and recommended resources.

"If you want to make the world a better place, take a look at yourself and then make a change.
Michael Jackson, *Man in the Mirror*

ARE YOU READY TO GET STARTED? GREAT! LET'S GET COOKIN! MEET OUR GROUP OF INSPIRING MENTORS, MASTERS AND AUTHORS!

Les Brown

Cynthia Kersey

Jack Canfiel

Ali Brown

Dr. Joe Vitale

Lisa Nichols

Alex Mandossian

Terri Levine

Wally Amos

Dr. J.B. Hill

Andrew Angle

Allison Babb

Regina Baker

Jayne Blumenthal

Beverly Boston

Dr Linn Bourget

Susan Brown

Bonnie Bruderer

Sharon Cadle

Traci Campbell

Cris Carter

Lawrence Cole

Mari Cooper

Dr. Sarah David

Bill Davis

Kelly Davis

Larry Davis

Raven Blair Davis

Tracey Doctor

Tyra Jones-
Franklin

Kelli Frazier

Angela Gagauf

Ellen Gaver

Elizabeth Gilmour

Monica Hancock

Cathy Hansel

Roberta Harris

Victor Holman

Dr. Renee
Hornbuckle

Leah Humphries

Rev Criss
Ittermann

Martha Johnson

Kimber King

Peggy Knudson

Christine Konopko

Diane Lampe

Diamond Leone

Anne-Marie Lerch

Arika Lewis

Laura Lopez

Deborah
McNaughton

Marcia Merrill

Ludolph Misher

Joelle Niedecken

Sheila Pearl

Mark Perkett

Angelika
Putintseva

Helen Racz

Caterina Rando

Kimberly Rhodes

Dawn Rickabaugh

Mary Rives

Eva Rosenberg

Robert & Vikki Rosenkranz

Lea Rutherford-Williams

Tina Scheiner

Kathleen Schulweis

Tuck Self

Lori Snyder

Shaun Stephenson

Kalin Thomas

Devin Tindall

Karen Tompkins

Terry Tribble

Ken & Gretchen Umbenstock

Dr. Taffy Wagner

Rita Wiltz

Raven

Grills

the

Guru's

Careers
from the
KITCHEN TABLE

Hosted weekly by
Raven Blair Davis

Talk Radio

ENJOY THESE EXCERPTS AND AUDIOS FROM PREVIOUS INTERVIEWS HEARD ON
1320 WARL, 1270 KLAV, CNN650 AND CBS TALK 650.

Be sure to also visit www.careersfromthekitchentable.com/audios to get over eight hours of downloadable audio interviews!

Les Brown

Author, Motivational Speaker, Speech Coach

You know from time to time we have to stop and think where we are at in our life. Is this where we want to be? Are we stuck in a job in a situation that, "Oh my goodness it's just hard to get up out of bed in the morning?" Well I am just excited today to have someone that we are going to be interviewing. Actually this is a dream come true interview for me because this person doesn't know it yet that he has changed my life tremendously 'because I used to be in a job that I hated. I used to be so unsure about what was next for me until I plugged into his audios and his teleseminars and then I finally had that wake up call. So without further ado, I am going to bring on this dynamic person. You have heard his name before, it's the Les Brown. He is Les Brown the motivator and he isn't messing around. He has got so much going on. Wow, Les! This is a blessing. Thank you for being here.

Les: Well, it is a blessing for me to be able to talk to you and I am so excited about the opportunity and the work that you are doing to help people to begin to take charge of their destiny, which is more important now more than ever before.

Raven: Yes and I am glad you brought up taking charge of your destiny because that's what I really want to discuss with you. Les, as I share with you. Careers from the Kitchen Table is about helping people wake up and realize that they have to take charge of their life. They can't wait until they get that pink slip or until that job makes them so sick, they can't go in. They have to start having a plan B, wouldn't you agree?

Les: Well, they can wait. They can do that, you know. They can be a volunteer victim, or they can choose to step up and take charge of their own destiny because when you begin to look at it, this is the age where Ralph Waldo Emerson called the Age of Self Reliance. All of us know that there is no such thing as job security and that the 40/40 plan is gone, where you can work for 40 years, 40 hours a week doing the same thing, and expect to retire on 40%, which wasn't enough in the first place. So okay, that's gold, darling. That's gold now..

Raven: That's golden than gold.

Les: That's real gold, okay. So what I'd like to share with people three very important steps that will, one help them to make the decision if they have not or two, take their business to the next level if they have already made the decision.

Raven: Okay. Now this is where everybody needs to grab something to write with because we're getting some golden nuggets from Les Brown the motivator. We are at the edge of our seat and waiting.

Les: Yes. Are you ready?

Raven: We are ready, Les.

Les: Well, there are three steps is very important. Number one is what you first said, mindset maintenance. Listening to motivational messages on a daily basis and what it does is, it begins to retrain your thinking that how people live their lives is the result of the story they believe about themselves. Now remember this, how they live their lives is a result of the story they believe about themselves and so when you begin to listen to motivational messages on a regular basis, what it does it overpowers the story in your mind and stretch your mind, challenges your thinking, and eventually, it goes from your mind, to your heart, to your spirit; and you start acting on what you hear. Faith comes by hearing and hearing and hearing. And so the reason that most people don't operate from their faith as opposed to their fears is because they don't feed their minds enough with things that can strengthen their faith and then cause their fears to starve to death.

Raven: Oh that's good.

Les: So taking the time to invest in your mind is so very, very important. Having a schedule that you put yourself on. Still to this day I listen to motivational messages everyday and I suggest that people take 30 minutes to listen to a motivational message when you first get up in the morning after you spiritualize your thoughts with scripture, whatever you read to help to empower yourself on a spiritual level and your meditation and prayers; then review the goals that you like to achieve and listen to positive messages for at least 30 minutes because whatever you hear the first 20 minutes when you get up in the morning, it will affect the spirit of your day. Do not wake up and have the news playing and don't play the news while you sleep at night because all that stuff goes right straight to the subconscious mind.

Raven: Oh yeah. You are a hundred percent right.

Les: And so now the next thing is, make it doable. Read 10 to 15 pages of something positive every day. Just make it simple 10 to 15 pages. If you just do that 10 to 15 pages of something positive everyday seven days a week, just like you'd brush your teeth or you should seven days a week. This is mindset maintenance and it will cause you to operate at a higher level. Now when I first heard this I said, "Yeah right." I remember hearing somebody say that all of us are just six inches from success. Well that was challenging to me because I was labeled educable mentally retarded when I was in the fifth grade as you know and put back from the fifth grade to the fourth grade and failed again when I was in the eighth grade. Having no college training but I remember hearing this speech once that they did a study to find top achievers around the world and they wanted to know what was the common denominator among them that enabled them to reach their goals. And here's what they have discovered, that 85% of them reached their goals because of their attitude, 15% because of their aptitude. Now that excited me. So I spent time working on my mindset, on my attitude. Oliver Wendell Holmes says that "once a man's mind or woman has been expanded with an idea, concept, or experience, it could never be satisfied to going back to where it was" and when I heard the words that "You don't get in life what you want, you get in life what you are," "As a man thinketh in his heart so is he", I took that seriously and I spent a lot of time, a lot of money on my mind. I suggest that people start a personal development library. If anybody told me that that would leave me from earning $10 an hour to earning now when I speak domestically $25,000 an hour or $55,000 internationally and I don't say this to impress people but to impress upon you "judge a tree by the fruit it bears". This works if you work it. The next thing that's very important is, is look at your relationships and ask the question, "what are my relationships doing to me?" MIT did a study and the study indicated that we earn within two to three thousand dollars of our closest friends. People rub off on you. Dr. Dennis Kimbro said, "If you're the smartest one in your group, you need to get a new group."

Raven: Now I've heard you say that before and when I heard that, let me tell you, I changed my group.

Les: Yes, because there are two types of relationships in life, there are nourishing relationships and there are toxic relationships. Nourishing relationships, they empower you. They bring the best out of you. They challenge you. They hold you accountable. They stretch you. So your relationships are very important. You want to upgrade your relationships and make sure these are people that challenge you, and help you to grow mentally, emotionally, and spiritually. The other thing and this is major. Put your money where your mouth is.

Raven: Ooh! That's a big one.

Les: Yes, because communicators, you look at the presidential election, speech matters, message matters. I'll never forget Mr. Washington who challenged me. He said, "Someone's opinion of you does not have to become your reality." And he told me the value. He said, "Mr. Brown, develop your mind and develop your communication skills because once you open your mouth, you tell the world who you are." He was absolutely right.

Raven: That is so profound. My goodness!

Les: If you are an entrepreneur, people hear you. I see people pass out their business cards; they spend a lot of money on business cards and stationery and no money on developing their communication skills. You pass out a business card or you have the impressive stationery or very expensive brochure; all that sets up the process of communication. People don't do business with you because of your brochure or business card; they do it because of how you communicate. Is there a connection? Can I trust this person? Are they credible? Can I believe in them? Your ability to communicate helps you to develop relationships and empower you to negotiate. It is very important in the negotiation process and most people they neglect that; which blows my mind.

Raven: You know what Les, everything that you have said you are so right on the mindset maintenance. I love the fact that we started out speaking about that today because it has truly changed my life.

Thank you for sharing that. Now Les, you had spoken earlier about goal setting so for those people that are starting their home based business and they don't have a boss around them, what tips can you share with us on working their business actively and making sure it's a productive day? Could you share your thoughts on that?

Les: Well I think if you are going to become an entrepreneur, it's very important that you one, find a business coach. Somebody that you've met, that you've interviewed, that you resonate with that can help you to begin to find out what are your strengths and what are your weaknesses. In order to be an entrepreneur and operate from home, it takes a great deal of discipline and focus.

Discipline is very important. Getting a coach, a business coach, someone that can help you stay organized and stay on point and keep the main thing the main thing and can help you to monitor your behavior, your execution, and see how well you're doing, and how you're operating in terms of staying on course. Are you on course? Asking yourself constantly the choices that you make because when you say yes to something you're saying no to something else in your life; when you say yes to someone learning to say no and to manage your time, manage yourself, and stay focused in the direction to where you're going and never give up. You must be patient. You must persist. You must be willing to persevere and understand and know a dream has its own timetable in many cases. Some things we can predict but some things we can't and it takes you on a journey and is okay with that and trust the process.

And in many homes, a lot of people have all kinds of distractions and some people are easily distracted. And so you have to be able to work around these so you have to have a coach and so I have to be corralled and keep me from working against myself.

Raven: Oh wow! You know what Les, we're going to get close to closing now but I wanted you to kind of touch on something. The big thing nowadays is law of attraction and before the big buzz word of law of attraction, you were actually attracting what you wanted in your life.

Les: Yes. Well here are two very important things that are missing from the law of attraction, which is a very good program and very good concept. The number one thing is - and one of the things that is not only missing from there but all the motivational books that you will ever read and that I've read and that distinguishes me from the rest is that no one talks about the beat down in life. "Think it not strange that you face the fire and furnaces of this world." You're going to experience a beat down. I mean life is going to wear you out. You're going to want to throw in the towel on yourself. You will experience the storms of life. It doesn't matter how positive you think. It doesn't matter if you tithe. It doesn't matter if you pray. Life's going to whoop you. Things are going to happen to you and people you care about. Why? I don't know. That's the way it's set up. The other thing is that they don't talk about to the extent that they should, is W-O-R-K work, you got to work.

Raven: Oh yeah. Les, I know people are going to want to find out more about what Les Brown's got going on, your teleseminars, your products and services. Can you share that with us? What's your website?

Les: It's http://www.lesbrown.com and also I encourage them because we got a tremendous special now going on. One of the products that I think can help people to make their lives recession-proof, *Create Your Greatest Life* and *Choosing Your Future*.

Raven: Oh that sounds wonderful. And last thing now, are you still doing your weekly teleconferences?

Les: Yes, that's on every Monday at 8 o'clock eastern standard time. They can go to our website and see the number.

Raven: And get a piece of Les every day or at least once a week.

Les: That's right. Live.

Raven: Dynamic! Well this has been a pleasure. Thank you so much. I want to respect and honor your time. I appreciate you.

Les: It's my pleasure and honor and I'm just very glad and just very thankful for the opportunity and supportive of the work that you're doing and God bless the day you were born. I appreciate you.

Raven: Oh thank you. Everyone, this has been a dream come true interview. I hope you got as much from it as I did. We have been speaking with the Les Brown the Motivator!

Les: Mamie Brown's baby boy.

Be sure to visit http://www.lesbrown.com.

Listen to the full audio of this interview:
http://www.careersfromthekitchentable.com/audios
Plus be sure to visit and subscribe to Raven's popular newsletter and get your free e-book *"The Real Power of Social Networking: Profit on Facebook"* by Regina Baker
http://www.careersfromthekitchentable.com

Cynthia Kersey

Author, Motivational Expert, Speaker

Cynthia Kersey is an awesome lady. She's a bestselling author as well as a leading performance and productivity expert. Based on her bestselling books *Unstoppable* & *Unstoppable Women*, she's developed proven strategies to help people develop an "unstoppable mindset" that enables them to move to the next level in their business and in their life.

You see Cynthia coached sales teams in the Fortune 500 companies' and she has trained thousands and thousands of entrepreneurs all over the world on how to get to the next level in their business. Cynthia is a business owner, national columnist and the National Foundation of the Female Legislators' 2001 Entrepreneur of the Year, contributing editor for Success Magazine, and she has been a guest on countless TV and radio shows including Miss Oprah! She is also Chief Humanitarian Officer of her non-profit foundation and her latest project in building 40 schools of substantial communities in Africa and Haiti.

Cynthia is going to be giving us some secrets to being unstoppable in your business, even during this recession. Just trust that things can change but for things to change, you must change. You've got to have the power in you and be willing to unleash that unstoppable power that I strongly feel we all have within us.

Cynthia: Hey, Raven. Thank you so much for having me and for that beautiful introduction.

Raven: You know your book *Unstoppable* is amazing and reading that book started me to open my dream circle again. It's because of the stories. Now I tell people to be inspired by other people's stories and then share your story so other people can be inspired by yours. So I got to ask you, what inspired you to write this incredibly amazing book?

Cynthia: Thank you. I was in corporate America and I worked for Sprint Communications. I had actually sold the Kinko's account, 900 and some stores, and I literally started as a secretary. I was fired from my first two jobs and then moved into sales which was a little more consistent with my personality and got to the top of Sprint in sales and national account manager and yet I wasn't passionate about my life. And how often are we on this track where we think well, when we get to a certain level, or are making a certain amount of money, or we get that house, or the corner office, or that husband then we're going to be happy? I had all of that and yet I wasn't passionate and so I started looking at what really inspired me in my life and I always loved weaving stories about unstoppable people, people like Walt Disney. He was on the verge of bankruptcy, every 18 months for 30 years and I remember reading his story and well, first of all, kind of shocked.

I thought that unstoppable people were more super humans. I didn't realize that unstoppable people had to go through so much to get to where they really wanted to go and I decided when I was in corporate America that I wanted to share these stories of people who'd inspired me throughout my whole life and so literally, in 1986, I cashed in my entire life savings, downsized my life to write my first book with the intention of inspiring people, with the message and the stories that I really had been studying and following their example for many, many years. That was the impetus of wanting more meaning in my life, wanting something that just inspired me to get out of bed which I think is so critical. If we want to create anything in our life look at what gives you meaning, what gives you joy, what excites you and then you tap into that energy. You become magnetic. You do become unstoppable.

Raven: When you unleash that unstoppableness in you, it feels great. We all have it. It just takes that something to help us unleash it. Can you give us a good definition of being unstoppable?

Cynthia: What I really believe is that unstoppable is simply having the courage to follow that divine calling, to find your inner purpose even to follow that meaning, that path and then not letting your own fear, circumstances, excuses or justifications on why you can't do it stop you. Every time you take a step forward, you've created an unstoppable moment and to live an unstoppable life is simply creating a series of unstoppable moments. Saying yes every day and literally it does come down into the moment of "I'm going to do this. I've got the courage just to take one step" and if you have the courage to take one step, then you can take ten steps and 100 steps and ultimately, you create the life that you really, really I feel are called to create and live and share on this planet.

Raven: Absolutely, and that's a key thing. You can't just take it and keep it. You got to share it! I want to read something out of your book *Unstoppable*. *"The greatest natural resource in the world is not in the earth's waters or minerals, nor in the forest or grassland. It is the spirit that resides in every unstoppable person and the spirit of the individual benefits us all."* Wow, tell us more about that, Cynthia.

Cynthia: I believe everybody has a dream. They have a calling. They have a unique way of expressing something that only they can do and so it's within us. The opportunity is to, as you said, tap into that and that's really been my life's work is helping people really get in touch with what is it? What is that inspiration? Because I think so many people allow their circumstances to dictate if they can do something. I can't start that business or I can't follow this calling or I can't really contribute until my circumstances change, until I get out of debt, until my kids get into college or out of school and what happens is we let our life pass us by.

And so for me, my intention is literally to help people, to help people listening to this call really know that we don't have time to waste. We can't wait for the recession to turn around. The reality is that we don't live in the consciousness of a recession and we're in our purpose and our passion, we magnetize people to us. We magnetize them because people want your product, your service. They want to make a difference. They want to contribute and so I'm encouraging all of you for the time that we're on the call together to suspend the belief or your circumstances or the reasons why you think you can't do it and be open to what would your life look like if you were living a life that you were passionate about and wanted to be unstoppable. You want it enough that it's like, "Wow, I have to be unstoppable because it's too important to me."

Raven: I think Les Brown says it best, Cynthia. He says you got to be hungry for a change. For things to change we've got to change and we have to recognize that and be willing to take the step and that's what you bring with these stories in this book. You mentioned courage earlier. You mentioned passion. Are those some of the characteristics, to have that unstoppable mindset?

Cynthia: Yeah, absolutely, you first have to have the courage to say yes. It's something that's bigger than us. It's like how do I contribute in a way that nobody else can do it? You have to be able to say yes and willing to risk, to take the risk and be positive. If you have the desire, you have the seeds within you to bring that to fruition.

So it's knowing that the calling is there, somewhere within you is the ability to manifest it and nothing happens until you say yes and you're willing to take that step and that's really my work is supporting people. My coaching program is helping people get clear on what is it, and then how do you get the courage. What is that first thing you need to do? What's the next thing you need to do because people get overwhelmed with the bigness of their idea, but it's a process!

Raven: It certainly is and we have to embrace the little steps along the way. Embrace them and recognize them and know it's okay to say, "Good job, Raven." Don't wait on nobody else because I think when you recognize that you made a giant leap, no matter how small that leap was, you got to look at where you came from. Can you share your thoughts on that?

Cynthia: Yeah, I really appreciate your mentioning that because we have to learn how to be our biggest fan, instead of our biggest abuser. I mean think about it, you think about people, a lot of people have been physically abused, sexually abused, emotionally abused but look in the ways of our own life how we do that to ourselves. And it really, it's stopping that. I mean I've been doing this work for many, many years and I still have to stop myself when I hear that inner critic that says, "Oh, you're too this or you're too that, or you're not enough or whatever" and it's like, "Stop!"

We have to learn how to love ourselves and to be our biggest fan because if we wait - it understands that we are the ones we've been waiting for. It's not for somebody else or it's not that man or that spouse to rescue us. It's like we are the ones and if we're willing and we have the courage to say yes, all of these resources, the universe, it conspires to support us in that calling but nothing happens until we say yes to that. That's right, we got to show up. I'm willing, God. Use me.

Raven: Yeah, and be ready to show up big time. It's your time to shine. Don't hide it. Don't be shy go on and let it out! Be unstoppable. Let's talk about unstoppable moments so some people can recognize it when they have one.

Cynthia: An unstoppable moment is anytime you get out of your comfort zone, anytime you honor your word to yourself, anytime you're ever willing to say yes. Unstoppable moments are every single time you say yes to yourself. One thing I'm doing this year is one thing I'm passionate about now and that's giving.

Communities in Kenya and Haiti - We're going to support over 4,000 students and teaching people how to give, how to make a living by giving, how to create wealth and abundance by giving and so one thing that I'm doing this year is I'm going to live a year of giving where every day it's like I look at, "How do I give?"

Raven: And you know what? Now you brought up a biggie. H-O-W! Too many of us get stuck in trying to figure that out and you're right. You're just going to trust what you know in your heart is right. Everything else will come, and put that action forward so you can make it happen.

Cynthia: Yeah, exactly and all of a sudden like for example, and I said, "Okay, great. I'm going to do it. I'm going to live this life of giving." So it's not like okay, I'm sitting, meditating and praying about it.

I'm in action! But you see, once you create the intention and the why you're doing it, all of the "how" starts coming forward. Once you say yes, it's like literally the universe conspires to support you but without the yes, you've got filters on and you're looking for how I can't do it. Before it was like asking yourself the wrong question. How do I make a living by giving? It's like no. How do I step into giving my gifts and then it will come forward? Do you see the difference?

Raven: I absolutely see the difference. Just say, "Yes!" and don't question the "how." Giving is so important. As business owners, don't take this lightly because when you give, you receive so much more in your business.

Cynthia: Absolutely, and you're magnetized. I have a thriving business with my coaching and I was reading, a friend of mine, Gay Hendricks', book *The Big Leap* and he's talking about how we have an expertise. I have an expertise in what I'm doing but truly my genius, my passion is in the conversation around giving. I wake up. I become alive. And so it's like instead of focusing on what I'm good at, and continuing that and my work to some extent, but the bigger picture is how do we live in our genius, that divine calling? Inspiration is in spirit. How do we come from that place of inspiration and when you're living that genius area, I believe that's the real opportunity to have an amazing life.

Raven: I would love it if you could give our listeners that are home-based business and enthusiasts some serious tips on how even during the recession they can become unstoppable in their business.

Cynthia: I want you to really look at what are you doing and why you're doing it and I'm going to give you some specific things that people pay me a lot of money to learn in my coaching program, all right? So I'm just going to give it to you so you can start immediately applying it. Number one is when you're looking to selling as entrepreneurs, as business people, are you coming from the place of "I have to sell something to them, I have to persuade, I have to manipulate? How do I overcome their objections?" Versus "How am I really going to be of service? Who needs this product in a way that I can be of service to them?" So when you come from the place of "I'm looking only for people who need, who have a problem that my product, my service solves." When you come from that place, when you're speaking to them, you're not coming from a place of desperation or manipulation. You have this desire, this problem and I have the perfect solution for you.

First up, look at what you're doing, why you're doing it, how it's creating a difference in the lives of your prospects. As you're out there talking to people, come from a place of who can I serve? In my program, I encourage people to create your day and literally you get in touch with, "What are you doing? Why are you doing it?" See yourself being of service to people who need what you have to sell so it's almost like a disservice not to share your product or service with them.

It's an injustice versus as women, we think, "Oh we don't want to sell something or we don't want to be too pushy." No, if you have the cure to cancer and somebody had cancer and you didn't share ...because you don't want to be pushy?

When you really get in alignment with what you're doing and why you're doing it, it gives you the boldness to really speak it.

Another thing is your belief system. This is really so critical. How do you believe in yourself? One of the things I wanted to share is one strategy I call "Tapping into your internal caller ID." We all have this conversation that's inside of us. We have a desire to do something and we're of two minds, right? There's one mind that comes from a place of faith that says, "I'm so excited about this. My product makes such a difference. Everybody's going to want it. It's so amazing. I'm so blessed to be in this business." The other voice says, "I've never been a business person before. I've never made seven figures or six figures. I don't know how to do this. People are going to think I'm too pushy." So we've got this voice of fear and the voice of faith.

Raven: We're going to talk about some action steps so we can create an action plan, okay? 'Cause you and I both agree, you just can't sit it, think it, and be inspired and read it. You got to put it into action so can you help us out?

Cynthia: The first step is to know what you want. Specifically what is it that you want to create? "I want to make a million dollars, a hundred thousand dollars, fifty thousand dollars" Something that's specific and measurable.

Number two is the why. The why's the motivation. Why is it so important? Why is it a must that you create this result in your life?

The third is to believe it's possible. I wanted to share a very quick process. Let's say the belief is where we get stuck. 75 to 80%, our researchers say, of our internal conversation is negative. It's limiting. It's looking for why it isn't going to work instead of how can it work? We have to learn to dispute these limiting beliefs. We've got plenty of evidence in our life to prove anything. What is the belief that's going to move you forward?

When you have that belief system then you take it down to, "What is that action step I need to take every single day that's going to move my business forward?" You have to persevere so what is that thing that you need to be doing consistently that's going to move that business forward?

Then the final thing is how do you create a structure that helps you show up for yourself? That's why coaching and accountability is so critical. You can know what to do, why to do it, but if you can't get yourself to do it... and that's the problem, because most of us are operating from a place of our past conditioning. As a matter of fact, studies show that one out of ten people can create a sustainable change in their life, even when their life depends on it. Only one out of ten people!!

You got to have a structure. You got to have something that forces you to show up for yourself until you create some momentum to really take your life to the next level.

Raven: Cynthia, we're out of time, but can you tell our listeners how can they get in contact with you real quick?

Cynthia: Go to Unstoppable.net to learn more. We also have something called UnstoppableChallenge.com. If you're feeling like you're in business and you need some support, you want a partner, or you want this accountability to really minimize your learning curve. Check that out and let us interview you and see if it's a fit for you.

Listen to the full audio of this interview:
http://www.careersfromthekitchentable.com/audios
Plus be sure to visit and subscribe to Raven's popular newsletter and get your free e-book *"The Real Power of Social Networking: Profit on Facebook"* by Regina Baker
http://www.careersfromthekitchentable.com

Jack Canfield
Author, Coach and Speaker

The Success Principles and How to Get from Where You Are to Where You Want to Be...as a Business Owner - that's what we're going to be talking about today.

Jack Canfield is an inspirational self-help author and success coach, famous for the popular book, him and his partner, Mark Victor Hansen, Chicken Soup for the Soul. He's a motivational speaker and has tons of books and audios out there. One of my favorites, we're going to be speaking about today, The Success Principles: How to Get from Where You Are to Where You Want to Be. I am so excited, Jack, how you doing'?

Jack: I'm great, Raven. Thanks for having me on your show.

Raven: Well, you're absolutely welcome. Thank you for being here. This is an audience that a lot of people, Jack, have not made that transition yet. They're still trying to decide whether they want to leave corporate. I always try to tell them, hey, plan a plan B. Just in case you don't have that choice.

I want to start out, if you don't mind, sharing just a tad bit of your story, about how you and Mark first began the Chicken Soup series. I know you went through a lot of no's.

Jack: Yeah, we did. We were rejected by 144 publishers before we got a yes. It took us over 16 months to find a publisher but had we stopped at number 100, I would not be talking to you or your audience today, so I would say the key to our success has been having a clear vision and then being willing to persevere through many, many rejections until we got a yes, and that one yes with the Health Communications, a little unknown publisher down in Florida went on to sell over 10 million copies of the first Chicken Soup for the Soul book, and now we have over 115 million copies of Chicken Soup for the Soul books in 47 languages, so if we had given up, I wouldn't be where I am today, so perseverance. And knowing, I think another thing I've been teaching people really is patience. A lot of times, we get very impatient. You know, we see a movie like The Secret, we think all you have to do is visualize and affirm, and one year later, I'll be a millionaire, and it takes a little bit of work and it takes a little of bit of time, and not to give up on your dream. You know, it takes a while to build a big building, and it takes a while to build a great life.

Raven: It does. I've got to ask you this 'cause I know a lot of people are stuck right here. So how do we begin to discover what it is that we really, really want to do in life and what we really are meant to be? How do we figure that out?

Jack: Well, there are several things I look at. One is do you notice yourself feeling jealous or envious of another person in their job or their career, or what they get to do for a living? That's often a clue. I remember I used to be envious of movie stars. They got a lot of attention. They got to travel around the world. And so I realized that those were aspects of what I want in my life. I also was envious of people, who were teaching like Oprah and Dr. Phil, and you know people like that, but back then, there would have been other people like, you know, that were running daytime talk shows like Merv Griffin and Johnny Carson, and so forth. And so I realized that part of what I wanted was to reach lots of people. There was a message in there that I wanted to reach lots of people in an entertaining, uplifting, and empowering way. The other thing to do is look back at the times you were happiest in life.
I used the story of Julie Lately in my book, The Success Principles where I talk about, she was a student at Ohio State University, and she was not all that happy, and she thought she would be 'cause she was studying veterinary medicine, and she had been someone who loved animals, and one day, she sat down and really examined her life. It was raining out. She was depressed. She said, "When was I happiest in life?" And she realized, it was when she was in student leadership positions in high school, when she was doing the chaperoning of the high school student leaders at Ohio State University, and she would, you know, be part of that process for them. She said that's when I was happiest, and she said, I get it, I love leadership.

So she went to the head of the university and she said I'd like to major in leadership instead of veterinary medicine. They said, we don't have a program on that, and she said, well, can I create a new one and I'll take courses in communication and then media, and then you know government, different things where I can learn a lot about leadership? So they let her develop an independent study course in leadership, and she went on at the age of 26, she was leading leadership training for generals and colonels in the military at the Pentagon. She became a leadership instructor at the Pentagon, and then went off to create her own foundation, and now teaches youth leadership all across the country. She is all of like 29 years old.

So the ideas if you look back over your life and say, when was I happiest, that's going to give you clues. There is a wonderful thing called *The Passion Test*, which two of my friends, Chris and Janet Attwood put together.

Raven: Oh yeah, that's marvelous.

Jack: And you just simply ask yourself. You say, you know my life is ideal when I am, and you list down 10 or 20 things that you love to do. So for me, my life is ideal when I'm teaching, when I'm learning, when I'm with spiritual people and hanging out and sharing, when I am developing new products, when I'm hanging out with my family, when I'm travelling, and so forth. So I list all those down, and then I go back and say, if I could only do one of these, which one would I do? If I had it like, like it said okay, all other 19 are impossible, you can only do one, which would I pick? And that tells you something very important about your passion, then you look at the next 19 and say, if I could only do one of these, which one would it be? And you just kind a do a little force choice test.

Well, when I first did that with Janet about 5 years ago, 6 years ago, I realized that my number one passion was hanging out with really conscious people, and I realized that I wasn't doing that enough. I was teaching all my students, but I was way ahead of them. So I started something called "The Transformational Leadership Council," where I invited 30 people, like John Gray who wrote *Men Are from Mars, Women Are from Venus* and those kind of people to come to my house, and we created an organization that now meets twice a year for 4 days in a beautiful resort location. We teach each other what we know. We share our latest breakthroughs. We have fun social events and now, I am fulfilling one of my passions and it's a way that I make money and it's a way that has led me to things like I appeared in *The Secret* because they filmed *The Secret* at one of our events, and that changed my professional life to a large degree. I was introduced to a whole new audience I've never been introduced before, but if I hadn't acted on that passion, I wouldn't have had that career breakthrough.

Raven: Speaking of *The Secret*, we absolutely loved that. I've watched that twice a week continuously. I love it. You know, you mentioned some very key things that I appreciate, and it took me back for a moment, and I got to tell you, Jack, the same kind a way you had that "enviness", I did too. Growing up, I loved Hollywood stars. I told my dad to build me a stage in the basement 'because I'm from Ohio and we had basements. And listen to this Jack, I used to sneak from high school up to the radio station, and the deejays called my parents all the time and tell them, "Come get your daughter. She's up here again."

Jack: That's funny.

Raven: And then after all those years, you know after all those years at the age of 55, I found my passion or I tell people, my passion found me. You know, while waiting for my mother to get well at the hospital, it was put on my heart to start doing a show to empower women, and I started my first show *Women Power* that way. So as I listen to you, it made me think, "Wow! He's right." This stuff kind 'a creeps back up in your life, doesn't it?

Jack: So there's something in us that we each have as a unique talent, a unique ability. You know most people; they have it wired up backwards. They go and do a job they don't want, so they can get enough money to then go spend it to do what they want. And if you can find a job and everybody can if you look hard enough, where you can do what you want to make a living. A friend of mine loves to travel. What does she do for a living? She takes people around the world to spiritual centers, like Machu Picchu in Peru or she'll take people to the Taj Mahal in

India, or to the Wailing Wall in Israel, or to you know Stonehenge in England, and so forth. And she has figured out how to make a living doing what she loves.

Raven: Wow! Amazing! It's absolutely amazing, and what a good feeling it is when you're doing what you're passionate about.

Jack: Well, it's true.

Raven: I got to ask you this because I know what you're saying about how to discover what we want and what we're meant to be, but a lot of times, once we discover that, we're having problems with staying focused. There are so many distractions around us. How do we get past that? How do we stay that laser focused?

Jack: Well, our environments are very important. I say that, you know, 50% of your life is determined by your environment and 25% is your mindset, and 25% is your skill set. So you need to know the skills, in your case, of you know, putting on a radio show. In my case, being a public speaker and a trainer and author and so forth, but your environments are critical, and your environments are made up of several things. One is the people in your environment, who you surround yourself with. A lot of times you surround yourself with people who want to go out drinking and get drunk, and you know, party, and so forth versus people who study and focus and work on their careers and are uplifting and encouraging and supportive of your dreams versus people who are naysayers and whiners and complainers and blamers. So that's a big piece of it.

Raven: I love the way you laid that out for us. Thank you. We're going to get a lot from that as we go back and listen to this replay, and you know, you really discussed some important things because we seem to sometimes make out that to do list and it overwhelms us.

Jack: Yeah, there are too many things on it. If you take that whole to do list, in fact it was important to get done and put it on a schedule, then if you just do your schedule, you can forget about the to do list until later that night before, and then you make your schedule for the next day.

Let's talk about the home business person being stuck in that procrastination mode. We talked earlier, we have to stay focused and we have to change things up, you know. Is it fear or is it really procrastination that's holding us back or the both?

Jack: Well, it's always fear. Fear of failure, fear of rejection, fear of looking foolish, you know all that kind of stuff. So basically, the way to get through fear is twofold.

Number one, do the thing you're afraid of. Do it in baby steps. Don't freeze yourself. Get that accountability partner to hold your hand and walk you through it. And then, there's something they call consequences. Make a deal that if you don't, you know, call ten people by next Friday or open up your store front, or whatever it is your goal is, by a certain date, that you're going to write a check for a $1,000 to your accountability partner.

That kind of consequence which no one wants to do becomes very motivational, and you make that a public declaration that lots of people know about.

Raven: And who wants to pay up a $1,000 even a $100, right? I like that. So, can you share some of the things you have and where everybody can go to get it?

Jack: Yeah, sure, we have all kinds of audio programs and video programs and DVDs. We got one called, The Success Principles DVD. You can show it to your staff. It's an hour long DVD. You know, it's a way to motivate your family and teach the principles. There's a whole, Jack, we call it, Jack in a Box. It's an entire course that I do in 7-day training. These are there's like 26 DVDs. It's huge but the point is, you can go from the very simple to the very profound, and just go to JackCanfield.com, and you can get all of that there under the Products and Books Section, but there's also a Training Section. We do trainings and I do public speaking and so forth.

And you can also go to TheSuccessPrinciples.com, and that's where that daily download that you're getting is coming from. There's also a Leader's Guide to do a 6-hour Success Principles Program, so you can learn this, take it into your own company or into your church, or your family, and lead your family through a 6-hour, could be 6 days, 1 hour each or all day at 1 day.

Raven: Thank you so much. I appreciate it. Alrighty, Jack. I just had to do that. Listen, this was an absolute pleasure. Thank you so much! Go check him out, JackCanfield.com. His book, *The Success Principles: How to Get from Where You Are to Where You Want to Be*. Sign up for his newsletter; you'll get uplifted like I do every day.

Learn more by visiting http://www.jackcanfield.com

Listen to the full audio of this interview:
http://www.careersfromthekitchentable.com/audios
Plus be sure to visit and subscribe to Raven's popular newsletter and get your free e-book *"The Real Power of Social Networking: Profit on Facebook"* **by Regina Baker**
http://www.careersfromthekitchentable.com

Ali Brown

Author, Entrepreneur, EZine Queen

Yes, Ali Brown is here! So if you're standing up, sit down. If you're sitting down, stand up 'because you're not going to want to miss anything this lady has to say. Let me tell you about Ali before we bring her on.

Ali is CEO of Alexandria Brown International Inc., a multimillion dollar company devoted to empowering women around the world with the tools to live the freedom-based lives of their dreams. Ali's journey into entrepreneurship was a natural one. After hopping from job to job like most of us do, in New York City, she found herself frustrated and unemployable by her nature of always, always, always wanting to change things and improve upon them. My kind of lady. After deciding to leave her final job in 1998 at a small New York City ad agency, she reviewed her options and chose the opportunity of owning her own business.

After that she immersed herself in books, audios, and courses on marketing, success and prosperity. And you know what? Using the power of online marketing to build her business, she quickly became known as the Ezine Queen where she got really, really good at marketing her business via emails, newsletters, and ezines. Some of her clients were New York Times Digital, Adweek Magazines, Scholastic Books, and Dun & Bradstreet. This lady is all that and then some. She has over 36,000 subscribers. Did I say 36,000? I sure did and get this – she currently has more than 800 solo-entrepreneurs enrolled in her high-energy coaching program.

Wow! Is this lady incredible or what? Help me welcome the lady the simply call by her first name and I'm not talking about Oprah. I'm not talking about Tyra. I'm not talking about Ellen. I'm talking about Ali! Hey Ali!

Ali: Oh, I'm having so much fun already. This is awesome! I wish all interviews were like you.

Raven: Oh thank you, Ali. I'm just so delighted to have you here. Thank you so much, girlfriend!

Ali: Yes, you're so welcome and I love you, Raven, because you're making business fun and we forget that this can be anything we want it to be. This doesn't have to be the old school way of doing business. This is the new women's way of doing business out there.

Raven: Yeah, and you know all about having fun and I know you have launched a magazine and we're going to share all that about with the listeners so we're going to hold that for later but I tell you, girl I took a glance at it and mmm, mmm, mmm, mmm, mmm. Oprah, get back. You're on your way.

Ali: Thank you. It's a big leap but everything I've done has been scary, a little scary and I think that's true for everybody especially when they're making their first step working at home.

Raven: Yeah, well I want to know this. Woman to woman. Talk to me now.

Ali: Uh-oh.

Raven: You just got out there and just pushed that old boys' club to the side. How did it happen?

Ali: Oh God. I want to tell all of you listening to this that if I were to look at myself from the Ali I was ten years ago, I would go, "There's no way I will ever be a multimillionaire. There's no way. I don't know how I could do that. I don't know the how, how this, how that." But all I knew is I was so frustrated working for someone else and I think that drives a lot of us to taking a risk more than wanting something to sometimes being so frustrated with your situation, you just say, "That's it. I can't take this anymore." I was working at this little ad agency for these, I call them the knuckleheads. These guys didn't know what they were doing and here I was way back then. I was like only 25, 26 and just so frustrated working with these guys. They didn't seem to care about their clients and I got frustrated and I just quit and I was in for a rude awakening because I didn't realize Raven that the most important part of owning a business is actually the marketing. So I started a business doing copywriting 'cause that's what I had learned doing at this little ad agency. I was writing some of the ads for the clients and helping them out and did an okay job and then I saw what you could make freelancing so I thought well, I'll give this a try. Well I had no idea how to get clients. I had no idea how to network. I was not good on the phone like you are. You're known as the phone diva, right?

Raven: Yes, ma'am. Thanks.

Ali: Ok, so I wasn't that good back then and I'm good now. It's taken a long time but I was really much shyer and when I would meet people I'd be terrified to follow up. So I was going around all these networking meetings and just getting through these breakfasts and lunches and dinners and have a stack of business cards and kept thinking, "I don't know if I can do this. I don't think I'm smart enough to have my own business. I'm going to get online and write my mom and see if I can move home." And this was in New York and gosh, it was just a scary time. There's a story I tell when I'm speaking on stage when I remember I couldn't take $20 out of the ATM. My balance was 18.56 and I will never forget that number.

Raven: Oh I've been there, Ali. I know that.

Ali: Oh yeah. And I would never, I'm not one of those speakers you know the story like I was living in my van or anything...

But I mean I had a little tiny apartment. I just scraped by and I did what I needed to do, but it was not happy and it wasn't pretty and I couldn't buy anything for myself but I didn't want to go back to have a job and I was fiddling around with email a little bit and I saw some of these email newsletters that we also call them ezines which is short for electronic magazine.

That's what I got good at, doing these little email newsletters. All this was, Raven, was if you can type an email and press send this is all it was. I wrote a little tip for the people that I had met that talked about how to market yourself with good communication such as what I did. I wrote brochures and web pages and things like that. So I wrote a tip to show them that I knew what I was doing and I put a little promotion for my business. Now I started with a list of ten people and that included my parents and it included my cat. I mean this was pathetic and from there, an interesting thing happened. People started forwarding that little email around and then people were writing me asking to sign up for it. People I've never heard of, people all over the world.

And within about six months, I started getting finally steady work and steady clients because what would happen is I hear from somebody at for example Dun & Bradstreet that said, "You know what? A friend of a colleague forwarded me your little newsletter and we need someone to write a brochure and we'd like you to come and then make a proposal" and this wild stuff started to happen and then I thought well I want to learn more about this email thing. So I looked around the bookstores. I looked online and I was just frustrated with what I found and I started to write a few articles on the topic and then I wanted to write a book 'cause I've always wanted to write a book but I didn't know how to get a book published and I learned about these things called eBooks which is really just a PDF file. It's just a digital file that you buy online and you download and I thought well this is great 'cause I don't have the money to get anything published anyway.

So I wrote a little eBook and at that time it was called *Boost Business With Your Own Ezine* and I put it online and I remember I had by that time I had an email list of about a thousand people which is pretty cool. I thought that was awesome. And I sent out an email to the list telling them about this eBook and I was scared to death. I'm thinking they're not going to want to buy this thing. They're going to get mad that I'm selling to them and I remember I pressed send and my heart was pounding and I just shut my computer and left. I ran out. I was so terrified.

Raven: I don't want to see.

Ali: Yeah, I'm like "I don't want to know what they're going to write back. They're going to hate me and I'm selling." I come back from the gym and I just like very slowly. I'm bringing my computer up and my email comes in and I see order, order, order, order, money, money, money and I said, "Ah! Oh... this is cool" because I did the work and I'm done doing the work and now I'm getting paid, paid, paid. It's passive income and I was hooked. I was so hooked because I was so used to working hours for dollars, hours for dollars and that comes from way back in the industrial revolution and then we were in the service age and now we are truly in the information age. We throw that term around but it's still so applicable. Now we get paid for results and the information that gives people results, they will pay well for. And from there I studied everything I could about online marketing. I started scraping up my change and going to seminars. I remember the first ten I had to buy a plane ticket to go to a seminar. I was just terrified but since then I'm just so in love still with the internet and the possibilities it gives you to work at home or to work from anywhere. This past year my dad passed away and I have to tell you.

Raven: I'm sorry to hear that.

Ali: Thank you. I have to tell you that when he was so ill it meant so much to him that I could grab my laptop and be there with him within a few hours and fly to Texas and am by his side and this is, it was so sweet. It just broke my heart. I remember him grabbing my hand and just trying to get the words out. He said, "But what about your business?" And I said, "Dad, my business is with me. It's okay." He still didn't quite understand that I could make money and still be there with him 'because that generation, they didn't have that opportunity and it's just an amazing place to be and today my business is worth several million dollars. We have a coaching company. We're launching a magazine for women in business. There's so much going on. My passion though is still helping those women get started from home.

Raven: And boy you help 'em. I mean everybody loves Ali and the reason I think so is just, you are just you. You're so authentic. You're so real. You're not about the hype you know, and that's important nowadays, don't you agree?

Ali: Absolutely, and I think people's BS detectors are a lot more sensitive nowadays too. I don't know about you.

Raven: Yeah. They want for realness. They just want you to talk to them. Talk to them, you know? And be for real. Let them know what the good, the bad and the ugly and let them make the decision.

Ali: Totally and I say this in a lot of seminars now too. People are getting a little tired of the men who are yelling at the audience and, "How many of you want to blah blah blah?" and you know...People want to be talked with and have conversations with and this is why anyone, and I do believe anyone can start a business from home on the internet because all you're doing is talking to people whether it's in type or on the phone or a recording that you do and it's just about communication and you don't have to act like this big company and in fact, one of the biggest advantages that solo entrepreneurs have is being people and that people buy from people. Big companies hire spokespeople to give their company a face and a personality. Well, you already have that so people listen to Raven because she's Raven. People come to Ali because she's Ali. I mean there are a gazillion other people teaching internet marketing but I have people coming to me say, "Ali, but I want to learn from you 'cause I've come to like who you are and what you represent" and so Jane Doe sitting in the kitchen right now, even with the kids all around her feet with Cheerios and all that, people would like to know that that's her life and if she can talk about and talk about a product or service that she uses, that's helped her in some way. It's just so wonderful for anyone.

Raven: Yeah you mix that really well. So let's talk about the ezine, because this is something that any business at any point can do. Correct?

Ali: Yes, absolutely.

Raven: Okay, and I know at one time you were really recommending it and can you tell us why and maybe give us a couple of tips in that area?

Ali: Yeah, and I still do. It's about the relationship. It's just like writing a friend with an email like with a friendly tip, and then your offer. And whatever your offer is whether you're selling a product, you could be a network marketing company; maybe you have an ebook or an infoproduct that you're selling. If you don't have a product, join up with someone else and be part of their affiliate program. You need to start with an audience so let the biggest lesson and this is an advanced tip to give but I think your audience would like this. *The who is more important than the what.* If you develop a readership of a certain type of person, your income will be accelerating for years to come because you have a market that you can bring additional products and services to. The problem that most people have when they start online is they have a product or service and then they go out and then they go out and try to find people. The thing I love about a newsletter is, if you have a theme for your newsletter and you attract readers who are interested in that theme, you can bring in additional products and services.

My biggest tip is: pick an audience first that you have a natural affinity with, or they're easy to find.

Raven: Okay, so don't go out there creating products before you do research on where your target market is, who they are and understand them and what they need, right?

Ali: Yeah.

Raven: Thank you, Ali, for joining us this week. We look forward to you coming back next week. Meanwhile, they can go check you out at where?

Ali: Check out the system at http://www.alibrown.com

Raven: Can they subscribe to your magazine yet or no?

Ali: They can. Go there and then click around and you can find out about all the other programs as well - the magazine, the Millionaire Protégé Club, and the new Ali Boutique which is going to have some work at home apparel.

Raven: Oh my God. The Ali effect. Look out, Oprah, you're a goner.

Learn more at http://www.alibrown.com

Listen to the full audio of this interview:
http://www.careersfromthekitchentable.com/audios
Plus be sure to visit and subscribe to Raven's popular newsletter and get your free e-book *"The Real Power of Social Networking: Profit on Facebook"* **by Regina Baker**
http://www.careersfromthekitchentable.com

Dr. Joe Vitale

Best Selling Author and Star of The Secret Movie

Guerilla Marketing King himself, Dr. Joe Vitale is an author of tons of bestselling books including Your Internet Cash Machine, The Key, The Attractor Factor, one of my favorites, Hypnotic Writing, and that's just to name a few. He's also author of several audio and DVD programs including two Nightingale-Conant bestsellers The Missing Secret and The Power of Outrageous Marketing. Dr. Vitale he has been interviewed on Larry King Live, appeared on The Big Idea and also starred in the famous inspiring movie, The Secret. You know that movie that shook the world.

He is the marketing guru Joe a.k.a. Mr. Fire Vitale. He is here. He's going to give you all the insider secrets tonight on having a successful internet marketing business.

Joe: Wow! I'm excited. What an intro. I love your language. I love your passion. I love that you had me on. I'm flattered. Thank you.

Raven: Oh thank you, Joe. Thank you so much. Well you know, I've been following you for a while so I know a little bit about your stories and you're just truly rags to riches story so to speak. Could you share just a little bit with our listeners first?

Joe: Yeah. I used to not talk about it but people said it's inspiring to hear that at one point in my life, I was actually homeless. When I was in Dallas in the late 70s, I was really struggling. I was in, it wasn't even poverty. It was below that. I was homeless. People will say, "What kind of car did you live in?" And I think, "Car? Gosh! It would have been so much nicer to have had a car." I didn't have anything and when I migrated to Houston, I was in virtual poverty for many years. As I was struggling, I wanted to be an author. I was working on myself. I was writing things, writing plays, writing books, writing articles, trying to make a living at it and it was not easy. It was not, my overnight success, if you call it that, probably took me 23 years to achieve.

Raven: Ooh, 23 years, wow! Well you know what? Sometimes we got to get through the bad to get to the good, don't we?

Joe: Well we do and I had to learn a lot about myself, about what I was capable about, about how to make money. I had to work on my self-image. I had to work on my beliefs. I had to work on my level of deservingness within myself. What I do today is teach people how to collapse that time so you don't have to take 30 years to get out there and make your own life and make your own living doing what you love, maybe do it in 30 days.

Joe: When attributed most of it from doing big things but also befriending the media. He would let the press, the newspapers of his time, know what he was doing and they would write about him, which would send traffic to his circus. So the parallel today is you do something on your website, you come up with something unusual, you do something a little different, but then you tell the media, and you tell the media online. You go to a service like http://www.PRWeb.com and you can send out a news release. You can send out a basic news release for nothing. No charge at all. You can send out some that go to more media, to more newspapers and so forth for maybe a hundred dollars and if the media does a story on you, they are freely sending new people to your website. So this is another thing that you can do, that anybody can do to bring more traffic to their site when they're online.

Raven: And that is cool. That is really cool. Let's talk about joint ventures. We've got a few minutes, I know you're big on that as well and I, before we go, I definitely want to touch on that *Hypnotic Marketing* of yours. So let's start with a little bit about joint ventures. What would you share real quickly on that?

Joe: That's a great question. Joint ventures is part of hypnotic marketing and even publicity, which I've just talked about as part of hypnotic marketing and this is all stuff you can do online. A joint venture is when you find somebody else to do a partnership agreement with. Let me give you a real quick story, a real quick example. Years ago, Pat O'Brien, Pat O'Brien was a struggling musician. He had five CDs out. He would tour Europe, but he was basically broke. Musicians don't make that much money especially where I live in the Austin, Texas area where there are musicians all over the place. And so he went to one of my seminars, he got the book about internet marketing, and he got this idea to create a workbook for the famous book, *Think and Grow Rich* and I thought that was brilliant, a *Think and Grow Rich* workbook and it was easy for him to write because there was a lot of blank pages saying what did you learn from chapter one? What did you learn from chapter two, that kind of thing. He wanted to sell it and I said, "Well that's okay but a better idea is give it away." If you give it away, people can give you their email address in exchange for it and you will build your own mailing list of which those people you can go to later and sell things to them.

So he came to me and I became his joint venture. I said, "I will promote your free workbook, the *Think and Grow Rich* workbook to my list." Why would I do this? Because I will look good to my list. My list will thank me. Why will he do this? Because my list is going to go to his website now, give him their email address, in exchange, they'll get the book to download but now Pat has a mailing list of his own. Once he did that which was very successful, he came out with 40 products of his own and he began selling those 40 products to his own mailing list but it began with a joint venture with me.

Now I'm not telling people to go and do joint ventures with me 'because I'm plenty busy. But the point is you find somebody who has a list of people that you want to be selling your product or service to. You go to them and say, "Look, if you promote my product or service to your list, I will give you and you give them some percentage. My rule of thumb is if it's a service, you give them 10%, if it's a product that's already done, you give them 50%, but you work out whatever is comfortable with you, for you but you have this win-win going on. The joint venture person is glad to do it. They're going to make money. They're going to look good to your list. You're glad to do it because you're making money. You're selling your product to a whole group of people that never heard of you before.

Raven: Oh sure. You are so right. Now what about affiliate? Can you touch on that real quickly?

Joe: Yeah. An affiliate is like a joint venture but affiliate person is somebody who said, "I want to be a sales person for your product or service." For example, I have a software program called *Hypnotic Writing Wizard.* It's at http://www.hypnoticwritingwizard.com. And you can be an affiliate for it. So you would go there, you would fill out the form to be an affiliate. Once you've done that, you get a unique website link. You give that out on your radio show. You give it out to whoever you want. Whenever somebody buys from it, you get credit for that sale. So you're like a registered sales person for my product. That's what an affiliate is. You don't have to come up with a product. You just go to somebody who has a product and say, "I want to help sell it."

Raven: Yeah, absolutely. Wow! Well, this has been amazing. I mean, you have given us a lot of good information and before we go, we have a couple minutes and I definitely want you to take some time and share with us how you can assist perhaps some of the listeners that want to jump into this internet marketing game, Joe.

Joe: Well that's, thank you for that opportunity. Well, first of all, I would invite people to go to my website, http://www.mrfire.com because there's a lot of free information that will help people. There are a lot of inspirational articles, a lot of informational articles. If people are looking for hands on coaching, I have a coaching program. There's also a link on http://www.mrfire.com so if you go to http://www.mrfire.com just look on the left and you'll see executive mentoring, and you'll see my blog, and all these other things, just click on it. And you can get information about getting a coach who has been trained by me to help you open your own internet business. And finally, I have a brand new book out. It's called *Inspired Marketing.* It's in Amazon, and that might help a lot of people about having the encouragement and the inspiration to do an internet business.

Raven: Well, thank you so much, Joe. You have given us a lot of your golden tips. We appreciate you so much.

Joe: Oh, thank you. You're doing great stuff. I love your energy and passion. God speed to you and everybody listening.

I came out with my first e-book. And again an e-book is like an invisible book. It's a book but it's only a text file that people buy online and they download. I had a book called *Hypnotic Writing.* A friend of mine, he was doing pretty well on the internet by the name of Mark Joyner. He said, "Let me take a book by you and let me sell it online." I was so skeptical inside, "Nobody's going to buy an e-book." I like real books. I want to hold books. I like those printed books. So who's going to buy an e-book? So I told him no for two years. When I finally said, yes, take this book called *Hypnotic Writing.* See if you can sell it." he put it up. He wrote a sales letter for it at http://www.advancedhypnoticwriting.com. I went and read it. It was so powerful I wanted to buy my own book. I was a skeptic. Well, he announced that thing and we sold 600 copies of that e-book overnight at $30 a pop. I woke up in the morning and I had made a tremendous amount of money while I was sleeping. And there it was, this is the beauty of internet. There was nothing to ship. There was nothing to print. There were no fulfillment costs, no warehousing cost. People would pay online and they get a download link, they go and download the book. It was instant gratification. I instantly got their money. They instantly got the book!

Raven: I know how fantastic that is! On the internet, you could be sleeping and you'd hear a sound saying ka-ching ka-ching.

Joe: Yeah, you got mail means you got money.

Raven: Absolutely.   Well I love that. You know I love the energy that you have and the passion and because I know like I said, I've been following you. I've seen you on *The Secret*. I love your book *The Attractor Factor* and everything that you're saying, how you talk about the importance of our intentions and also the importance of having a plan because a lot of us, that's one of the things where we miss mess up, isn't it? We truly didn't have a plan.

Joe: Well, I find that having your passion is even more important than your plan, isn't it?   As a first step, I'm a great believer in inspired action, which is the action that comes from within. It's the thing that's coming from your intuition that tells you what to do next. But before you can have a plan, before you could follow your intuition, before you can take inspired action, you got to be coming from your passion. If there's any one secret to my success, any one secret that I hear from very successful people, it's that they do what they love. They do their passion. Joseph Campbell said, "Follow your bliss." I say, "Follow your enthusiasm; follow the thing that really excites you. Do the thing that you would do even if you weren't getting paid for it." Just find a way to get paid for it, and that's what I do on the internet. I've changed so many lives including my own by telling people find what you're good at. It could be your own hobby, your vocation, something that you do for fun. It could be gardening. It could be guitar playing. It could be, I don't know, making hand puppets for kids. Whatever it happens to be, you know what it is. Everybody's got something that they enjoy doing. They can make money at that online, just by transferring it over from a past time or a hobby or doing it out there on the street and do it on the internet because that's where the gold is, baby. There is gold in cyberspace.

Raven: Let's talk about that. I'm a true believer in the passion, and that's for sure. I can tell you this, Joe. I've certainly found mine.

Joe: I can tell it in your voice. You've got that energy. You've got that vibe. I tell people go watch Donnie Deutsch on TV at night. He's on CNBC. And I say, "Watch him, he's on I think five days a week." And I've been on the show once. One of his things that always shows up, he has said there is never, ever been a successful person on his show, who didn't get their riches from following their passion. That's what, I mean, when you hear something like that, that's a no-brainer. You don't want to work for your living. You want to go and play for your living and if you play for your living, it comes from your passion.

Raven: Absolutely. Well, let's talk about this internet marketing 'because you're right. It is a gold mine.

Joe: Well, the beauty of the internet is that it's so easy to take a chance. There is no scarcity. Even if there's competition, because online, there are so many people trying to buy so much stuff, you don't need the entire market to come to your door to make money from that. You just need a small sliver of that market to come to your door.

Raven: And there's plenty for everyone. And I'm glad you brought that up because I was just here thinking; I bet a lot of listeners are wondering, Joe, how do you make yourself stand out, like a cut above the rest?   You have any suggestions there?

Joe: Yeah, that's a great question. There are several things to do to make yourself stand out and you definitely want to stand out. One rule of thumb is simply "do something different." That's it right there. Do something different. So if everybody else is just putting up a plain website, maybe on your website you can have a little bit of an audio or you can add some more photos or you can add a little video clip. You're doing something different.

Keeping in mind and I don't want to confuse people but there's search engines out there that are always going out there and cataloging all the different websites and so if you put content on your website, content meaning good information, the website will be registered by the search engines and you'll go up in status.

So when somebody goes to Google and they type in gardening or they type in Polish cookbook, or they type in, you know, the puppet socks for kids, you will be more likely to come up higher in rank so that people will find you. But I also believe in thinking out of the box and sending out news releases. This is one the things I learned from writing about PT Barnum. I did a whole book on the great circus promoter and he was one of America's wealthiest people and he Learn more about Joe at his website: http://www.mrfire.com

---

Listen to the full audio of this interview:
http://www.careersfromthekitchentable.com/audios
Plus be sure to visit and subscribe to Raven's popular newsletter and get your free e-book *"The Real Power of Social Networking: Profit on Facebook"* by Regina Baker
http://www.careersfromthekitchentable.com

Lisa Nichols

Author, Speaker, Coach and Charismatic Teacher

You've seen her on Oprah and in the movie *The Secret*. You've seen her on Larry King and she speaks all over the world. She's amazing and she is a powerful woman with a powerful message and she says, you know what? You can be successful. You can bring out your greatness that's within you no matter what. You have to have that "No Matter What" attitude. She is the author of *No Matter What!*

Lisa Nichols is our guest today. She is a bestselling author, a popular public speaker, a powerful coach, and charismatic teacher! If you haven't seen her in *The Secret* you need to go out and get the movie. Strong message in there but she's way beyond that. Lisa Nichols has reached millions, both nationally and internationally with her powerful message of empowerment, service, excellence and gratitude. In addition, Lisa is the founder of *Motivating the Masses* and CEO of *Motivating the Teen Spirit, LLC* and her transformational workshops have impacted the lives of 210 thousand teens and over 1 million adults. Now, we want to think about that. Our teens need some serious guidance, right? And Lisa is the one. I mean she's going to get them straight. If they're a little crooked, she's going to go straighten them out! I love that about her.

Her new book, *No Matter What!* hit 6, not 1, 2, 3, 4, or 5 but 6 bestsellers lists, including the New York Times, in the first 37 days of being released and has already been sold in 20 foreign languages. Lisa, you're all that bag of chips and some M&Ms on the side girlfriend. Welcome to Careers from the Kitchen Table!

Lisa: Thank you, Raven. Thank you so much for your generous, generous introduction. I'm so excited to be with you. We've been talking about this for a while.

Raven: Like the last time you were on *Women Power*, we had an almost two-hour interview. I still get emails about that. That is powerful but today, I appreciate you coming to talk to our business audience, 'cause we need some help up in here.

Lisa: Yes, yes, well I have some. There's so much opportunity in home-based business ownership that I am so, so excited about. I have just recently launched back into doing just a couple of extra projects and the possibility. This is the time for entrepreneurs and home-based businesses to thrive the most, believe it or not, so I'm really excited to be here.

Raven: Yes, I love that. To thrive the most. How exciting is that! Hello, everyone, did you hear that? We can thrive. We don't have to get sad. Right, Lisa?

Lisa: Right. You're not even just surviving the time. This is the thriving. Do you know more millionaires are built during times like this than ever before? This is the time for the creative mind. This is the time for the entrepreneur. This is the time when you can get the distance between you and everything you want is simply possibility and perseverance and so this is that year where all deals are off, all bets are off. It doesn't matter whether you have a PhD or a GED. All that matters is the possibility that you carry. So this is the perfect time. I kid you not. It's the perfect time. I have worked with probably about 150 people in the last six months and helped them to generate and create over a quarter of a million dollars collectively and none of them saw it before we started working together. None of them. So I'm super, super excited.

Raven: Oh, yes! Boy, I'm getting excited. Girl, I'm ready to leave out of here and go pick up the phone and make some sales!

Lisa: Right, right. Reach out to me. One of the things that I understand is that money isn't given and money isn't earned. Money is created. You find the need and you meet the need and you simply put a quantifiable dollar amount to the service that you've provided and then you find your market and you let your market know that you exist. When you can do that and that's not a difficult equation. It requires some creativity but that's how millionaires are built and what I love is that millionaire, the best story of a millionaire is the millionaire that comes from an ordinary woman, an ordinary man choosing every day to make extraordinary decisions. So you don't have to start out extraordinary. You can be ordinary. I was just in Atlanta speaking to about 1400 people and I said, "Listen, you want to make me extraordinary but I'm an ordinary woman who chooses every day to make extraordinary decisions." But what it does, Raven, is it equalizes the playing field. It makes everyone available to play.

I love it. I absolutely love it. I had a woman come to me in March and she said, "My back is against the wall. I don't know what to do. I just started playing with this new home-based business." I said, "Well, you know what? Why don't you play in this?" She went, "I don't have the money to join." I said, "Okay, I'll lend it to you." That was March 3rd. Fifty-seven days later she had generated close to $30,000.

Ordinary people choosing everyday to do extraordinary things and boldly saying, "no matter what." Boldly saying, taking every other option off the table. Most people still have the option of, "What if I don't make it? What if it fails?" See, whenever you slide that "what if, what if" - What if we don't hit our mark? What if my family doesn't…? What if? The moment you start that "what if" then you just decreased your power by like 20%. Every time you say it, 20, 40, 60, 80, and 100. Now you have a deficit of 250% of lack of energy. When you take all the "what ifs" off the table and you say, we're going to build this home-based business no matter what. We're going to produce abundance for our family no matter what and then everything in your body, your fiber, your mental and your spiritual being is in alignment with the no matter what mindset. Remember a no matter what mindset, most people are determined but they haven't gotten a no matter what mindset yet. People ask me, "How can you be so successful, Lisa?" I say, "I take every other option off the table."

Raven: There is no other option but just to go and get it. Hey you got to be in the game to win the game and when you start mentally killing yourself and just setting up failure, you're blowing it big.

Lisa: What's amazing is that most people, they don't even realize that it's unconscious.... it's not a conscious decision to sabotage your success. It's an unconscious reaction because we've been hit so hard with the perception of failure. If something doesn't work, we failed. We've let people down. If your home-based business doesn't work..."You're less than the next person who made it work." When we get that failures lead to success and that you and I have a right to do it all wrong before we ever do it all right, then we welcome those breakdowns. We welcome the systems that aren't working. We welcome the fact that we don't know what we don't know until we know it. We welcome the fact that we need constant coaching. We welcome the fact that we live in a dysfunctional society, in a dysfunctional family and that we're imperfect and that none of us will ever be perfect. The only thing that we have to do is perfectly manage our imperfections. I'll say that again 'because that's a biggie.

We don't ever have to be perfect. We don't ever have to get it perfectly. All we have to learn how to do is perfectly manage our imperfections. When we begin to get all of that and we give ourselves permission to go through the journey, to be in the journey and to have the experience of getting it all wrong while we get it all right within the journey. We give ourselves permission to also be immensely successful, to celebrate abundance, exceed our expectations, over hit our goals, step into a new life, and change our mental, our physical, and our emotional zip code and our financial zip code.

Raven: Lisa, let me ask you this. Okay, that all sounds good. Some people are saying but how the heck can we stay positive and building our business during the time when so many businesses are closing down and people are losing their jobs, how can we do that?

Lisa: Well, first of all, don't make someone else's situation yours. So cut the umbilical cord to everybody else's chaos.

Raven: Cut it! Get the scissors. Cut it off.

Lisa: That's number one and that's not the same move selfishly but to say, "I stand with you, I hold this space for your healing and I am not going to own this experience in my fibers." I didn't sign up. I'm not subscribing. I'm not clicking yes to the invite about the economic situation. My son was being interviewed by a newspaper and the woman who was interviewing him, said, "So how do you feel like the recession has impacted you and your mom?" And my son said, "Oh, my mother doesn't let the recession in our front door."

I am not subscribing to a conversion of lack, scarcity and deprivation. I am not subscribing to that. In this crazy time, I've generated more money in the first quarter of this year than I've generated in the first two quarters of last year. Why? Because I've become more creative. I didn't do the same things I did last year. You can't do the same things and expect to get a different result. Stay focused on what you're creating versus what you're trying to avoid.

So work towards something versus trying to run from something. So don't work because you don't want to be broke, don't work because you're trying to avoid not being able to pay your bills. Work to create abundance, work to create prosperity. You're never going to find prosperity reducing your bottom line, which means cutting out your expenses. "I'm going to stop getting my hair done. I'm going to stop going out to dinner." That's going to put more money in your pocket because you're saving money but it's not going to create abundance, and versus reducing the bottom line, you want to increase the top line. What answer are you to someone else's problem?

If you have a weight loss project then who's looking for someone to be with them? Here's the marginal difference right now between you and any other business. It's going to be your customer care because the first thing that's left in every business is customer care. If you haven't seen customer care gone, you go fly on a couple of airlines and you'll see that you got a seat and that's about it and a seatbelt and the care but all the extra fringes have had to go because they're reducing their costs to do business versus increasing their customer service.

So right now, you want to increase your customer care. You want to take care of your people more. You want to spend a little more time with them. Yes, your days are going to be longer; however, you also get to increase your top line and so the answer to it is be creative. Work for what you are creating versus what you are avoiding. Be willing to reinvent yourself. Be willing to meet your consumer in their current day need, not the 2007 need 'because their 2010 need has some extra things to it. So find out who is your customer and how do you get to them and how do they know that you are the answer to their problem.

Raven: One thing that I have to say something about and that is the customer service part. We do have to really, really get into being, I like to say back in the old days when customer service people walked people to the door and all that kind of stuff.

Lisa: Absolutely. What I do is as a businesswoman, I simply provide my consumer with information, education, and inspiration on multiple platforms. Be it live trainings. Be it workshops. Be it radio like this. Be it a book. So as an infopreneur I'm looking for different ways to meet the needs of my customers. I know for me, my USP, my unique selling proposition is intimacy, closeness and connection. So what I wanted to coach each person, what is your unique selling proposition that makes you distinctively different from everyone else? Find out how to serve the market like it's never been served before at a time that the market says we need you.

People are no longer spending $3 in three different directions. They spend $1 and they're choosing between three different choices so you want to be that choice. How do you rise above the rest? What do you do? It's not a big huge costly shift. Most of the most valuable things that a customer wants are actually free for you to give.

Raven: Right. Now Lisa, I want you to go ahead real quickly, share your website.

Lisa: We have several different trainings that are really powerful. I focus on entrepreneurs, women, and teenagers and so number one is a *No Matter What!* mindset teleseminar that I do. I spend 12 weeks with you, helping you to stand aside your power, push past your limiting beliefs and really take your personal life and your business life to the next level.

The second thing that I really love for those of you who are face to face learners is to invite you to come up to San Diego and join me for the *No Matter What! Mindset Training*. The *No Matter What! Mindset Training* is all about moving the velocity. The final training is *Speak and Write to Make Millions* for anyone that's a speaker, a writer, an author or you have a bestseller in you or you have to speak for a business this training shows you how to build a bestselling book, build a bestselling tour behind it, and lastly, how to make your brand into a multiple revenue stream generator. I teach you the secrets that I wish people would have taught me a long time ago.

That's all on my website at http://www.Lisa-Nichols.com. However, if you're interested, email us at Margaret@Lisa-Nichols.com.

Raven: Oh, thank you so much for being here. I love being with you. Thank you so much from the bottom of my heart.

Lisa: Thank you so much and you continue to be a blessing to the world, girl.

Visit http://www.Lisa-Nichols.com for more information

Listen to the full audio of this interview:
http://www.careersfromthekitchentable.com/audios!
Plus be sure to visit and subscribe to Raven's popular newsletter and get your free e-book *"The Real Power of Social Networking: Profit on Facebook"* by Regina Baker
http://www.careersfromthekitchentable.com

Alex Mandossian

Entrepreneur, Trainer, Improver and Internet Marketing Expert

Boy, do we have a dynamic, just dynamic show. Back in 2005, I stumbled across the name Alex Mandossian and I found out that he taught teleseminars and I said, "Oh, this will be pretty cool. I've been in sales. I can get people on the phone and do teleseminars and make a lot of money" 'cause Alex you see, he makes a lot of money doing this, in his pajamas relaxing, or however he chooses to dress at home, and he teaches thousands and thousands of others to do the same. How cool is that? Well, at that time I was only making a couple of hundred a week so I didn't have much you see but you know what? My husband Larry and my daughter Jamie, they pitched in and we got Alex's course Teleseminars Secrets on a payment plan, and I was so thankful he offered that because that's all I had at that time. Little did I know that just a couple months later 2006 in February to fast forward this story, my mother would be in the hospital getting aneurysms removed and what was supposed to be ten days turned into three weeks in the ICU unit. Well that's -- that's when, my friend, I had my wake up call. Yes, I woke up because I looked at mom and I looked at her situation. I wondered "Oh is she going to make it? Has she lived her dreams? Did she do everything she wanted to do?" Then I quickly started asking myself those very same questions and sadly the answer was no. You see I was settling. I was just going day to day, not dreaming anymore. My dream circle had shrunk completely. Yeah and then I took this course Teleseminars Secrets. I downloaded everything that I could from the previous weeks into my mp3. I took it to the hospital. I prayed for mama of course and when I wasn't praying, I began to work on my plan. I began to work on my dream.

I heard one person Alex interviewed I think the second or third week say rather than do teleseminar, he was going to do a radio show. Well, he did radio shows where he interviewed people, that was the format, and that hit a dream, a buried dream that I had years ago in my teens to be a DJ. But now instead of music being my format I would do interviews, because I learned from Alex if you're not an expert, you go out there and you interview experts and guess what, my friend? That makes you an expert. That's how my show *Women Power Talk Radio* was born and four other shows after that. It started from a Teleseminars Secret's course, went to internet radio show, and now terrestrial radio on CNN radio news. Don't tell me dreams don't come true. Don't tell me you can't do it because you can. That's Alex Mandossian.

Now let me tell you about this man and bring him on because he's got some exciting news to share so let me tell you this, go grab a pen, and be ready to take some copious notes. You're not going to want to miss this. Since 1991, Alex Mandossian had generated over 233 million in sales for his clients and partners via electronic marketing and teleseminars, radio, TV, and the internet. Did I say 233 million? I certainly did. Hoo-hoo chi-ching, chi-ching! Alex personally consulted Dale Carnegie Training, NYU, 1ShoppingCart Corp., Mutuals.com, Trim Spa and Sam's Club. He has hosted teleseminars with many of the world's top thought leaders such as Mark Victor Hansen, Jack Canfield, Steven Covey, Les Brown, T. Harv Eker, Donald Trump, Brian Tracy, Harvey Mackay, and so many more. He is the CEO of Heritage House Publishing Inc., a boutique electronic marketing and publishing company that repurposes written and spoken educational content for worldwide distribution. Alex lives in San Francisco Bay area with his lovely wife Aimee, and his two children that he always talks about, Gabriel and Brianna.

Ladies and gentlemen all across the world help me welcome, my number one mentor, Alex Mandossian. Alex, welcome to Careers from the Kitchen Table. Thank you.

Alex: Well Raven, thank you. It is so good to be here and I'm so proud of you. I just can't believe how far you've come in so little time.

Raven: Oh thank you, my friend. It has definitely been your course. I know inquiring minds just wants to know, "How did you ever get started online?"

Alex: Well the way I started was on television infomercials. I was in the TV infomercial business back in the 1980s and it was so fast. You could get results so quickly and I thought, "Wow, this is fascinating." It's not like direct mail or postcards. You get results back and you know if you're failing or you're succeeding, and you can stop the media buys and then one day I think it was 1998, I'm sitting in front of my computer and I'm just hanging out on a website and I thought to myself, "Wow, I've been here for about an hour. That would have been over $60,000 in media buys for an infomercial. You know what? I got the skills. Why don't I go online?"

And I did it and from that moment on, I started marketing online, both as a communication medium and as a distribution medium and because I'm at home, I mean one of the things that happens when you work out of your home, you get colds when the kids bring it from school but the nice thing is you got a 17-second commute. So if you got to go back and sleep you don't have to drive back home. So there are pros and cons but I love working from home and the internet and teleseminars allow me to do that. This is kind of a teleseminar in a way. It's an electronic web radio show and it's not social media so it's kind of a teleseminar but the one too many approach is I think what you really set into and you are a good interviewer so this is going to be fun. Take it easy on me, alright?

Raven: I sure will. Alex, one of the things I know that many people that know your success including me have always wondered you know, "Did Alex ever hit any bump in the roads? Did he have any challenges? Because you're just a smooth operator."

Alex: Well, I mean you get to see the result but the evolution of the result, I was on a park bench in 1989 and I was $242,000 in debt but most of it wasn't mine. My friends didn't want to have anything to do with me because I wasn't you know fun to be around. My family was disappointed and I was wondering, "How am I going to get out of this hole?" And you know I know what it feels like to go hungry. I know what it feels like to be on a park bench. Now, I love to say that it was snowing and it was brutally cold but it was in Los Angeles. It was in McArthur Park so it was a little bit comfortable but you know I was on a park bench and I couldn't pay for gas. I didn't have enough money.

And on that bench I was there about a week, I watched this woman, this heavyset woman. She walked up to a bird feeder. You know those bird feeders that you put some change in and then you turn the knob and then seeds come out, you know what those look like? Well she went to a bird feeder and she wanted to feed pigeons and she was walking towards the pigeons and the pigeons were walking away and then she showed them the bird seed and they were walking towards her when she turned around to walk away. And then when she turned around again to walk towards them, they walked a little slower and then when she turned around again the distance became closer and closer and closer until they had enough rapport with her 'til she got down on one knee and started feeding them from the palm of her hand and that's where I learned how to sell, that's where I learned how to promote.

If you do it too hard in the beginning you know, you're going to shoo people away. If you do it too passively, then they're not going to come and feed from you but if you are willing to go back and forth and do the dance and court them like you do, then you can have them feed from your hand. And that was the turning point. I'd love to say that, "Hey, the next day I became a multimillionaire but it took me ten more years before I had that seventh zero on my net worth and it turned an annual income into a monthly income and then into an hourly income several times within a five-year period and I'm just grateful because it's the students that helped fund all the new marketing ideas and I love being generous with new ideas because we have strategic alliances just like this. I mean here, I'm the interviewee but you were a student so the tables have turned and I just love the way that that works out.

Raven: Oh yeah. How sweet it is. How sweet it is. Thank you for sharing your story because I heard a little bit of it I think one day in your car, we were talking about you know that you were on a park bench and I knew that the audience would want to know that. I think it's important that people know where we came from because they know that they can do it. If you can do it, I can do it and I'm always inspired by other people's stories. Alex, your toughest, toughest challenge, you know one of those rough tough don't start no stuff challenges you know what I mean? What was it?

Alex: Just disappointment. You know my family being disappointed in me. I was a great athlete; I was a great student, and my first attempt at building a business I just completely failed. I mean fell flat on my face and I didn't get out of it for seven years. I never claimed bankruptcy but it was like a seven-year period where sometimes I'd wake up three o'clock in the morning and just, you know weep because there was just no way out and I think the darkest moment was when I gave up hope.

Now we're going to talk about productivity. You know hope is the beginning of confidence. You know hope and faith are so important. Hope isn't knowing how to get from point A, where you are now, to point B, where you want to be. Hope is simply knowing there is a point B and I gave up for about a week and I'll never forget that and you know, I'm disappointed that I did give up because that was a wasted week and you know things happen but it's how we respond to those things that make all the difference so pain I think is inevitable but suffering is optional. I don't know who said that but I believe it to be true and oftentimes you know, the last thing that we're willing to give up is our own suffering for whatever reason.

So once I was done with it and I was done with the "poor me" period I just got back on my feet and I said, "Hey you know, I can't go any lower than this. I'm at the bedrock. There are no, there's no space between my shoulder blades and the wall so you can't even you know put a piece of paper in between. I might as well just move forward so I just burned the ships behind me and moved on and seven years later, it all worked out. Very fortunate.

Raven: Yeah, boy did it work out. You sure brought up some key things 'because you're right. Sometimes we get so disappointed in ourselves for letting family and friends down, or for letting our self down, that we just give up. So I understand which you were talking about you know and it's so important for us to just kind of push past that pain, I call it, Alex, that we can unleash that unstoppable power that I truly feel we all have within us and you certainly did. And I'm glad you did and thousands and thousands of other people are glad you did because you certainly have changed not just my life but many people across the world life.

Now *Teleseminar Secrets* is just huge. Everybody knows about it. What inspired you to say, "I'm going to do this on the phone?"

Alex: Well, I wanted to be a professional speaker but I didn't want to travel. I wanted to stay home so I could catch my children's colds when I came back home. So what I did instead is I just stayed in my, you know I converted a bedroom into an office in the first home we had and started doing teleseminars which is better than one to one, even one to two people you get 100% more people on the line. I will get 100, 200, 300, and what would end up happening is I have a lot to say on how to create a business through teleseminars. So I was doing teleseminars and as you know, *Teleseminar Secrets* is a teleseminar series on how to build teleseminars into your marketing mix and it's more than just teleseminars. It's about professional speaking. It's about marketing. It's about web pages and blogging, and now social media but I just use it as an excuse because no one owned that brand. No one had that niche of teleseminars.

It just, it changed my life so the spoken word is very powerful. The Gettysburg Address was spoken before it was written; the Sermon on the Mount was spoken before it was written. The sayings of Lao Tzu were spoken sayings before it was written, and so I think the spoken word, whether you are an auditory learner or visual learner or tactile learner, I don't think that has a lot to do with it. The spoken word is so flexible that you could be listening to me anywhere and it doesn't require a hundred percent of your attention. You could be in traffic, you could be on a Stairmaster, in a gym, you could be walking your dog, or mowing your lawn, or you know taking your kids to the school and still get a little piece of marketing advice and recommendations on a pre-recorded teleseminar so that's why I love it and it's highly leveragable.

Raven: There you go. Love it. Love it. Okay, so let's go into detail about your definition of productivity. Go ahead and give us that definition.

Alex: Well it's five words: maximum results in minimum time. The goal is just to achieve more. You got 86,400 seconds a day. You can't manage time. You can manage what you do with the time you're given. You've got 168 hours a week. Everyone has the same amount of time. It's how productive you are during that time that makes the difference. So the results, what you're actually getting in minimum time, that is productivity and that really is what a teleseminar is and the reason that I started to move towards productivity is because that's what I've been doing all along. Teleseminars just happen to be one spoke in the bicycle wheel of productivity. The hub is the message, the spokes are all the different ways to get to the wheel and the wheel is the market so productivity is maximum results in minimum time. Five word definition.

Raven: Yeah, hear hear. Wow! This has been amazing. You have really given us some tips. Thank you, Alex Mandossian! This has been great. Alex, you want to ahead and give me your website so they can be Googling that right now.

Alex: Yeah, you can go there and just to go to ProductiveToday.com or if you go to Google, type in "the productivity guy" and you'll see I'll pop up number one.

Raven: Alex, thank you so much for being here and making another dream come true. Thank you for just being a part of my life and for all that you do for me and all the thousands of people all over the world. Thank you so much.

Alex: You're welcome. Is it okay if I said I love you on the air?

Raven: Yes. Yes, it is.

Alex: I love you, Raven.

Raven: Oh thank you, Alex. I love you, too.

Listen to the full audio of this interview:
http://www.careersfromthekitchentable.com/audios
Plus be sure to visit and subscribe to Raven's popular newsletter and get your free e-book *"The Real Power of Social Networking: Profit on Facebook"* by Regina Baker
http://www.careersfromthekitchentable.com

Terri Levine
The Guru of Coaching

Our guest today is Dr. Terri Levine and she is not only a dynamic speaker but she's also an international Master Certified Coach as well as the founder of *Coaching Institute*. Check her out. Her program is world renowned as the number one place for coach training and she has trained over 4,000 coaches. Terri has also authored bestsellers including *Work Yourself Happy*, *Stop Managing, Start Coaching*, *Coaching for an Extraordinary Life*, and *The Successful Coach*. Her newest book due out in a few weeks is called *Coaching is for Everyone*.

I met Terri a couple of years ago and was so impressed with her genuineness, content and expertise that I invited her to be a co-host on my Amazing Women in Business show. She is a phenomenal talk show host. She has her own radio show as well and she's going to be speaking today about *"7 Step Process to Generate New Clients at Incredible Rates"*, no matter what kind of business you're in." Hey Terri. How are you doing?

Terri: Hey, it's great to be with you. I'm doing spectacular!

Raven: Well, thank you very much. Coaching is such a great business to transition to from your job, isn't it?

Terri: It really is and what it allows you to do is take the skills, the brilliance, the talent that you already have, bring it into the field of coaching, learn coaching skills, and then not only make a lot more money 'cause you will, but you get the opportunity to use your brilliance serving others and really sharing your passion with the world and hey, that's what life's about.

Raven: Absolutely. For those people that do not know you can you just maybe share just a tad bit of your story before we jump into our questions?

Terri: Well, I'll be honored to. Thanks for asking. I was like most people working at a J-O-B, and I was miserable. I have to be honest and just tell people right up front I was miserable. I didn't like the work. I didn't like the people and it wasn't using my brilliance. It was president of a national healthcare company and it was all about laying people off and meeting budgets and it just wasn't me. I knew what was me was helping people, being with people, and connecting with people and the minute that I found coaching which is gosh, it's 11 years ago now. The minute I heard about this profession, I have read that it was the fastest growing home-based business in the United States, the number one money-making home-based business, immediately I quit a high six-figure J-O-B and walked away and I said, "This is what I'm supposed to be doing" and Raven, you know I have never for an instant looked back and I'm so happy. My life is so abundant, so magnificent and ever since I've become a coach, I have a spiritual connection. I have great finances. I have more free time. I devote more time to community, family, and friends and you know what, I'm living a magnificent life.

Raven: Hmm, that sounds so good, living a magnificent life. That's awesome and you're so right, Terri, 'because that's one of the reasons I always love to interview you and just speak with you because you're so uplifting. You're always in a great mood. You can tell that you're definitely living your passion. Okay, let's jump to the questions 'because I know time is going to fly. We've got so much ground to cover so let's start with what is the 7 step secret process to generating clients you're talking about?

Terri: All right. I'm going to share these and I call them the seven step recipe for success. Number one, create a compelling vision. Let me just explain what I mean. You need to imagine your ideal clients or customers. You need to picture them coming to you so fast and so easily and so effortlessly that it makes your head spin. So you need to create those visions and then you need to spend about 10 minutes a day reviewing this vision.

Second part of our recipe: Record what we call inspired actions. An inspired action is something that comes to you at any time. Mine come in the shower. I'm in the shower like, "Oh! This is a great idea" or maybe when you're driving your car but it's always a surge of energy and inspiration. You know what I mean? You get this like, "Oh! That would be a great idea" and take the actions that the universe reveals to you and write them down. Record these actions so you don't lose them and these are the actions that help you feel on fire. We have to grab them. We don't want to lose them.

Number three is script your day. I'll explain it. Script your day before you even start your day. So I get up first thing in the morning. I mentally think about the end of my day. I look backwards and I script everything. I script how I want to feel, what I want to do. Everything. And this exercise, Raven, is incredibly powerful because if you have a very big vision, that can feel like a pipe dream but when you script it, it brings it to your reality and here's a secret. I'll tell why. You can't tell the difference. The human brain simply cannot tell the difference between reality and fantasy. This is a cool secret. This is a biggie. You can actually reprogram your mind by repetitively seeing and feeling whatever you want as a reality now, and I have to tell you, scripting has changed my life. Highly recommend people do that. It's fun too.

Number four. Complete five things. Just five, okay? Five things everyday to attract clients - just five. The problem with a lot of entrepreneurs is they try to do everything at once, but that really isn't the way to do it. It's continual, consistent action that makes a difference so here's what I want everybody to do. Just pick five things and do them no matter what. They're your priority for the day. It could be writing letters, sending postcards, doing an email campaign, having lunch with someone. Five things every single day. Make sure those things are fun 'cause if you don't like doing them you won't do them.

Raven: That is good 'cause you're right, Terri. So many of us, I know I do, you wake up. You feel so overwhelmed and you don't know which direction to go so you start trying to go it all a little and the day's gone. You haven't accomplished anything.

Terri: Number five, you take all of the things that I'm giving you kind of the assignments from everything that I'm teaching you right here in these secrets and every single day, create a list of how you are making progress on them. Every single day, make a list of how you are creating progress on them. Because sometimes you know what? We don't even think we're making progress. We don't get it. We don't know we're making progress and it's really important that we do this. So even your tiny baby steps and you know me, I'm a big fan of baby steps. Very, very important.

Raven: Okay, number six.

Terri: List your results and not just your results in terms of, "Oh, I got this. Oh, I got that." but how you are feeling - your thoughts, your feelings, your words, your actions. Make sure that you list your results and how you were feeling in each and every moment. So when I go through a day and I do my five actions, I take a look at how I was feeling during that time frame and kind of amp it up, getting more of those great feelings.

Number seven: This is an easy one. Read your goals before bed. You know everybody's heard this one but do we do it? We don't do this. We need to do this. Right before bed, read your goals. Spend some time with them. Really feel your goals and then I also suggest to all of my clients to make a mental inventory of what's working. We're human beings, right? So what our brain likes to do is it likes to focus on what's not working and whatever we put our attention to expands and it grows even more. So instead, you want to take some time and you want to say, "Oh! What's my day like? What happened today? Let me feel my day again. Oh, I had a great conversation. It was really important. Let me write down that conversation."

Let me share this tip. I call this, Raven, keeping your evidence. Keeping your evidence, so what you do is you write down all the evidence of things that are great, that are happening, that are working and I'll share this with you. I collect what I call driftwood. Are you ready for this? I've never talked to you about this one.

Here is what driftwood is. You're out there floating around on a boat. You're lost. You don't know where the island is. You think you've disappeared. And what can happen is you start to notice, "Hmm, there is a little piece of bark floating by me and my boat. That means there are trees somewhere. I'm near land." Its evidence and it begins to show you that it's coming.

You're getting there. You're getting there. So keep those driftwoods every single day. Collect them and notice them. Driftwoods are coming to you.

Raven: Driftwoods are coming to you. I like that one. Terri, you always come up with some good ones. That's a good one. Wonderful. I want to go back to where you were talking about reviewing your goals and visions. Why is that so important for this process?

Terri: You know everything that happens, happens because of feelings, okay? And when we don't review our goals and our visions and we kind of get down about things then we think, "Ah, it's not happening. It's not coming." The negativity sets in, and when the negativity sets in we just can't get ourselves feeling good and into good action. We get stuck. We have got to make sure that we constantly review what we want, what's important to us, and we get ourselves amped up over and over and over again. So review it and I'll say it again, feel it.

Raven: Feel it. Yeah, now that was my next question 'because you talked about feeling a whole lot so why do you talk about feeling so much? Is that that big of a part of everything?

Terri: Oh Yes! Here's the deal. We are human feelers. We are not beings. We feel everything. Everything in our experience happens because of feeling. So there's a law of the universe, one of many, and it's called the law of resonance and the law of resonance says that everything vibrates. Everything has a certain frequency and vibrates. So if you're sitting in a chair right now, that chair is vibrating. Your telephone is vibrating. You are vibrating. Everything is vibrating and when we vibrate, we vibrate and attract things to us.

Raven: Don't want to attract the wrong thing, that's for sure.

Terri: And you need to make sure that you're vibrating to attract the right thing just as you just said. So what you want to make sure that you're doing is that you are constantly and I ask myself this question. It may sound quite of weird but it's a great question. How am I vibrating? How am I vibrating? Okay, so if I'm vibrating, "Oh, things are not coming to me" and "I'm not doing so well" and those kinds of things, guess what's going to happen?

Raven: You're going to bring all the bad things, the things not going so well to you.

Terri: Right, and so then your energy is more negative.

Raven: It's negative. It's lower. You start stressing more, eating more 'because your stressed out and doing all the wrong things. So you have to shift that, huh? Have that quick paradigm shift.

Terri: You have to very quickly shift it. Very quickly shift it or you will be in a state of saying, "Things aren't working. Things aren't going well. It's not good. It's not happening." You won't be noticing the driftwood, and when all of those things happen, you now are attracting exactly that. So you're attracting what you just said you don't want to attract.

Raven: Be careful how you vibrate. Be careful how you think and be careful what you speak about, huh? Okay, so now we know why feelings are so important. How can you tell if an action is the right action because a lot of people they get up and they have so much to do and they do just a little bit, a little bit, a little bit and they're not quite shifting, making the right move, doing the right things that's going to bring out the opportunity because that's what we need, right? We've got to stay productive.

Terri: That's a very good question and I recently said to a client, an inspired action is not like a burning bush. It's not like, "Ooh! I'm on fire!" An inspired action shows up and you feel good about it. You go, "Oh that would be easier. Oh, I'd be aligned with that." I'll give you an actual one.

I have my new book coming up. I'm all excited and I'm trying to think of whom can I tell and who can I share it with? And my inspired actions come in the shower so here I am showering this morning and I think to myself, "Oh my gosh! I know exactly what to do. I'm going to tell everybody on my social networks" and I got out of the shower, came to the computer and this is going to be so much fun and that was an inspired action.

Now how do I know if it's a good one? I check myself and say, How does that feel? Does it feel good? Does it feel like, "Oh, that'd be fun; I can hardly wait to do it"? Then it's perfect.

Raven: I like an inspired action. I think that's the first time I've heard about that, Terri. Another good one you threw out. All right, we've got a couple more questions but I want to talk a little bit as to those people that are sitting at home and they may really know this coaching thing or really know how to cook or fix cars whatever it is. How can they take that passion, and begin to say, "This could be a home business?"

Terri: Make a list of the things that you love to do that are your passion, whether it be catering, cooking, baking, teaching, writing, hiking. I don't care. Just make a list. Don't worry about how you make money from it. Then think about coaching someone to do that. So if you're great at making brownies and you're great at baking cakes, there are tons of people that want to learn that. If you know great techniques and strategies for eating well, being healthy and getting motivated, you can coach people around that. So just begin to think of, "Hey, what comes natural to me? What am I good at?" Think of it as sharing your compassion with the world.

Terri: It's just amazing to look at the diversity of students we have. We've got people who are massage therapists who are adding coaching. We've got teachers, chiropractors, dentists, stay-at-home moms and dads, parent coaching, sales coaching, just forget this whole thing that the government loves to instill fear in us and loves to tell us, "Oh my gosh, recession." "People are losing their jobs. Gas prices going up." Gang, take control of your own life and say, "My attitude of gratitude makes me a wealthy individual." So I just start coaching and serving other people. I'm not going to rely on a J-O-B, just over broke. I'm not going to rely on the government. I'm not going to care if gas goes to $5 a gallon because I can create my own abundance.

Raven: Can you share one of your success stories using this process that took a passion or a job that they did and turned it into a business?

Terri: I have one that I'm so anxious to share so thank you for asking. It's just so exciting. This person was working as a physical therapist until she was about 36 and she had a car accident and it's created a lot of stress and trauma on her back and she found that when she was doing physical therapy it just was too much for her. So she thought she was going to be on disability. She was really depressed about it, got coach training and she said, "I don't know what to do with this because I only know how to do is be a physical therapist" but we found out she absolutely was stellar at creating programs for people where they could get fit without doing any strenuous exercise. Stuff they can actually do like sitting at their computer during the day. I call it like yoga at the computer. It's very cool. It's amazing stuff. So what she does is she coaches people on how to break their day into segments where they get about 100% more movement than they're getting right now. They get more fit. They lose weight. They create more energy and they get healthier. All the things that she was able to do as a physical therapist she's now doing by telephone with clients around the world and by the way I have to share this. When she was a physical therapist she said she made below $60K. I think$ 62 or $63 thousand. She's only been a coach for seven months and she's made $130 something thousand dollars at home coaching people and working like 20 hours instead of 50 a week.

Raven: Where can people find out more about you and your program?

Terri: www.TerriLevine.com and www.CoachInstitute.com

Wally Amos

Cookie Man, Inspirational Speaker

Our featured guest is Wally. His name has been a household word since he's been in the public eye for over 30 years. As a professional speaker, Wally is highly valued for his charismatic, warm style and his inspiring "do it", positive attitude. He is an author, motivational speaker, lecturer and entrepreneur. Best known as the founder of The Famous Amos Cookie Company which pioneered the gourmet cookie industry, he is a man of many causes. Wally Amos is living proof that the success principles he lives by actually work! He has the experience of multiple entrepreneurial endeavors to share with you so sit back and relax...but don't get too comfortable. Get ready to take some copious notes 'cause it's not about what you hear, it's about taking action after you hear it.

You were responsible for opening the world's, I believe, first store selling chocolate chip cookies. What inspired you to start Famous Amos Cookies?

Wally: Well first of all I wanted to do something that I really love doing and I loved chocolate chip cookies since I was 12 years old. I've loved baking them since 1970. So I'd been an agent and a personal manager in show business for a combination of about 14 years and got tired of doing that and wanted to do something else and didn't know what it was. But one evening the latter part of 1974 I was having dinner with a friend. Her name is B.J. Gilmore and she'd been Quincy Jones' secretary, and we were good friends. My office was next to Quincy's at A&M Records. And somehow the conversation got around to cookies and she said "You know, Wally, you and I should open a store selling chocolate chip cookies together." And then she immediately followed that with, "I've got a friend that I could get to put up the money."

So Raven when she said that she had my full attention. And it was at that moment that I made the commitment, that I made the decision to open one store selling chocolate chip cookies. B.J. never found her friend but I found mine and Helen Reddy and Marvin Gaye and Artie Mogull. In five months I was selling cookies because I was motivated, I was inspired, I was excited, I was enthusiastic. All of those things create wonderful results.

Raven: I caught what you said at first you said you made the decision and it all starts there, doesn't it?

Wally: It does and I think that's even more powerful than making the decision what comes as a package deal is making the commitment. Commitment is "I will". It's not "I hope", or "I guess", or "Maybe", or "I'll try". No, when you commit to do something you say, "I will do this regardless" and once you have that commitment in hand nothing can stop you.

Raven: I know starting out there had to be a lot of challenges that you faced. So can you share with us how you got past any of the particular challenges that you found yourself facing?

Wally: Everyday was a challenge because I had never opened a retail store before so for me it was all a challenge. But I'll give you another definition of challenge. Challenge is just an opportunity for growth. When you confront what it is that is challenging you, you will go through it and usually it's just getting past the fear. There is a friend who sends inspirational messages everyday and the message that I got today is so powerful.

Raven: Can you share it?

Wally: Yes. It was by actually Eleanor Roosevelt.

"You gain strength, courage and confidence by every experience by which you really stop to look fear in the face."

The thing that stops most people is fear. They fear that they're not good enough, they fear that they don't know what they're doing, they fear that they can't do stuff. It's just one fear after another. When you confront that which you fear the most, you can't help but succeed because you do gain strength, courage and confidence. But there's a great thing about fear also. The word actually says False Evidence Appearing Real. What you fear, it doesn't exist and if it does exist, it only exists in your mind, not in someone else's mind. So when you can grow beyond your fear and know that you can do anything that you set your mind to, regardless of your lifestyle, regardless of your education, regardless of your experience, but you are capable of doing whatever you think of because if you couldn't do it, you never would have thought of it because everything starts with a thought.

And thank God for me that I didn't totally understand that at that time but I've always been a relevantly positive person and I understood that I could open one store selling chocolate chip cookies. I'd been baking cookies for five years clearly. I knew how to make 'em but I didn't know how to have a retail store but it was just one thing after another. It's common sense. If you think about what you want to do, the answers will come. If you start figuring it out, the answers will come. You can't sit back and say, "Well I don't know how to do this." And then there's the thing is people start calling everybody asking them, I get so many people asking me how to do stuff. I don't know. I mean I didn't know how to open a retail store but I figured it out. I am a high school dropout.

Whatever it is that you want to do, you have to start. You have to just go do it. And don't let the economy bother you. Don't let anything stop you. Be positive regardless and move forward with your idea. That's the key, man. That's all I've done. That's all I continue to do.

Any business, any idea that you come up with, how will it get done if you don't do it? You're going to wait for somebody else to do it? You're going to wait for your husband, your wife, your mother, and your friends. You're going to wait for somebody to tell you when is the best time to do it? You're going to look at your astrological chart and see when is the perfect? No, the best time to do anything is when you get the idea. I mean that is the only time. When you get the idea, that's the time to do it. See here's the thing people don't understand, ideas do not come to you exclusively.

More than one person can tune into the universe, the ideas in the universe. So if you don't respond to them, someone else will and then what will happen later, when that idea becomes a reality in someone else's life? You will say that person stole my idea. You can't own ideas if you don't respond to them then someone else will. So that's why it's important to do it when you get the idea because you're just one of maybe millions that got the same idea.

Raven: You're so right and I've heard that over and over again, and that makes the difference of the successful ones, the inventors actually having the invention and the other person's just thinking about it.

Wally: Exactly. And you say, "Oh, this person stole my idea." No, you don't own this. You can't own an idea. No. You don't own anything really. Listen, you come in the world buck naked, you're going to leave buck naked. You will take nothing with you. You've never seen a U-Haul following a hearse. So the idea is to use yourself up while you are here. You know don't be saving stuff because you're going to die and leave it. People got tons of stuff saved in self-storage places. They die and there it is. So the idea is to do it now. Don't wait. Do it now. The best time in the world to do anything is right now.

Raven: Right now. Figure out the how along the way.

Wally: Absolutely, and you got to rely on something spiritual. Influence I think also because the reality is ideas come through you and not from you. They come from a much higher source than you, but they are channeled through you. So you are just a channel for ideas. And you want to be an open and clear channel to realize that there is a greater force in the universe than you and that all ideas come from that source. I think it's a great secret to one being successful, but our ego gets in the way and we want to believe that we're doing everything and we can't do anything. All you can do is fail. The only thing you can do by yourself is fail. So you're going to need a team of people and you're going to need God on your side 'cause God is always on your side. If you think that God is no longer with you, guess who moved?

In five months I was selling cookies. When I decided, when B.J. and I had that meeting that night and I made the commitment, that's the power in commitment. Can I share a poem with you?

There's a poem that is written by Goethe. It's in my book *The Power in You, and* Commitment is on chapter 4, page 75. First of all, it's called "The Power of Commitment" written by the German writer, Goethe.

"Until one is committed, there is hesitancy, the chance to draw back-- Concerning all acts of initiative (and creation), there is one elementary truth that ignorance of which kills countless ideas and splendid plans: that the moment one definitely commits oneself, then Providence moves too. All sorts of things occur to help one that would never otherwise have occurred. A whole stream of events issues from the decision, raising in one's favor all manner of unforeseen incidents and meetings and material assistance, which no one could have dreamed would have come his way."

Are you in earnest? That's asking, "Are you really serious? Are you really committed?

"And seek this very minute whatever you can do. Whatever you can do or dream you can begin it. Boldness has genius, power, and magic in it. Only engage, and the mind grows heated." Begin. Folks, *"begin now, and then the task will be completed."*

Ah! That's a powerful piece. If you know that that's the way life is, if you know that you are the cause and effect of everything in your life, then it's not unbelievable. It is incredibly believable! But you know, the thing also it works every time. So commitment worked for me 34 years ago when I started Famous Amos. Commitment also worked for me four years ago when I started a company in Hawaii called Chip and Cookie – chipandcookie.com.

Yes, cookie dough, chip and cookie dough. We got two retail stores here in Hawaii and we sell our cookies online. This is my original cookie. This is my personal recipe. This is the same recipe that made me famous. This is not the recipe that Famous Amos cookies use today but this is the recipe that I used to create Famous Amos. So I'm resurrecting, I have resurrected that recipe.

Raven: Hey, Wally, I want to talk to you about the economy because you know a lot of people are really having a hard time dealing with this. My thing is cut the TV off. Don't listen to the negativity.

Wally: And don't read the papers. And you know, Raven? I'm not interested in the economy. I have no control over the economy. Control the controllable. Control the things you can control in your sphere of influence. I'm not in control. I'm not in charge of the economy.

Raven: Yeah, and I like what you said because that's what I was going to ask you what's the biggest suggestion you can throw out to those listeners that are worried about their business and the economy right now? You just said it. Don't worry about it.

Wally: Two things, maybe even three things. First of all, stop worrying! Because the literal translation of worry is "to strangle" and guess who you're strangling when you worry? Yourself. Yeah, so quit killing yourself. Stop worrying. Start focusing on answers and solutions. That's the only way you will save your business, by focusing on answers and solutions and doing it every single day. And here is the kicker though, above and beyond everything else, be positive regardless, every second of every single day, folks.

No one has ever created a business from being negative. No one has ever written a great piece of music by being negative. No one has ever built a skyscraper by being negative. You create other things from being positive. You grow your business by being positive.

Focus on answers and solutions. What do you need to do today to get your business going? This Chip and Cookie business? I am skating on thin ice because I've run out of money a couple of times already, and don't know where the next batch is coming from. But the one thing I do know, it is not necessary to print any additional money for me to get the money that I need. It is already in circulation. Another thing I do know in order for me to get the money I must stay in business. I must keep the doors open somehow, some way. I don't need to know the answer.

Raven: Wally Amos, give me your website one more time.

Wally: http://www.ChipandCookie.com. It's one-stop shopping. So it's not only about cookies it's about food for the soul, food for the mind.

Dr. J.B. Hill

Grandson of Napoleon Hill

Today I have the pleasure and honor on having a very special guest. His name is Dr. JB Hill, the grandson of Napoleon Hill. Now let me tell you a little bit about him. Dr. Hill was born in Morgantown, West Virginia. He's the son of David Hill, the youngest son of Napoleon Hill and Florence Hornor. He graduated from high school in 1966 and spent time in the Merchant Marines until 1969 when he was drafted into service as a private with the United States Marine Corps.

Now by 1973, he had been promoted five times to the rank of staff sergeant and given the opportunity to attend Vanderbilt University, where he spent three years earning a Bachelor's Degree in Mechanical Engineering. At graduation, he was commissioned as a second lieutenant and commenced service in the Marines as a field artillery officer. He later earned a Master's Degree in Mathematics from the Naval Postgraduate School. As an officer, he held command twice. Led a team of military advisors into Southeast Asia, briefed the Soviet General Staff, served as aide-de-camp to two Marine Corps generals, taught mathematics at the U.S. Naval Academy, and served in many critical billets at the battalion, and regimental level. He is certified in scuba, mountain, cold weather, and jungle warfare and is a graduate of the Army's Command and General Staff College.

JB is a wonderful guy. You're going to enjoy listening to him because he's a man that's authentic. He speaks from the heart and if all of you that have followed all my shows, you know I'm really big about having people on that are authentic, you know inside that you can trust what they're saying because they speak from their heart and I love that about him. So without further ado JB Hill! JB, welcome to Careers from the Kitchen Table.

JB: Thank you, Raven. I hope I can move up to that introduction.

Raven: Sure you can. Careers from the Kitchen Table is all about assisting our listeners with having a plan B and to get into the mindset of what it will take to have a home-based business. We have lots of listeners JB they have had a home-based business for a while but they're finding themselves going through ups and downs and ups and downs and of course you know the economy's beating them up. So we are just thrilled to have you here 'cause I know we are going to be talking about some of your grandfather Napoleon Hill's principles and how people can start applying this whether they're working a career, a job, or a home based business. But since we're a business show, we'll talk in that aspect. Before we get going with our questions, why don't you share with the listeners just a little of your story I know I told a little bit but we want you to have an opportunity to share as well.

JB: Okay. Yeah, I'm the only son of my father David Hill who's the youngest son of Napoleon Hill. I have two sisters. My dad, much like Napoleon in that he had incredible looks and incredible brain bar. He also is like Napoleon Hill in that he had a large number of failures as well and neither one of them achieved success of the path. My dad's greatest success probably was marrying my mom. He met her during the war. He was flying bombers out of England. He met my mom and they had the kind of a romance that they write love stories about. He could have rotated back to the United States after 25 missions but he stayed and flew 55 combat missions and every time he flew his chance of dying was one in eight. He'd take a 12-hour train ride to see her for 15 minutes in the station and then ride all the way back on the train and then the next day fire. They had that kind of love affair that sustained them for 60 years.

Napoleon Hill

Raven: Just hearing about your dad in the military, is that obviously where you picked that up?

JB: My ending up in the marines was a culmination of my own poor decision making as a young man. I ended up being drafted like a lot of young men, you start off in life, you want to be independent, and independence really means financial independence and until you are financially independent, you really cannot make your own decisions. Once I discovered that, I became financially independent and the way I did it was through the service. So I was out on my own making my own decisions from the time I was 18 and a half probably.

Raven: Well, it sounds like you always had a strong mindset. I've read that you once said that you certainly did not receive any of the success genes from your granddad. Elaborate on that.

JB: Well, I don't think there's such a thing. I really don't and if there was, my dad didn't get it so how could he pass it on to me, right? And Napoleon himself, I mean his life had its ups and downs. I mean he started Martha Washington's Candies for example. That was my grandmother's recipes.

JB: In Chicago and he lost that. He started two magazines and lost them. He started a number, a college for to teach his philosophy of success and a number of things came into play, the depression and the war. During the war, people weren't trying to get ahead. They were trying to survive so the success industry just wasn't there and so he had a large number of failures. And ask my dad. My dad flunked out of school three or four times and finally, when he did go back to school, he's had a wife and three children and he drove a taxi cab to support himself while he was going to school after the war. But it took a long time for my dad to reach the point where he you know, as brilliant as he was and as handsome as he was that he realized that his life was up to him, and he had to do something. And I think that was part of my dad's problem. He was the youngest son and the poorest relative of the richest family in town. Does that make sense? The expectations that you're going to be better than you are but you're only what you are and what you produce and Dad didn't produce.

Raven: Yeah. I remember it I guess it was grade school when I first heard this little saying, "if it's meant to be, it's up to me." So that's kind of true, isn't it?

JB: That's exactly right. When Napoleon gave me the book when I was 12, I wasn't ready for it. I read the book and I said, "It's a pretty good book you know but it wasn't until I was ready to receive the book and even at that point, I had to accept it on faith to make that commitment. You have to do that at times and whether if you want to develop spiritually and you have to accept the things on faith and then proceed as if it's true and then the inalienable truth, if it's there, will become apparent to you.

Raven: You brought up a key thing when you said I was ready, meaning open to it at that time. Yeah, because if we're not open to things, we miss opportunities.

JB: That's absolutely right because our mind shuts down because we don't want to do this. It's hard to do this and there's only when we're forced that, we reach that point when we know we're forced to do it, that we have to do something, right? And then we start looking for other things and the possibilities of other things start to become open to us when we start seeing clearly, this is what we have to do. Understand that our own happiness is really depended upon ourselves. It's not dependent on other people. It's always depended upon ourselves and the same thing is true with success. What we do in life is dependent on what we do in life, not what someone else does for us.

Raven: That's a big one. I know one day when we were speaking, you were talking about that you thought, was it applied faith was one of the strongest principles in the book?

JB: Well it actually depends on where you are in your life. For me at that time, it wasn't applied faith. I mean that was certainly part of it because I had to accept it on faith. But I had to choose a goal and definitive purpose because if you don't have something you working toward and it may not be your life's ambition but you got to have some goal that you're working toward. Otherwise, you're a piece of wood drifting in the tides controlled by forces instead of being in control of the tides. And so that was the biggest step for me at that time. Certainly the mastermind principle that that wasn't something I needed at that time. I'm on the position where I needed the outside skill, I needed to control myself. I didn't need a group of people to control me or provide me information.

Later on in life, when I decided to go to medical school, the success I achieved in accomplishing that goal was probably cosmic habit force because I had been successful as I needed to. I knew that the philosophy of success would work if I applied it and so I applied it and it was just kind of on automatic. It was a cook book by that point. Just follow the recipe and it's going to work and I knew it was going to work but back in the early days, it was, "Well, gee! I never made this before what it's going to taste like?

And along the way, when I became a senior officer, a field grade officer in the military, you make decisions but you actually have a mastermind group. You have input from your operations officer, your logistics officer, your intelligence officer, and you bring in everything they have, put together a plan and you make that plan and then you supervise. That's all a mastermind, you know. It's a military concept I mean at that point but you have it in the business as well where you have to bring in a marketing specialist, or you bring in productions specialist or internet specialist. Sooner or later, you're going to need to bring those people in because they all have skills that you don't have and so the mastermind becomes more important to you then. So you use these principles. You don't use them all at the same time and some become more important as you go through life.

For me, when I was 23, it was definitive purpose, now I didn't say definitive life's ambition, I said definite goal.

Raven: Definitive purpose.

JB: And later on, cosmic habit, the sustaining force I think is cosmic habit force, applied faith was important in the beginning because I had to accept it on faith to make it work for me.

Raven: Did you find when you started reading the book and practicing the principles helpful for you to write your goals down and did you write them that far ahead?

JB: Oh yes so I mean I didn't. When I chose the goals, I wrote them down and I read them every day. When you pray at night okay and you go over the things that you did bad that day and the things you did good that day, that's kind of reconciliation, okay? And you make the promise, well, I'm going to do better the next day that you make up for the bad thing I did. It's a process of reconciliation and that's what people need to do to develop spiritually. The same thing is true when you have a non-spiritual goal like a personal goal that you want to achieve. Every day, you need to focus on that to think about what you did that particular day to achieve that goal, what you're going to do tomorrow to achieve that goal, what you didn't do today, what opportunity came your way that you missed this particular day. And you do that so that you can maintain your focus so that you can accomplish your goal. That's why you're doing it whether it be to develop spiritually or your goal in life. And this conscious keeping you focused is essential and that's what writing your goals down and reading them aloud to yourself several times a day, put them in your pocket, take them out because you'll see opportunities that'll come your way if you're focused and alerted and ready to receive them. If you don't have it, you don't see those opportunities so I really believe in writing your goals down and rewriting them and writing new steps and crossing off steps and it's a dynamic process to achieve that goal. That's why you win when you do it.

Raven: Absolutely. And as business owners, like you said going through that list of what we did and what we didn't do at the end of the day and what needs to be done the next day and writing those specific goal is going to help us achieve a very profitable day versus us just coming to our desks and you know nowadays unfortunately, we have the computer, JB, so first thing we're doing is we're puttering on the computer and then we're lost in that and the day is gone.

I can tell from you talking about your practice and how you talk to people that you're huge on customer service. You know as the years go by, the value of customer service has somewhat dwindled. I'd like to see people go back to the old days when people really serviced you at their best.

JB: Cleaned your windshield and pumped up your gas.

Raven: Walk you to the door. I really miss going to the store and people would walk especially if it is a small boutique or something. They would actually walk you to the door and stuff you know.

JB: Sure

Raven: But it made you come back. It made you come back and it made you tell all your friends so I always share with my listeners, JB, to you know be the best that you can, go an extra mile, give that little extra "uh!" that maybe your competitors are not giving. And you'll be so glad you did.

JB: I think probably for the independent businessman going the extra mile is the essential thing because the competitors that are larger don't have to go that far and so if you can go a little bit further than they are, and then you're going to be successful.

Raven: Absolutely, wow! So glad that you came on to share with the listeners. I guess I want to close it out with one of my favorite quotes, "What the mind of a man can conceive and believe, he will achieve." Does that ring a bell at all?

JB: Well, I've heard that a few times.

Raven: That's one of my favorite quotes. I have it on a couple of my business voicemails and I always keep that quote by Napoleon because I really believe that and I think of all of us, business owners, just believe that regardless of the recession, regardless of the economy, you do as JB and I had started out talking about today, you do have the control that you need to change the direction of your life and if you haven't read *Think and Grow Rich*, get it. Stay plugged into those principles that Napoleon laid out and all the other different people that you have read and listened to. Don't just listen to good tapes, read good books, take action. That's when you really start to see things change.

JB: Absolutely.

Listen to the full audio of this interview:
http://www.careersfromthekitchentable.com/audios
**Plus be sure to visit and subscribe to Raven's popular newsletter and
get your free e-book** *"The Real Power of Social Networking:
Profit on Facebook"* **by Regina Baker**
http://www.careersfromthekitchentable.com

Be sure to join award winning talk show host and celebrity interviewer **Raven Blair Davis** each week for insider secrets, tips, strategies and formulas for success to help you grow your business faster rather than slower!

"Careers from the Kitchen Table"

America's Hottest Home Business Show

Hosted weekly by Celebrity Interviewer and Award Winning Talk Show Host Raven a.k.a. *The Talk Show Maven*

Visit http://www.careersfromthekitchentable.com *and listen to nearly three years of archived audios from these experts, sign up for the free newsletter and receive copy of "The Real Power of Social Networking: Profit on Facebook" including a full-fledged marketing strategy! By Regina Baker*

Want to have "your" own radio show and interview your favorite thought leader, author or celebrity?

Now you can get my easy to follow step-by-step formula for creating and launching your radio show and land that dream interview! You'll get exact steps to go from zero to launching your first show in less than six weeks!

Raven Blair Davis Presents Kitchen Table Radio

How to Produce, Post and Profit From "your" very own talk show

Discover the real secrets to:

- *Just how easy it really is to create and launch your show without having to buy expensive equipment*
- *How being a talk show host can be a great platform for you and your business*
- *What type of format is best for you and how long your show really should be*
- *The easiest way to create content for your show that will keep your listeners coming back for more*
- *How to get the guest of your dreams without paying them anything*
- *The fastest, easiest and simplest way to attract and build a worldwide audience*
- *When you should do a free vs. paid internet radio show or podcast*

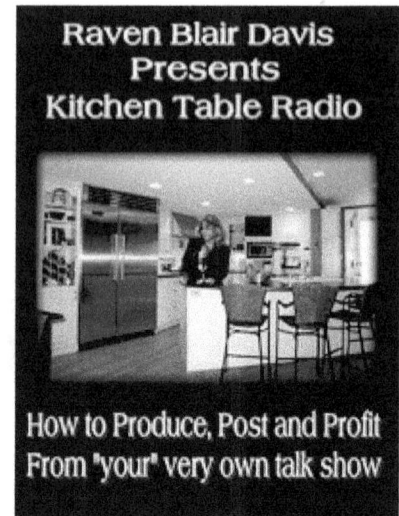

Why be mentored by Raven? See what others have to say...

BONUS AUDIO: Join Raven and many celebrities as they congratulate and celebrate Graduation with the students! http://www.audioacrobat.com/play/Wfrz1xSh

---

I have appeared on more than 800 radio interview shows in the past 20 years, and my time with Raven Blair Davis on her show "Careers from the Kitchen Table" was one of the most enjoyable ever.

She is a rare combination of dynamic, spontaneous and fun, as well as thoroughly prepared, deeply insightful and a great listener who responds with great follow-up questions as well as her own experiences in a way that moves the conversation forward without stealing the focus. I would highly recommend being on her show to anyone who is serious about getting your message out to more people—and enjoying the process at the same time.

Jack Canfield
America's #1 Success Coach
www.JackCanfield.com

2010 National Business Directory

The Kitchen Table Radio Personal Broadcasting Course, was a god-send for me. As the widow of, radio legend, Earl Nightingale, many of my customers today first heard of Earl over the airwaves of early radio. His, "Our Changing World", radio show was heard daily around the world, but it was always his desire for the two of us to have a radio show together one day. In the mid-eighties, we came close to seeing that dream come true when we were approached by a group of people who wanted to start a "success radio station" with Earl and me as their main commentators, however the incredible costs involved with starting a new radio station were prohibitive and we saw our dreams dashed.

Through the years, many station managers have confirmed the need for positive programming, and could see a program hosted by myself as filling a great yawning need in radio, but said that "sponsors won't pay for that kind of programming".

When I learned about, The Kitchen Table Radio Personal Broadcasting Course, I just about jumped for joy! The Course, is incredibly informative and provided me with every tool I needed to be on the air and sharing the Nightingale messages. The only thing Raven asked me to bring, "to the table" was, my own personal desire!

Raven, thank you from the bottom of my heart!

Diana Nightingale,
Speaker/author
Nighingale Radio, Host
http://earlnightingale.com

KITCHEN TABLE RADIO
INSIDER SECRETS TO PRODUCING, POSTING AND PROFITING
FROM YOUR OWN TALK SHOW

Unleash the power of your voice! Order your copy today!
http://www.kitchentableradio.com

FREE CONSULTATION

Call or email Raven today to schedule your no cost, no obligation 15 minute consultation!

Email: Raven@Womenpower-Radio.com
Call 800-431-0842

OR Visit http://www.kitchentableradio.com now!

Stories from the Kitchen Table

Enjoy these engaging stories from Entrepreneurs, Solopreneurs, and Founders of Non-Profit organizations as they share their challenges and how they've come to where they are today!

Andrew Angle

"If you fail to plan, you plan to fail."*
Unknown

You Can't Do It All Yourself

After years of sacrificing precious time as an underpaid freelancer, raising fantastic kids while working nights to grow a business, I started diving into the "guru" business courses. The people and ideas I met were awesome; but, I knew something was missing.

Some people I met through the guru courses were earning decent incomes, but felt trapped by their own businesses. Most others just were NOT making money! That's a problem.

Get this...I was a work-from-home dad. My wife still had her corporate job while I only carried *memories* of a corporate job that downsized me. That was the world where I <u>trained corporate Human Resources departments</u>, won <u>big clients</u> for my bosses, proposed the creation of new products that my employer patently rejected – ideas that later proved to be worth *billions...* it was a world where executives referred to me as "Executive Material" shortly before *laying me off* in a corporate buyout. That corporate "pink slip" (kindly handed to me on my birthday) was my ticket into *freelancing*.

Business can be tough, especially for solo entrepreneurs. We constantly hear buzz phrases like, *"work your own hours"* and *"unlimited income potential."* Get real! Those statements often mean "work *ALL* hours" and "unlimited income *risk*".

Over the years I have studied and even met face-to-face with top entrepreneurs including founders of Pizza Hut, Microsoft, Dell Computer Corp, Turner Broadcasting, and many others, all to find the answer to the question, *"What makes your business <u>so successful</u>?"* The #1 answer? "<u>It's our *PEOPLE*.</u>" Ah HA!!! It's *people* designing the *systems*. Its *people* that DO the work of identifying needs, building products, selling, delivering, and supporting the stuff that we open our wallets to consume! So... if it's *people* turning ideas into successful *companies*, <u>WHY are we working *solo*</u>?

Outsource your weaknesses! Do *you* have *PEOPLE* helping to build *your* business? Will taking a day off work set your business (and income) another day behind? Do you blaze through every task in your business painlessly? What aspects of running your business do you hate? If you are a solo entrepreneur, *you* may be capping your own success. Ask yourself this...

Do you own your business, or does your business <u>own you</u>? When you recognize that it's time for your business to grow, you can *out-task*, outsource, crowd source, or hire W2 employees. Your recipe for success depends on you finding the right people and being skillfully ready to maximize the profitability of their contribution in your business. If <u>you are the boss</u>, be a good one!

= Make time to learn how to plan more effectively

Andrew Angle,
Master of Business Acceleration™
http://NetGainAssociates.com

Andrew Angle's

Recipe for SUCCESS!

2. Know yourself.
3. Know your market.
4. Don't innovate... improve!
5. Outsource your weaknesses.
6. Always be recruiting.
7. Remember that people can read minds.
8. MAKE BACKUPS!!!

⟪header⟫

IMPORTANT: You must read this!

They say, "Pursue your passion". If your passion is in "building sand castles", you should find a more reliable way to make a living. Too often, entrepreneurs eagerly sacrifice careers on niches that just won't work. Others trap themselves into businesses they don't enjoy. If YOU want to become one of the wildly successful entrepreneurs, learn how to pick a niche. Before you spend another day or dollar on your business, read the diagram below and use the online version to explore whether your niche provides a solid foundation for future success.

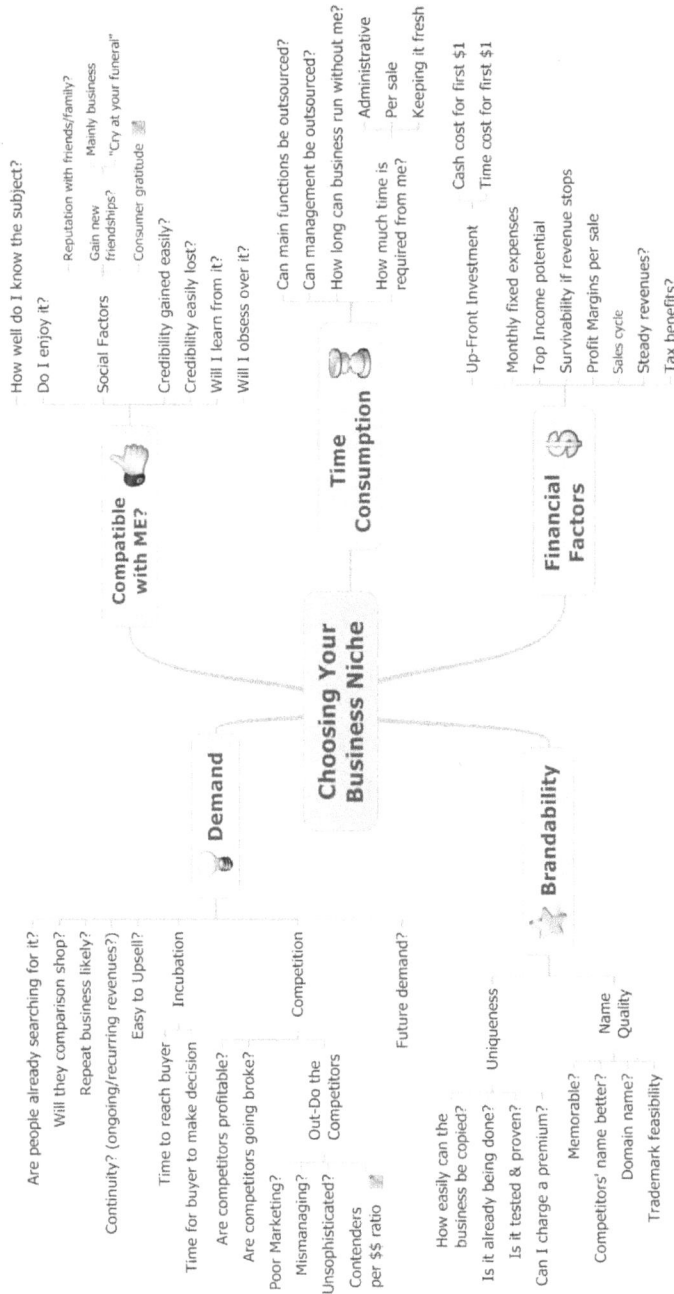

Choosing Your Business Niche

Compatible with ME?
- How well do I know the subject?
- Do I enjoy it?
  - Reputation with friends/family?
- Social Factors
  - Gain new friendships?
  - Mainly business
  - Consumer gratitude
  - "Cry at your funeral"
- Credibility gained easily?
- Credibility easily lost?
- Will I learn from it?
- Will I obsess over it?

Time Consumption
- Can main functions be outsourced?
- Can management be outsourced?
- How long can business run without me?
- How much time is required from me?
  - Administrative
  - Per sale
  - Keeping it fresh

Financial Factors
- Up-Front Investment
  - Cash cost for first $1
  - Time cost for first $1
- Monthly fixed expenses
- Top Income potential
- Survivability if revenue stops
- Profit Margins per sale
- Sales cycle
- Steady revenues?
- Tax benefits?

Demand
- Are people already searching for it?
- Will they comparison shop?
- Repeat business likely?
- Continuity? (ongoing/recurring revenues?)
- Easy to Upsell?
- Time to reach buyer — Incubation
- Time for buyer to make decision
- Are competitors profitable?
- Are competitors going broke?
- Competition
- Poor Marketing?
- Mismanaging?
- Unsophisticated?
- Out-Do the Competitors
- Contenders per $$ ratio
- Future demand?

Brandability
- How easily can the business be copied?
- Is it already being done? — Uniqueness
- Is it tested & proven?
- Can I charge a premium?
- Memorable?
- Competitors' name better? — Name
- Domain name? — Quality
- Trademark feasibility

Check out the interactive version at http://NetGainAssociates.com/Raveniche

About Andrew Angle

Andrew Angle started his first business at the age of 16 doing singing telegrams. It cost nothing to start and he found a big demand for it. It was a story quickly landed in local newspapers. Since then his passion for business took him to college where he became President of the Association of Collegiate Entrepreneurs, launched successful fundraisers, paid his way through school by selling academic study guides door-to-door, and eventually entered the corporate world of Human Resources software before launching a web development consultancy firm. He has been a work-from-home executive dad for a decade, listing both business and family as his greatest passions.

As a web developer he created the online presence for a wide range of companies representing billions of dollars in annual sales across industrial, real estate, pharmaceutical, automotive, and "mom & pop" shops. When work piled up, the solo freelancing model proved to be inadequate structure for getting work done and still have time for family. That was when he began outsourcing, realizing that he should started that way from the beginning.

Today his experience covers deep levels of niche selection, marketing, SEO, PPC, Social Media, Public Relations, e-Product & Project Management, plus the hiring, managing, and firing that goes along with it.

Andrew Angle, Master of Business Acceleration™
www.NetGainAssociates.com

Phone: 800-651-9027

Allison Babb

"Do not go where the path may lead, go instead where there is no path and leave a trail" ~
Ralph Waldo Emerson

Failure is NOT an Option

Allison's journey into entrepreneurship was an interesting one. After climbing the corporate ladder and becoming a successful senior manager at a software company, Allison began feeling quite unfulfilled.

Allison spent over 2 years wrestling with the idea of leaving the security of her 6-figure corporate paycheck. But as a single mom with two kids, Allison finally decided that it was time to step into entrepreneurship (petrifying as it seemed at the time).

But success was not instant. While still employed, Allison realized that her true passion and calling was in her natural abilities as a gifted coach. She completed training at Coach University and started her first business as a Life Coach. Although she had some clients, without a mentor and without any business-building knowledge, her Life Coaching business eventually failed.

Allison quickly reflected on this experience and knew that to fulfill her self-employment dreams; she *must* discover what it took to create a truly successful business. As a single parent, she knew that **failure was simply not an option** in her quest to become self-employed full-time.

Allison's prevailing belief was "*Someone out there HAS the recipe for building a successful business and I intend to find it.*" And with that, she made the decision to **study 6 and 7 figure solo entrepreneurs**.

To the tune of well over $150K, Allison invested her own money in discovering exactly what it took to create a successful business.

In her time as an Executive Coach, a funny thing happened. One manager after another began asking Allison for help in making their own transition from unfulfilling corporate jobs to self-employment. This prompted Allison to create GoodbyeCorporateJob.com coaching "corporate captives" on how to make a successful transition to entrepreneurship.

From there, more full-time entrepreneurs were drawn to Allison's authentic, motivational, action-oriented, and results-focused coaching. This led to the launch of GreatSmallBusinessAdvice.com where Allison now spends her time.

Allison is an upbeat and very down-to-earth single mom who likes to keep life simple. When she's not taking her relentless high-energy to speaking gigs, or escaping to warm Caribbean vacations, Allison is usually kicking back at home with her two kids.

Allison Babb - Small Business Coach
http://www.GreatSmallBusinessAdvice.com

Allison Babb's

Recipe for SUCCESS!

1. Build your business with your lifestyle in mind.

2. Choose clients you love to work with.

3. Systematize your business processes to create a well-oiled income-generating machine.

4. Always have a coach or mentor to guide you and help you avoid costly mistakes.

5. Get help. No-one can build a business all alone. Be ready to delegate so you can focus mostly on income-generating tasks (vs. administrative tasks).

6. Always be marketing. Marketing is the gas in your business engine. If clients seem few and far between, check into how consistently your marketing is happening.

7. Stay in alignment with your passion and vision. Remember why you started on your self-employment journey in the first place. When the passion is gone, the success is harder to come.

About Allison Babb

Allison Babb is recognized as a leading expert on self-employment success. She is the founder and CEO of GreatSmallBusinessAdvice.com, and also the creator of the Ultimate Clients & Cash System. Allison has taught thousands of business owners around the world how to attract more clients and close more sales in the shortest time possible.

As an award-winning author, national speaker, and Small Business Coach, Allison has appeared on television, radio shows, in magazines and in news articles sharing her own secrets on how to create a client-magnetic business - one where customers are chasing after you vs you chasing after them.

Known for her upbeat and down-to-earth style, Allison consistently provides a rich source of unique, revenue-generating insights on how to create the success they envision for their businesses.

Allison Babb
http://www.GreatSmallBusinessAdvice.com

Regina Baker

"You may never know what results come of your action, but if you do nothing there will be no result."

Gandhi

A Story of Trust and Giving

After enduring several years of Corporate America, Regina Baker tapped into her true purpose of empowering others by example.

Being laid off due to downsizing and through the passing of her husband Ruben to cancer in 2002, she has learned to rely and trust in the wisdom and will of God.

Regina believes that everyone has a purpose and journey to travel. While it may not always be easy, making a commitment to unravel life's mysteries can be challenging and fulfilling – even through the struggle.

She made a decision to seek the Bible for understanding the complexities that life brings. Making a commitment to realize the power of self-growth, uncompromising faith and a positive attitude, helped her through 'the process' of being sole care-taker to her husband as he gradually slipped away.

Aligning herself with like-minded individuals, mentors, continuing education, reading, listening to tapes and researching the power of entrepreneurship, she realized her purpose and passion is to assist others.

Regina says: "I knew there was something for me to continue to live for, to empower others and to have a profound effect in giving instead of just receiving."

In doing so, she made it a point to become a Certified Biblical and Business Consultant. In this role, she is able to consult individuals on the importance of a suitable ecommerce software solution for their business while answering all of their questions concerning internet and affiliate marketing in an easy to understand language.

Known as "the keep it real" consultant, Regina stomps out hype by writing down to earth, call to action messages on her popular blog, "Keeping It Real," at ReginaBaker.com

Having various roles in computer technology led her where she is today as the Co-Founder of Wahmcart.com, a full ecommerce software solution for work at home moms as well as the small business community.

When my partner, at the time, and I first talked about Wahmcart, we wanted to provide a full ecommerce software solution for work at home moms BUT without the huge price tag. Our goal was, and is, to reach the masses with our full ecommerce solution as opposed to only those who can afford a high ticket service comparable to what we offer.

We believe that small businesses dominate a large portion of the market place however, a huge percentage of small businesses miss the opportunity to provide a secure environment like Wahmcart due to the lack of funds. Therefore they settle for free carts and not as secure or easy shopping options for potential customers.

This is why Wahmcart was born. Our goal is to educate the small business individual (sole proprietors) and companies with ecommerce solutions that will allow them to work smarter, not harder while at the same time providing an affordable solution that the "average" person can afford.

Regina says, *"Meeting the needs of others is the best gift I could have ever received!"* She loves traveling, meeting people, hanging out with family, listening to music and reading.

Regina Baker – Entrepreneur
www.wahmcart.com
www.ReginaBaker.com

Regina Baker's

Recipe for SUCCESS!

1. Seek god to reveal your gifts and talents.

2. Consistently renew your mind commit to personal growth by reading, listening to audios, etc.

3. Hire a coach, consultant and or/mentor.

4. Keep notes write down every thought.

5. Refuse to comprise our integrity & character just for money.

6. Research your target market.

7. Network with a listening attitude.

About Regina Baker

Regina Baker is a computer geek at heart. Her background is in Procurement and Information Technology. After being laid off due to downsizing and even through the passing of her husband, Ruben, to cancer in 2002, she has learned to rely and trust in the wisdom and will of God.

Regina knew there was something for her to continue to live for, to empower others and to have a profound effect in giving instead of just receiving.

Having various roles in computer technology led her to where she is today as the Co-Founder of Wahmcart.com, a full ecommerce software solution for work at home moms as well as the small business community.

Regina is also a Certified Biblical & Business Consultant at ReginaBaker.com, where she consults small business on how to move away from lack into prosperity, not only in business but in every area of their lives.

www.ReginaBaker.com
www.Wahmcart.com

1.800.294.1461
email@reginabaker.com

Connect socially
www.facebook.com/reginabaker
www.twitter.com/reginabaker

Jayne Blumenthal

"Unless you start doing something different, you are in for more of the same."
Author Unknown

From Burnout to Bliss!

Jayne's journey to become a BetterWay Coach™ emerged after launching and growing a garment manufacturing company with her husband Brahm from concept to $10 million over 20 years, while raising three toddler sons successfully to adulthood along the way.

Guiding employees to step into their greatness to fuel her company's progress was among her first sign posts to indicate that while personal success was fulfilling, it was much more rewarding to help others create their own success.

Jayne's employees often said...." **You showed me how to take back control of my life and future.** You showed me how to have the freedom to call the shots, set my own schedule, be healthy and spend time with my family and myself while doing things I love to do."

Jayne has lived the challenges of parenting and co-parenting five children while managing a successful growing business. She has felt the pain and heartache of missing her son's school concert while away on an overseas buying trip. She understands how easy it is to continuously eat fast foods. She has felt the struggle to maintain an exercise routine without sacrificing time away from family and work commitments.

Do you have the same challenges and struggles?

Although successful people often have the ability to live in big houses, buy fancy cars and send their children to private schools, they forget to play, to find the fun in their lives and feel the sand between their toes. Jayne believes that success is more than just making a living; the quality of how you are living is just as important.

Today, she leads **Solo-preneurs, Executives and Professionals** who have already achieved a measure of financial and life success to **step into greatness** that takes shape beyond the balance sheet.

With Jayne as their accountability partner and BetterWay Coach™ clients are lead on the secret path to taking back their life. Through thoughtful, mindful and deliberate steps the door opens for them to achieve success in priceless ways that show up in their health, spiritual path, joy for vibrant living and quality of their most important personal relationships.

Successful clients suffering from the **side effects of success - overwhelm, overweight, family disconnect, a life spinning out of control, burnout and more** - welcome timely and lasting relief as they recalibrate their "Wheel of Life" to shift focus toward a sustainable way of contributing to life and work in equal measure. Perfect clients to benefit from Jayne's results-focused approach are those who feel compelled and committed to finding a BetterWay™ in their lives, consistently over time, to welcome the bliss that has - to this point - remained too many steps beyond reach.

If the wheels on your life bus are locked, stalled or spinning, recalibrate the balance and get moving in a BetterWay™ by following Jayne's secret path from burnout to bliss and start today.

Jayne Blumenthal
BetterWay Coach™ to those on the Secret Path from Burnout to Bliss

www.jayneblumenthal.com

Jayne Blumenthal's

Recipe for SUCCESS!

1. Make your goals S.M.A.R.T.

2. Choose healthy, energy building food habits.

3. Be clutter free and organized.

4. Take a break, Rejuvenate!

5. Just say….No!

6. Hire Out – to Help Out!

7. Take a deep breath, work flexible hours and engage a "BetterWayCoach™.

About Jayne Blumenthal

Jayne Blumenthal leads **Solo-preneurs, Executives and Professionals** on "The Secret path to Health, Wealth and Sand between Your Toes" so that they can experience the joy of taking back control of their life and future while having fun and learning to play.

A trusted employee once said," Jayne quickly helps people grow and transform both personally and professionally. Her greatest asset is that she truly cares and personally invests herself and her talents in others.

Jayne is helping successful people live the life they are designed to live. Her clients are clearly on the secret path from Burnout to Bliss.

Connect with Jayne on Facebook: www.facebook.com/jayneblumenthal

Follow Jayne on Twitter: www.twitter.com/jayneblumenthal

Jayne Blumenthal

BetterWay Coach™ to those on the Secret Path from Burnout to Bliss

Beverly Boston

"Devote today to something so daring even you can't believe you're doing it."
Oprah Winfrey

From I Love Lucy to Wake Up From Autopilot Expert!

Beverly's story begins several years ago, when she started working as Master Coach with one of North America's largest coaching companies. The company provided her with top quality coaching clients who wanted to take their small businesses to high 6-7 figures and beyond. Between growing her private practice and serving clients with this coaching company she started to recognize some amazing patterns.

She soon saw that the slow results some of her coaching clients had was partly a result of their fears, self-doubt, and blocks in relationship to sales and growing their businesses. **While they were experts in their fields, they possessed an attitude that many business owners have, which is "I don't deserve success.", "I am not worthy of success." or they simply could not ask for the money.**

Can you relate?

As any business owner would, they loved getting increased sales and business, but were leaving money behind with their limiting beliefs, blocks, and fears. Beverly believes a large percentage of us have some sort of fears, and yet so many people she works with allow those fears to hinder their ability to think bigger, play bigger, make more money, and have renewed excitement about life . They are unaware that their fears can be removed easily and permanently.

Beverly mentored people and coached them all the way up to high six and seven figure incomes, and one of the things she learned about during this time is that regardless of the size of the business, or the size of the blocks, she needed to find a way to get to the core of the blocks and barriers in order to remove them so that they never came back again. This would allow her clients to become the best version of themselves. She also realized that she had some of the blocks holding her back as well.

She began to study what could shift people from being stuck in the "maybe" position, where people are frozen in their tracks and no action takes place, to the "definitely" position, where a bigger future than their past becomes possible!

Her "A-ha" moment!

One weekend, while attending a business seminar about money, thinking and beliefs, she started to recognize why some of her coaching clients were struggling. And where she was struggling in playing small in her own business as well! She became curious about what it would take to step into unknown territory and coach people to take a leadership role while becoming the best version of them, and building her tolerance for "bigness" at the same time.

She decided to study everything that she could get her hands on and hired expert coaches, the best of the best, to help her start exploring how to do that.

As she began attending seminars, tele-classes and training, she quickly noticed that there were so many more small business owners working their heart and souls out but unable to break into a higher income level. They were leaving so many opportunities behind.

Beverly's coaching, mentoring, training, speaking and programs started with a desire that by now is almost a synonym for "classic model." They got that way by doing all the things that others weren't doing, or thought they weren't supposed to do, to create a sustainable and profitable business. Beverly thought outside of the box like they did on the I Love Lucy Show in It's time. "You couldn't have a female star that was both attractive and funny. You couldn't have her male lead be an urban Latino—playing those devil conga drums at that!—whose Cuban accent was thicker than a platter of ropa vieja. You couldn't for God's sake build a storyline around a (gasp!) pregnancy. The shows are still watched and modeled around the world. ***Beverly modeled the show using unique thinking and imagination, tenacity, playfulness and broke away from the typical way business is done to create a sustainable and profitable business model for others and her.*** She learned to take imperfect action just like Lucy. And that was just simply unheard of in the coaching and mentoring industry.
It didn't take long for her to realize that she had a gift in combining the Law of Attraction with solid business principles, and helping people become the best version of them. **Her clients consistently say, "I wish I had found you years earlier" because what she offers is so powerful and makes such an impact on their lives.**

Today, Beverly is fortunate to enjoy a full and thriving practice with extraordinary long term relationships with clients who have unprecedented results using solid business building blocks combined with the next generation of Law of Attraction principles. ***She loves working with clients who are "committed to making a contribution" globally.***

Beverly Boston-Master Coach for BIG Thinkers
www.BeverlyBoston.com

Beverly Boston's

Recipe for SUCCESS!

1. When free is much too expensive in your business...when you have the wrong mentor, wrong information, and wrong strategy for YOU!

2. Put your business attraction on speed dial. Give 'Em something to Crave!

3. Throw away your "back- up plan" in your small business and instead just play full out to win.

4. Client attraction straight talk. Take out "me" and add "you" to your conversations.

5. Go back to what matters. Your mission, you're meaning, and your purpose IS what sells.

6. Deeper fulfillment in your small business comes by asking powerful questions, such as: What matters to me now? What makes me happy & fulfills me now?

7. Is your small business being perceived as, "No laughing matter?"- BE more fun, to have more fun, client retention, & client attraction will MASSIVELY improve!

About Beverly Boston

Beverly Boston champions the success of Solo-preneurs, Coaches, Consultants, and Spiritual Teachers so they can wake up from autopilot in their lives, and become the best version of themselves. Her clients consistently say, "I wish I had found you years earlier", because what she offers is so powerful and makes such an impact on their lives. Beverly is a Master Coach, Mentor, blogger, writer, inspirational speaker, the creator of the "Big Thinking, Big Mind, Big Heart & Big Life™ as well as "Wake Up From Autopilot-Your Life is Waiting™"programs! *These personal transformational programs have impacted the lives of small business owners; stay at home mothers, and even multi-millionaires.*

With an emphasis for Solo-preneurs to wake from autopilot, Beverly's work is helping people feel more highly physically energized, emotionally connected, mentally focused, and spiritually aligned. Beverly was an accomplished multi-award winning top salesperson in real estate, small business owner, and had a 6 year stint as an independent off-site coach with one of the top coaching companies in North America. *Beverly helped people find the courage and confidence to build sustainable businesses that multiplied their income 10 times time over.* She can also show you how to contribute your areas of strength; substantially increase your quality of life, and long term vision.

Follow Beverly on Twitter: beverlybostontwitter@gmail.com

Beverly Boston-Master Coach for BIG Thinkers

www.BeverlyBoston.com

Dr. Linne Bourget

"Without full knowledge of your best, you have only half the truth—the worst half."
Dr. Linne Bourget

How I Gave Birth to A New Field—Positive Greatness-Based Business Growth

Despite being disowned by my father for going to the University of Chicago because I was too smart for a girl, my intuition guided me there, so I went. A 4th generation intuitive, I trust my intuition. My purpose was revealed there in my M.B.A. program, after my B.A. in Economics. I had to work my way through 4 degrees with no support.

In my Ph.D. program at Boston University in change and leadership, my stomach kept crunching because of how people were treated in the name of change. It hurt.

One day, I prayed for guidance about why my stomach hurt and why I was the only one questioning what famous mentors taught. I trust my intuition--it came in a clear flash: What was wrong? What was I to do? Answer: **There was no focus on appreciation of strengths, which should be the basis of all change and leadership**. It made sense!

Change was based on the medical/problem-solving model 30 years ago, "Find out what is wrong with you and fix it." But no one wants to be the "what's wrong," so no one likes it. I had to do my literature review for my dissertation on <u>negative</u> feedback because there was <u>no</u> research on <u>positive</u> feedback and change!! Colleagues told me I was wrong. But how would this work with clients?

I gave highly skilled appreciation to a client team. They transformed from terrified to excited—physiologically, mentally and emotionally--in 20 minutes! This was huge! What You Say Is What You Get®, my trademark, came later, but I saw its power then! Words make or break your success! They went on to huge success.

My boss, the V. P., fired me for doing that with this client team - for being positive. That was my main income so I fought back. He offered me a full-time job and I turned him down. Soon I had a Fortune 100 New York client while still in my Ph.D. program. My work on positive communication turned around teams in trouble for several years.

A Fortune 10, 50, 100 Consultant, I built practical positive systems for clients, based on their greatness and strengths, e. g. team building, fun and fast planning, delegating, time management, clarifying roles and responsibilities, the positive language of change, etc. My Master Intuition System joins me, saving clients much time and money and bringing them better solutions and more peace of mind. My small business clients love this too. It strengthens them and speeds their success. They love FAST, POSITIVE systems!

This is a radically opposite approach to focusing on and overcoming problems to succeed. Client teams were transformed so fast, their businesses had such success, and they enjoyed it so much, that their great results inspired them to ask me to create books and products. Some took our work home and saved their marriages.

This was a huge challenge, to persuade clients to accept the positive leadership approach when they were addicted to the problem-solving "what's wrong approach."

Now I have over 40 books, manuals, e-books and articles, (with audios to come) in my trademarked What You Say Is What You Get® Positive Business Leadership Series.

When you know and own your strengths, you don't feel jealous of others. You know you have the right strengths for what you are here to do.

Dr. Linne Bourget MA, MBA, Ph.D
www.whatyousayiswhatyouget.com

Dr. Linne Bourget's

Recipe for SUCCESS!

1. Know Your Strengths Extensively and Deeply—this should be top priority for every woman, but women are conditioned to under-value themselves and thus make less money. No more!

2. Understand and release anything that blocks your knowing your greatest strengths.   Keep the best and release the rest!!

3. Associate only with people who see and appreciate your strengths, and release negative people, they harm your health, spirit, business, family and wallet.

4. Build your business and career based on your strengths, not on trying to overcome your limitations. More gain, less pain!

5. Passion and purpose are necessary but not sufficient. Without marrying them with your greatest strengths, applied in your business/career, you will always under-serve and under-earn. Not what the Universe wants for you.

6. Skills matter! Learn the positive business/leadership systems and skills you must know and apply for solid FAST business growth—Frameworks, Attitudes, Systems & Tools!

7. Always hire the best mentors! We all need help!

About Dr. Linne Bourget

Dr. Linne Bourget MA MBA Ph.D., ATM-G, "Dr. Appreciation"

- ♥   Giving you power to predict & profit

- ♥   Founder/CEO, ITLC, The Institute for Transformation Leaders and Consultants, and www.whatyousayiswhatyouget.com.

- ♥   Pioneer, strengths-based leadership "Build on Your Best" positive systems, Master Intuition System for Business Owners/Leaders.

- ♥   Expert in Business Turnarounds without Tears, Master Organizational Healer.

- ♥   Integrates nine fields of knowledge for clients, including metaphysics.

- ♥   4th-Generation Intuitive, expert business, science & technology intuitive.

- ♥   Fortune 10, 50,100, Small Business consultant, strategist, speaker, trainer.

- ♥   Co-author w/ Mark Victor Hansen, Deepak Chopra, Amazon #1 Bestseller, Wake Up Live the Life You Love-Finding Personal Freedom.

- ♥   Author, What You Say Is What You Get® Trademarked Positive Leadership Series, including

- ♥   The Secret Language of Great Business Results, endorsed by Mark Victor Hansen, Co-Creator, Chicken Soup for the Soul® Series

- ♥   Positive Quotient PQ® & Appreciative Quotient AQ® Questionnaires

- ♥   Secrets of Powerful Appreciation for Parents and Children, 2 CD Audio by "Dr. Appreciation"

- ♥   Appreciation: The Secret Key to Magical Marriage.

- ♥   B.A. Economics, M.B.A., University of Chicago, M.A. Psychology,

- ♥   Ph.D. in Positive Change Leadership, Boston University, Harvard & MIT.

- ♥   Spirituality in Business Expert since the early 80s.

- ♥   Lifelong singer, dancer, hot swing and Latin dancer.

http://www.whatyousayiswhatyouget.com

Susan Brown

"Our chief want is someone who will inspire us to be what we know we could be."
Ralph Waldo Emerson

From Cancer to Success!

Susan Brown is frequently asked about how she has gone from being a breast cancer survivor to an entrepreneurial thriver. She says that it was the diagnosis of breast cancer at age 42 that was the catalyst for the eventual launching of her coaching company, Impact Coaching LLC. Her experience with cancer revealed many things about herself which inspired her to become an entrepreneur. In fact, Susan emphasizes in her coaching work with entrepreneurs and rising leaders the importance of knowing oneself.

She discovered three key things that provide the purpose and energizing force behind her company. She states:

First, my passion to make a difference in the world was rekindled. As a former teacher and school administrator I have always loved transforming lives and igniting the unlimited potential in people. Impact Coaching was founded on this passion to help others maximize their ability to grow and transform others.

Secondly, cancer reawakened a strong desire to embrace life. I discovered that as my relationship with God got stronger, so did my enjoyment of life. My waking thoughts became "This is the day the Lord has made; let us rejoice and be glad in it." (PSALM 118:24) This intention to live joyfully and to be of service is the energy fueling Impact Coaching.

Thirdly, I learned that during times of despair, I could count on my courage, faith, and determination to prevail. Knowing that I had these key traits reassured me that I had the emotional resources to become an entrepreneur.

As soon as Susan launched Impact Coaching she faced these three obstacles quite common for beginning coaches without a background in business and entrepreneurism.

1) Susan missed the benefits of working with a team of people. She formed her own "Success Team" made of people who offered creative, moral, and intellectual support. She notes that her team constantly changes based on her evolving needs. For example, Susan added a radio show expert to her team to help turn her program, "Awaken the Leader Within," into one of the most popular leadership programs on internet radio.

2) She lacked key skills in the areas of marketing and sales. Susan traded her coaching services for marketing expertise.

3) Susan struggled to identify her ideal clients by starting out in a niche that did not reflect her true passion and purpose. She realigned her career objectives with her values and purpose. She also utilized the skills of a professional coach for clarity.

Susan Brown – Coach
http://www.impactcoach.wordpress.com

Susan Brown's

Recipe for SUCCESS!

1. **Reflect on the challenges of your life and notice the character traits you used to overcome them.** Use those same qualities to grow your business. I found that I used courage, hope, tenacity, integrity and humility to name a few.

2. **Define your niche.** Be patient but do it as soon as you can. Take the time to interact with a wide variety of people with a diverse set of needs. You will discover that "I'm home" feeling when you are with the people you were meant to be with.

3. **Identify your passions and priorities.** This will help make decision making so much easier when it comes to deciding how you want to spend your energy, time and dollars.

4. **Find mentors and trusted confidantes.** These are people who believe in you and will support, guide and nurture you. They are your earth angels who have your back and heart covered.

5. **Be persistent and aggressive about restoring your balance.** How you manage your energy affects your level of success. If you are not leading a joyful and balanced life, your energy sags and your effectiveness and relationships suffer.

6. **Draw bulls-eyes on a daily, monthly, and annual basis.** It doesn't matter whether you call them targets, objectives, goals, dreams or outcomes. What is essential to your success is that you are intentional in your thoughts and actions.

7. **Stay hydrated.** Connect with God by praying, reading scripture, singing, taking nature walks, meditating, serving others, etc.

About Susan Brown

Susan Brown is a 12 year breast cancer *thriver* and advocate for living a significant, spiritual and joyful life. She guides the maturity and development of leaders who want to increase their impact and not lose their soul doing so. She helps you develop a personalized plan that not only develops the skills you need to influence others but also balances the needs of your body, mind and spirit. Susan is a former school administrator and teacher specializing in coaching leaders of not-for-profit organizations.

Susan Brown, Ed.S.
Certified Leadership Coach
www.impactcoach.wordpress.com
susanbrown.impactcoaching@gmail.com

678-787-2406

Bonnie Bruderer

"Perseverance and determination were not only valuable skills, they were mandatory."
Bonnie Bruderer

Peaks and Valleys

Peaks and Valleys is an understatement when you are an entrepreneur working from home. If you have heard the term "trial and error," I built my business mainly on those two words, and they seem to come as a pair. Whatever I tried, for a long time, resulted in error.

The one thing I learned (well…. actually I learned thousands of things) was that perseverance and determination were not only valuable skills, they were mandatory. As lonely as it can be, being a careers from the kitchen table solo-preneur, I think it was lucky to not have anyone to commiserate with.

Although the tone of this story may be starting off a bit dreary, the important thing is that I learned. Each time I had tried something that didn't work, I would ask myself, how can I improve my approach? When you have a business or have a product, it is always about testing the market, finding out what is working and readjusting as needed. Below is an article I wrote that encapsulates what it takes to create a successful business:

How I sold my couch to pay a bill, and ended up giving 300 women a job…

I am always someone who has a plan B. Yes, being a go-getter; I do push the envelope, as most do, however I am smart and calculated in my efforts. This time, I had pushed too far. I was at the end of the line, so much so, that the stack of bills on my entryway table was too overwhelming to look at.

I am a woman of action, so I looked at my "resources" and what I had to work with, and literally it was the contents of my studio apartment. My parents had instilled the fear of God in me, about always having insurance, and since I had a medical bill to pay, I had to do the unthinkable.

I placed an ad on Craig's list, and sold my couch for $375. This was by far one of the lowest moments in my life. I cancelled the rest of my plans for the weekend, as I had no money, and I spent the weekend, tearfully in my apartment, trying to figure out what to do next.

By Sunday, with swollen eyes, and having exhausted the possibility of selling anything else, I decided to create a plan.

I have always been a big fan of the Vision Board, and the ability to attract in anything you desire. I scrounged up my change from every place in my apartment. I went to the local Walgreen's and bought a poster board and some magazines. I came home and began to cut out pictures of everything I wanted in my life.

I had so much fun, and felt so fabulous looking at all of the great things I wanted to attract in. Then it hit me. This is my next step. I launched a business teaching women how to train other women on how to create vision boards, using my *"Remember Forward"* technique which teaches you to act as if you already have everything you desire in your life.

During this weekend, that was one of the lowest of my life, I realized that there was such a lack of hope and inspiration in the world, and such an abundance of fabulous talent, so the Vision Board Party business created a solution for all of this.

Just a few months later, we now have 20 reps that are up and running and teaching many others. We have goals to hire 280 more reps between now and the end of the year. It is so exciting, and it all came out of the fact that there was no other option.

One thing I know for sure is that Vision Boards really work, and the satisfaction of helping women that are in a similar position as I was, that weekend, is one of the greatest experiences I have ever had.

The Vision Board Training now offers private label vision board products to companies all over the globe to help bring their venture to the vision board.

Bonnie Bruderer - Creator & Founder Vision Board Training
www.TheVisionBoardTraining.com

Bonnie Bruderer's

Recipe for SUCCESS!

1. Know your outcome.

2. Know your needle drivers.

3. When overwhelmed, ask "does this contribute to my bottom line" and only do that first.

4. Learn the delicate art of "no thanks".

5. Have a powerful inner circle.

6. Celebrate others successes as if they were your own.

7. Always be learning and improving.

About Bonnie Bruderer

Bonnie Bruderer is the founder and creator of The One Coaching. Co-Founder of VISS International, Vision Board Training, and the "Be The One" Brand.

Bonnie offers books, products, and subscription based motivational phone calls, coaching programs and speaking engagements, a weekly radio show, and television channel on the nValeo (www.nValeo500.com) network.

V.I.S.S. International offers in-home Vision Board Experiences, and allows women (and men) to teach the vision board training as a business opportunity, and earn an income on the product line of motivational books and DVD's.

Vision Board Training offers a private label and licensing option to create your own Vision board Kit for your organization. She has worked with some of the top thought leaders, MLM companies and sales organizations in the world to create product lines.

Bonnie is the author of: Becoming: "The One", Staying "The One", Be The Psychic, Tiny Morsels, and has two more books coming out this next year. "Be The One" also has a full line of candles, mugs, clothing, gifts and products coming out later this year.

Bonnie is trained in multiple modalities including a Practioner of NLP, Ericksonian Hypnotherapy, Holistic Health Practitioner, Results Coach, Neurological Re-patterning and five other holistic certifications. She uses a blend of all of the modalities in her work. She grew up in Marin County, California. She attended California State University, Chico, where she received a BA in journalism and a minor in sociology.

She is a leading innovator and expert on coaching on how to create abundance in their lives. With her holistic background, experience as a coach and mentor, and life experiences, she has created a series of books that are easy to read with powerful exercises that can guide any woman toward what she truly desires. She has had a unique set of circumstances and training including traveling on tours with Tony Robbins & Christopher Howard.

Bonnie Bruderer
VisionBoardParties.com
www.facebook.com/VisionBoards

Sharon Cadle

"If you cease to see life as a learning process you have disconnected from the Journey"
Sharon Cadle

Have You Changed?

Sharon's story begins with the sense of knowing that life consists of growing from where you are until you leave this planet. She is a person who also believes that transformation takes place, when you are helping others become transformed. The recognition of this reality started when she was much younger, a student, living in a neighbor where crime and drugs were all around. Sharon once wrote "If you cease to see life as a learning process you have disconnected from the journey." This quote came to her when she realized that after finishing college life's containment of daily living doesn't stop there, but in every faucet of our lives we are to be consistently learning, and growing from the adversity, and from the positive areas that life brings.

When growing up her parents were both strong willed individuals. Sharon's dad was this intelligent multi-gifted person who loved to play the guitar, ride his Harley, and bring home the bacon. Her Dad has since left this planet but he lives on in her heart. Her mom, the resourceful homemaker, social worker, and advocate for her community, she makes her life issues seem achievable. Sharon abstracted from her mom, a woman who knows what she wants. They both subscribed to the old fashion rituals that kept a girl confined. Sharon spent a lot of her time sitting on the front porch daydreaming about the wonders of life, and its beauties just looking at the skies. She envisioned visiting far away destinations. These dreams would take away the loneliness she sometimes felt. But little did she know that these very thoughts were transforming. Once grown up she realized that holding someone back can in fact bring about hindrances. She began to see the lack of life skills, fearful of challenges that were unfamiliar, letting opportunities pass her because of self-doubt. Sharon had settled for life as usual no change just doing what was comfortable the same old, unknowingly, sabotaging her thoughts with feelings of inadequacy.

But the good news is Sharon would keep questioning those negative doubts, with objections like why not keep on dreaming about change? Why not turn my dreams into a reality? Sharon heard a quote that says "Your past doesn't define you but your present will." She began reading literature like the Bible, The Greatest Salesman in the World, and The Purpose Driven life. These books were transforming because they all share a common denominator, they were about people with faith that transformed not only their lives but the lives of others. These were highly unlikely individuals that through the worst of circumstances and the good, were empowered to carry out the journeys set before them. Living life through the quest of these powerful individuals set her on the path to seeking out truth, increased faith, and gave her insight into recognizing the creativity inside. These key elements of empowerment would lead her into the future. She felt that while certain roads of life are not easy, you must take one day and step at a time. But also remembering that investing in others is the most rewarding, and fulfilling purpose anyone could have, the rewards will come back to you in more ways then one. She felt awesome in accomplishing the goals, and found with faith you can accomplish the impossible. In the process of this journey transformation will occur in your own life. Sharon recommends remembering that "If you cease to see life as a learning process you have disconnected from the journey" means, keep abreast of the path you are on, never quit, and realize life was meant to be lived it's like a breath of fresh air you have just inhaled, there are first, second, and third chances, never stop learning you can change.

> "There are no lonely ships out there, everyone is waiting to get on board somewhere, or at some time in their lives on a specific ship in life. It has just docked the harbors of your life, which ship are you going to board, and it's about what kind of boarding pass have you purchased. Is it going to be First class or Cargo?" (Sharon Cadle)

Today, out of a desire for continuous change SC Health Solutions was born. Seeing smiles on women's faces inside-out, head to toe became my mantra and model for success. Sharon feels she is truly a blessed woman, happier, healthier and fulfilled by the Power of Living in the encounters of change.

Sharon Cadle, CEO/Founder
SC Health Solutions
www.LeSharonbeautiboutique.com

Sharon Cadle's

Recipe for SUCCESS!

1. Write out a Strategic Plan it can start with a Things to do List the night before. You need an agenda for daily success. Create contacts; join networking groups, associations and power teams. STAY FOCUSED!

2. Invest time in prayer, yourself, family and friends. Read inspiring and upbeat messages of hope and faith.

3. Exercise your mind, body and spirit. Detox your life get rid of the garbage that is weighing you down.

4. Never stop asking questions of yourself or others. Gaining communication skills requires engaging in meaningful dialogue for real answers to be delivered. Don't be afraid! Speak

5. Remember life was designed for living and learning. Love yourself and others your life depends on it.

6. Think Big, Live Large in the life you were created to live.

7. Be Tenuous in your follow-up of clients and keep your promises. Good customer service is very important.

About Sharon Cadle

Introducing the Women behind SC Health Solutions

Sharon Cadle, CEO and Founder of SC Health Solutions was born out of believing in and demonstrating that change can happen in a women's life inside out, head to toe. Her dream was realized in 2003, when she began searching out skincare solutions for herself and wanting to see results for others. She spent years trying various regimens, and asking questions of health and skincare experts across the country. Her journey began with research becoming a graduate of Business Management, and laser/Skin technological institutes. The passion for skincare and the health wellness industry became a lifelong learning process.

Born and raised in Chicago, Illinois, Sharon currently resides in Scottsdale, Arizona where her dreams have become a reality. She aspires to reach women globally with insights, regimens and expert advice for spiritual and personal care. She has trained medical spa directors, aestheticians, and numerous individuals.

Sharon Cadle, CEO/Founder

SC Health Solutions

www.LeSharonbeautiboutique.com

Traci Campbell

"There is no such thing as coincidence"
William S. Burroughs

Us Against the World

Author, Coach, Public Speaker, Interviewer, IT professional. Those are some of titles I have been blessed to possess throughout my career thus far. However, my life did not start out nearly as impressive or promising. I did not come from a privileged background. Instead, like many families today, everyday was a struggle to survive.

Fortunately, education was the key that unlocked a whole new world for me. It was the golden ticket out of a life that could have easily turned into another statistic having come from the crime-ridden area where we lived in west side Baltimore. It was an area filled not only with crime, but with the unfortunately common issues we still see so much of today: gang violence, teen pregnancies, and drug dealing.

On top of these challenges to avoid, I had the challenges I faced at home. I was going through the normal issues that teens face as they mature including insecurities, depression and self-loathing. This was further compounded by a single parent who was also dealing with the same issues. We were a team. We relied on each other to survive in the world.

However, the issues I faced as a teen, coupled with my mother's, would later spawn the epiphany that led me to help tweens and teens growing up in similar situations.

Life started out very unkind to my mother who grew up in rural South Carolina. She was forced to leave school after the 8th grade to care for two ailing parents. She never got the chance to finish her education, and, being a single mother, she constantly struggled to make ends meet. This meant always having two or three jobs at a time so I could have the advantages that she never had.

By her early 50's, her health started deteriorating and she was forced to stop working altogether and collect disability pay. At age 18, I became the head of the household. I attended college and worked full-time to provide for my mother and myself.

For years I traveled as an IT consultant, but when my mother's health started to worsen, I stopped traveling so I could care for her. My mother lived her entire life just surviving. She harbored deep-seated insecurities and anxieties that she obtained as a child and was never given the proper nurturing and support from her parents in order to overcome them. As a result, she suffered from a deep depression that gradually consumed her. In August of 2007, my mother passed away after 13 years of battling congestive heart failure. She died without realizing any of the personal goals she had in life. She was 73.

My mother's story and personal struggles are the motivation behind *Heroes at Home Radio,* which showcases those single parents that had managed to be just as successful as others as they pursued their own careers and dreams.

The C.H.A.M.P. Within program was created to enrich the lives, specifically, of children from single parent homes, but the program can also benefit all tweens, teens, and their parents

With teenage pregnancy back on the rise, teen usage of anti-depressant drugs increasing, gang violence more prevalent than ever, and the unhealthy obsession many teens have with celebrity today, the need is great to equip single parents, as well as two parent households, with a way to start working on the emotional and mental health of teens.

While my life growing up with my mother was essentially "us against the world", it should never have been that way. No single parent home should feel that they are in the battle alone. The battle to save our tweens and teens falls on the shoulders of us all.

Traci Campbell, Host
Heroes at Home Radio
www.HeroesAtHomeRadio.com

The success "stew" below really helped me as I built and grew my business and organization. I am sure it will benefit your venture as well.

Traci Campbell's

Recipe for SUCCESS!

1. First and foremost, believe in and rely on a higher power. Strength and wisdom for success comes from not only your natural ability, but from having a healthy spiritual life as well.

2. Be as knowledgeable as possible about your business or project. Make it a weekly habit to take time to research and study trends, current events, and news related to your venture. This info can not only help your customers or clients trust your expertise, but it may also help you develop new ideas for your business.

3. Stay organized. Use spreadsheets, charts, or lists to keep track of tasks, deadlines, and new ideas. Use a spreadsheet or database to keep track of customers and client contact information. If necessary, seek help in using these tools as they will benefit your business greatly.

4. Set deadlines for your tasks and goals and most importantly, keep them! Setting time limits for task completion will help you to overcome procrastination and begin to see real progress. Also, avoid the temptation to move these deadlines once you set them.

5. Don't go it alone! Seek help and obtain help from other resources. Things like document transcription, database help, and website development can easily be outsourced to others to save time and allow you to continue focusing on acquiring customers and building your business.

6. Create a brain trust. Surround yourself with people and advisors that can offer you sound advice and/or give you honest opinions about your ideas. Keep the number small, but frequently communicate with use these trusted individuals to keep the well of ideas flowing and to possibly avoid going off in the wrong direction.

7. Be consistent! Be diligent in following item 1-6 above daily and weekly. Repetition is the key to success.

About Traci S. Campbell

Traci S. Campbell has been an IT consultant for over 15 years working for high profile corporate clients such as Sears, IBM, and McDonald's Corporation.

In 2003, she obtained her certification in life and business coaching so that she could be instrumental in helping others work through their personal blockages in order to live the life they desired.

In 2005, she co-founded a non-profit organization that aimed to help single working poor mothers. She launched her talk show program, "Heroes At Home Radio" in 2008.

Currently, she excels as a coach, author, and public speaker. She is regarded as a top advocate for single parent families, tweens, and teens. Her newly created self-help program*, "The C.H.A.M.P Within"*, has proven very successful for teens and tweens as well as parents.

Learn more about Traci at www.traciscampbell.com

www.thechampinyou.com

Cris Carter

"We are what we repeatedly do. Excellence, then, is not an act, but a habit!"
Arisotle

Mission – Vision – Passion

For more than 20 years, Cris was what you would call a vicious shark of a litigation attorney. And she was GOOD at it. The more vicious she was, the more people wanted her and the more people paid her. Luckily, that wasn't the key to her success. The key was running her business so effectively and efficiently that from the day she hung out her shingle, she was profitable. Cris set goals each and every year no matter what. Once she mastered a goal, Cris set new goals.

Before the age of 45, Cris was able to realize the great American dream: Retirement! For the first year it was fantastic; she enjoyed sleeping in, traveling with her husband, working out with a personal trainer every other day. Cris enjoyed studying for real estate and securities licensing. But she kept looking for more stimulation, more education, and more resources. That is when she realized that perhaps the Great American Dream might not be so great; for her, that is. Cris still had so much she wanted to do and so much she wanted to give to others.

You see, Cris wasn't one of those privileged youngsters who easily trots off to college and law school with a silver spoon and an attitude of entitlement. Cris was poor growing up. Struggling, and surrounded by every cliché of bad decision making and dead end life choices imaginable. She figured out that if she wanted something different (which she absolutely did) then she was going to have to figure it out for herself. Cris was going to have to work harder and be better. So she dug deep, fought hard for what she wanted, and made it happen!

Something that always frustrated Cris was that we have limited time so that meant she could only make an impact with the clients she could see one on one. That's how attorneys work and for 20 plus years she was stuck in that mindset. Once retired, Cris had the time and energy to devote to devising a way to reach more people than one on one allowed for. Cris loves psychology and systems and found a way to help other aspiring business owners discover their purpose, become excited, motivated, and yes - passionate about their life. Cris bring years of practical legal experience to the training, explaining what a business really needs to know to be safe and successful in our litigious society.

Cris found success by following her heart and what she learned along the way allows her to show others the way to success. Sticking to her beliefs is the very thing that not only led her out of poverty, but is a system that propelled her to the top of her occupation and led her to pursue things that were important to her and that she aspired to achieve.

As Cris says…"Everyone knows that MVP stands for Most Valuable Player. And YOU need to be the Most Valuable Player. Becoming an MVP doesn't come easy. But I have found a way to insure that MVP status: You see MVP to me doesn't just mean Most Valuable Player, but it also means Your Mission. Your Values and Your Passion aligned and in synchronicity. Without that alignment, you are just going through the motions like a lot of Americans; the same Americans that wake up one morning when they are in those senior years of reflection and feel like they blew it; that their life was not as significant as it should have been. Goals and dreams become your Vision and your Passion, but they need to be thought out and researched so you pick the ones best suited to become your Mission. I did it. I want to help others do it too."

Email: Cris@CrisCarterLaw.com
www.CrisCarterLaw.com
www.CrisCarterMVP.com

Cris Carter's

Recipe for SUCCESS!

1. **Have the Courage to Think Big:** When you can identify your essence and align that with a belief system that engages you, then your steps no longer are tentative but filled with the determination that you can achieve what you have the courage to implement.

2. **Let Your Passion Set Your Goals:** To have a meaningful and fulfilling life not only must you discover your passion, you must begin to live your passion. Your passion will be your guide to uncovering who you are meant to be and what your mission is today.

3. **Develop Systems: Organize and Manage your work, your office, your time.** Well considered work space and work flow allows you to better enjoy your work environment and puts you in position to tackle time and task management so you can move towards your goals more efficiently.

4. **Develop Your Drive From Within:** External motivation is never as powerful as internal. If your passions become your driving force you will never be at a loss for direction and motivation.

5. **Always Be Learning and Improving:** Begin the education process now. TODAY. Don't just think about it. Don't just talk about it. DO IT. Think how today you can be better than you were yesterday.

6. **Be Proactive:** Part of becoming empowered, my friend, is protecting yourself and your loved ones by being proactive with a safety net to avoid heartache, financial distress, and legal problems.|

7. **Expose Yourself to the Best:** Determine the 'best and brightest' in whatever you pursue, be it books, events, or people. Your time is the most limited of the resources you have, spend it on the best resources you can access.

About Cris Carter

Cris Carter has spent decades not only learning about legal entanglements but more importantly about people and their psychology. She now focuses on her MVP Coaching Program (Mission, Vision, Passion) that allows her to share her wealth of knowledge and experience. Cris is a natural at developing success systems; delivering her experience through public speaking and presenting meaningful programs and seminars. Her MVP program is designed to help others develop and achieve their absolute best, personally and professionally.

In her law practice Cris used her ability to make a difference in her client's life by teaching them how to not make mistakes, and when they do make mistakes how to overcome the problems caused and learn from those mistakes. Cris is excited to work with business people who are looking to take their business to the next level based on concrete systems and solid processes.

Contributing to her community is very important to Cris. While in Florida she served on the Board of Directors for Project Response (Aids Support Group) and Yellow Umbrella (child abuse prevention). Although Cris only moved to Colorado 3 years ago, she jumped right in and serves on the Board of the Senior Resource Council, is an Ambassador for the Alzheimer's Association and was the Charter President for several women's business groups including the American Business Women's Association.

The community awards which have been most meaningful to Cris are:

➢ **Tobias Simon Award** from the Florida Supreme Court (for providing legal services to people that were unable to afford legal services)
➢ **Woman of the Year 2009** (American Business Women's Association)
➢ **Athena Nominee 2010** (Chamber of Commerce)

Lawrence Cole
The Xtreme Marketing Guy

"Don't ask yourself what the world needs; ask yourself what makes YOU come alive, and then go do that; because THAT's what the world needs"
Howard Thurman

Mentoring – Can It Be The Key To Your Success?

Lawrence Cole never really felt at home in Corporate America. Perhaps that was because he learned the pitfalls of depending on a company very early in his career. At just 23 years old he was laid off of his very first corporate job during the "dot com bomb" of 2001. Ironically, he got the boot on the 1 year anniversary of having graduated from college with honors.

After having spent his entire life doing everything that he was told to do, from being on The National Dean's List, earning an honors degree, interning at NASA, and finally landing a "good job" for a major internet service provider he found himself not much better off than a beggar on any street corner in America.

Due to a strong independent streak Lawrence had been dabbling in the home based business arena since he had been a senior in college but he had never really taken it too seriously. After several months of trying to get another job to no avail, he went to his mailbox one day to discover that he had just received his last unemployment check for $230—in Los Angeles, one of the most expensive cities in America.

Several weeks later he found himself face-to-face with an eviction notice on his door. Meanwhile, he had nothing to his name besides the lint in his pocket, his beat up Jeep from college, a desk top computer (his internet service had been cut off), and a cupboard with a few cans of tuna. He had hit rock bottom. Knowing that it was time to get serious about making his own way, he quickly cut his losses, moved into a friend's spare room, and got to work building his own business.

Over the next several years he tried one home business after the next. With each enterprise he had a small to moderate level of success, but just could not achieve the momentum that he needed to break free from his need for a job. He worked 9 to 5 in corporate sales by day while building his businesses during his nights and weekends. He worked extremely long hours longing for even a glimmer of success; but time and time again it eluded him. The success that he wished for seemed right in front of his face, yet miles away at the same time.

To add insult to injury, he was living a nightmare in Corporate America. Having to answer to people he did not respect, being told what to do, and back-biting company politics had sadly become a part of his daily routine. He felt stuck in a rut, restless, and frustrated.

Eventually Lawrence became friends with Craig Duswalt, creator of the Rockstar System for Success™ who's brand he had personally watched go from inception to earning nearly 7 figures in less than a year. When Lawrence inquired about how he had accomplished such quick success Craig revealed that he had invested as much money as he could afford in 2 or 3 key mentors who were helping him build his business step-by-step. He advised Lawrence to do the same.

Being Coachable, Lawrence began to invest in one-on-one coaching with proven mentors who were already drawing 7+ figure incomes. It was then that everything began to turn around for him. He was able to quickly discover the mistakes that he had been making building businesses over the years and at last began to taste real success. The icing on the cake was that it was happening for him faster than it ever had before.

Today Lawrence is on a mission to show thousands of home based entrepreneurs and entrepreneur hopefuls how to cut their learning curves and build the successful, profitable businesses that elude 99% of everyone else who starts out on the path of business ownership. Lawrence understands exactly what it is like to be "searching for the holy grail" and coughing up stacks of investment money for half-baked basic principles packaged as "million dollar solutions" and being taken for a ride. He is passionate about demystifying the "secret sauce" that helps every day men and women to create their dream lives by becoming insanely successful in their businesses.

Lawrence Cole
Winning at Life International, LLC
http://www.xtrememarketingguy.com

Lawrence Cole

Recipe for SUCCESS!

1. **Find a Lake of Hungry Fish.** So many entrepreneurs make the mistake of forcing their ideas onto the public. Instead, look for an already hungry market of consumers with an insatiable desire to have a specific problem solved. Solve that problem, and then build your business around your solution.

2. **Niche and Grow Rich.** Don't attempt to appeal to everyone. Profile a specific target market and then create your solution to be exactly what that target market wants. You will increase the demand and the perceived value of your product or service offering

3. **Build a Consistent, Recognizable Brand Identity.** Disney. Coke. FedEx. IBM. When building your brand, make sure that the very mention of your name or business name creates an immediately recognizable vision in the public's mind. Then make sure that your brand is completely consistent in everything that has to do with your business from your website, books, eBooks, products, business cards, colors, and even the way that you dress.

4. **Invest in Proven Mentors.** Find several people who have already achieved what you wish to achieve and pay them for their time to show you exactly how they did it, step by step. Recruiting a mentor will help you to cut your learning curve and accelerate your success. Having several mentors as opposed to just one will help you to gain multiple perspectives and broaden your arsenal of strategies and tactics.

5. **Start or Join a Mastermind Group.** Having camaraderie with your peers is just as important has having mentors. All successful businesses incorporate the mastermind principle; think Board of Directors. Your mastermind group will help to hold you accountable with friendly competition, provide a wealth of shared information and resources, and also become an emotional haven where you can gain strength and inspiration in the safety of a team atmosphere

6. **Create Maximum Leverage.** Without leverage, you may as well just get a job. In everything that you do in your business, build it from the beginning with a strategy of how you will eventually remove yourself from every possible aspect of running its daily activities. Ultimately your goal as a business owner is to have people and systems working under your direction. Have a written process for EVERYTHING in your business so that you can eventually teach someone else how to do it as your profits slowly make it possible to outsource almost every aspect of your business, one-by-one.

7. **Develop Multiple Income Streams.** Set a goal to develop multiple income streams no matter what business you are in. This can be done via books, eBooks, "how to" products, membership clubs, taking coaching clients, or even hosting live events. Commit to getting 1-2 income streams up and running in your business each year until you have at least 10; then market and position all 10 streams day and night and watch the "0's" add to your income each month!

About Lawrence Cole

Lawrence Cole, The Xtreme Marketing Guy, shows small and home-based business owners how to dominate their niche with attraction-based branding and competition-crushing internet marketing strategies. He founded his company, **Winning at Life International** in 2004 with a vision of becoming a game-changing agent in the lives and businesses of entrepreneurial maverick types like himself.

After a decorated career in corporate sales, Lawrence wanted nothing more than to break free from the "rat race" and lead a more fulfilling life as a corporate refugee "beyond the gates". Lawrence is also dedicated to reaching back into the 9 to 5 world and showing aspirant entrepreneurs how to successfully transition from the drudgery of Corporate America to the freedom and fulfillment of full-time business ownership.

Lawrence currently resides in Los Angeles, CA and enjoys reading, mixed-martial arts, yoga, health and fitness, live music, USC and Miami Hurricane football, watching The Lakers, and various cultural events.

Mariana M Cooper (Mari)

"To Thine Own Self Be True."
William Shakespeare

You Deserve To Love What You Do For A Living!

I am grateful to have learned 2 vital things very early in my life. I began dancing at the age of 4 and rode my first horse at the age of 6. Both of these activities turned into lifelong pursuits and I consider myself to be very lucky to have learned what having a passion was about at such a young age.

As I grew up going to the stable to ride I began to take note of the fact that while my parents were working hard at their day jobs the other kids parents were at the stable watching their lessons in the afternoon. I asked the parents why they were not at work. And they told me that they indeed were working. They were "entrepreneurs" and had the flexibility to work at whatever time they wanted. Most arranged their schedules to be available for family activities, events, etc. and had staff to delegate to and/or the option to work at off hours. They also had A LOT more money as their kids had their own horses, and some had a horse for each kid in the family!

By the age of 13 I knew that I wanted to have it all. To be able to work at something I loved AND to have the time to train and compete at my two beloved passions which each required serious time and financial commitments. I also knew that working at something you hate just was not necessary or admirable.

Fast forward 15 years with a BA in psychology and an MBA in marketing I was recruited into a big Fortune 100 company and moved with my horse, cat and dance shoes to New Jersey for work. On the one hand I was thrilled to be in the state where the US Equestrian Team trained, but I had also turned down an opportunity to dance with MTV to do it.

I was on my way to what I call "Life's Boot Camp" also known as "Corporate America." I watched my colleagues become robots each morning and deny their true selves day in and day out. I personally could not succumb to what I coined "Corporate Anesthesia" and I went about getting as much experience and training as I could with the full plan to leave and start my own business.

A few years into my 7 year stay in corporate I had the tragic loss of my fiancé passing away. I was of course devastated, but his passing made me pursue my already growing interest in intuition and manifesting with a much greater focus. I wanted to understand the greater meanings of life as I knew that there was a lot more than the physical world. As I developed the intuitive gifts that I actually inherited from my Mother and Grandmother, I provided spiritual consultation and intuitive readings to clients. At the same time I had a marketing consulting practice with major corporations and eventually began assisting entrepreneurs in building businesses in their passions that made profits too.

What was interesting was that the Intuitive Clients would figure out their passion and need help with the marketing of their business. And the marketing clients were realizing that they needed to develop a keen sense of intuition in order to be successful. The two sides of my business merged and gave birth to what I have coined "Enlightened Entrepreneurs." I now have Aha! Moments, Inc which provides education, inspiration and motivation to entrepreneurs in the areas of marketing, manifesting and making a profit in their passion based businesses.

While the sacrifice of time and resources may be necessary to get a business up and running, sacrificing passion is never an option. You absolutely deserve to LOVE what you do for a living and the financial and time freedom to go along with it. With focus and balance I truly believe that you can have it all!

Mariana M Cooper (Mari) - Marketing and Manifesting Strategist for Enlightened Entrepreneurs
www.trustyourahamoments.com

Mari Cooper's

Recipe for SUCCESS!

The Aha! Action:

1. Focus on your passion that you are willing to earn income from (some passions are just meant to be sacred to you without the pressure to earn money).

2. Ask the question "How may I serve?" Often. It always gets answered!

3. Make a list of the top 40 characteristics of your Ideal Target Client.

4. Figure out what top 3 problems that your Ideal Client needs to be solved that YOU have to solution to.

5. Create a plan, and market to what they need not to your own comfort zone.

6. Focus on building a solid foundation – Your List, Your Core products, services or programs and your communication strategy.

The Aha! Attraction:

7. Make sure to meditate, reflect, journal and master your Intuition. It is by far your very best built in decision making tool and it is never wrong!

The Action + The Attraction = The Aha! Moment
Consistency is the key to success!

About Mariana Cooper

Mariana M Cooper (Mari) is a Seasoned, Internationally recognized and formally educated Marketing Strategist and Spiritual Intuitive who is equally fluent in both the languages of Executive Level Marketing and Advanced Manifesting and Intuition.

Mari has an MBA in marketing and a BA in psychology. She is also an Angel Therapy Practitioner with Dr Doreen Virtue for over 7 years, as well as a Teacher and Kabbalist with The Modern Mystery School.

In addition to providing over 15 years of Marketing Strategy, Advertising, Promotions, Film and TV production and Entertainment Marketing Consultation to Fortune 100 companies, medium and small businesses, Mari has provided spiritual consultation and Intuitive Readings to over 1000 clients privately and in dynamic intensive workshops and coaching programs.

Mari is the author of several business building and intuition development products exclusively designed for "Enlightened Entrepreneurs" including The Intuitive Living Oracle Cards, The Intuition Toolkit and The Intuition Mastery Home Study System and The Virtual Dream Team Building System.

She was invited to do readings for a private event at Neiman Marcus and has appeared on both radio and television as an expert in both business and spiritual topics.

Mariana Cooper

www.trustyourahamoments.com
www.trustyourahamoments.com
www.ahamoments.tv
www.facebook.com/ahamomentsinc

Dr. Sarah David

"Our deepest fear is not that we are inadequate. Our deepest fear is that we are powerful beyond measure. It is our light, not our darkness that most frightens us. We ask ourselves, Who am I to be brilliant, gorgeous, talented, fabulous? Actually, who are you not *to be?"*
Marianne Williamson

Knowing Your Passion and Personal Brand is Key to Success

Dr. Sarah David is the Chief Empowerment Officer and Founder of the Empowered Women's Institute for Entrepreneurship™. Through this global association set for pre-launch activities early in 2011, Dr. David uses her passion for connecting with others, drive, "go-giver" attitude and over 13 years' experience in professional development to help others understand their purpose and powerful personal brand and get inspired, get focused and get connected in business, career and life! Within this network she is able to provide a platform to inspire the development of others in their career advancement, leadership development and entrepreneurial learning. She specializes in strategic planning, strength's coaching, personal branding and professional presence. Often referred to as the "Go to Guru," and a "Social Butterfly," Dr. David is a career and reinvention strategist who understands the needs of the entrepreneurial-minded woman and the desire to connect with other like-minded individuals in designing work around life instead of life around work. As a serial entrepreneur herself, she understands the desire of this special group in crafting a work life that satisfies independence, security, validation and freedom to pursue what is most pleasing to the entrepreneurial palette. She has lived internationally from North Carolina to Japan and has a thirst for connecting with others to develop rich relationships to facilitate powerful, personal, brand building.

Described as "good for the soul," this "make it happen" strategist uses her diplomatic leadership style to create a shared vision and assemble a team of resources to assist entrepreneurs whether they are working for themselves or someone else, aspiring or entrepreneurial minded women to create, connect, and craft their work around their life in achieving their goals. She realized that many people whether they are a small business owner, executive, careerist, individual trying to advance in their current careers or re-inventing themselves for new careers or business opportunities are trying to discover what they are built for and what unique qualities make them stand out.

In her work as a national certified counselor and certified career management coach, Dr. David realized that people were feeling stuck in unfulfilled jobs or situations, being defined by job descriptions or clients that restrict them creatively, or trying to identify what they want to do when they "grow up" no matter what age! People are trying to figure out how to get from where they are to where they want to be and she is committed to facilitating that process.

With a degree in speech communication and successful background in education and training, Sarah uses these skills to help others understand how to identify their strengths and talents and then match those talents to a business or career they love. This starts with identifying the mission, vision, values and passions that make up an individual's core…their PURPOSE. She took her interest in professionally developing others further by obtaining a Master's degree in Counseling and training in image and personal branding certification which has enabled her to pinpoint the potential in others and identify what makes them unique. Ultimately, she earned a doctorate in leadership which has allowed her to incorporate leadership development into her professional development offerings for a more holistic approach to client development.

Dr. David has counseled and coached multitudes of success minded individuals across multiple industries throughout her career in identifying their passions, leadership abilities and unique personal brand.

Sarah has been sought after by entrepreneurs, business executives and professionals to provide leadership and professional development coaching and training for them personally and their teams.

She is an energetic and action oriented strategist that has been a contributor to a variety of magazine articles, cover features, pod casts, conference events and live seminars. To keep things exciting, she also incorporates her love for connecting with others in her work in voice-over and commercial acting. Her upcoming "Empowered Women" book series is set to launch early in 2011!

Sarah empowers others in identifying their purpose and discovering their personal brands so they can live life boldly and transform their passions into a life they love. She is committed to facilitating the professional development of others via powerful empowerment strategies.

Balance is Key.

Sarah is a very active member of her community. When she is not busy coaching or speaking, she enjoys traveling to warm destinations and spending time with her family and friends.

Sarah David, Ph.D.
www.empoweredwomensinstitute.com

Dr. Sarah David's

Recipe for SUCCESS!

1. Trust God; be grateful daily

2. Dare to believe

3. Think out of the box

4. Have a positive CAN-DO attitude

5. Think out of the box; Take strategic risks

6. Tap into your "success" network

7. Celebrate your YOUniqueness

8. Know that you are worthy of success

9. Weave your passions into your work

10. Seek out the wisdom of a coach

About Dr. Sarah David

Dr. David has a passion for assisting others in academic, business, career and professional services. As a lifelong learner, she is fascinated by innovation and entrepreneurialism. She has a special interest in leadership, professional development and coaching. Originally from North Carolina, Dr. David moved around as an Air Force dependent. She has lived internationally in Okinawa, Japan and currently resides in Houston, Texas.

She has worked in a variety of industries from business to institutions of higher education. Her experience includes working in various capacities including business owner, 13 years in higher education in leadership and professional positions in community colleges, private colleges and universities across the country in the following roles: Assistant Dean of Student Success, Professor, Career Counselor, Resident Director and Internship Coordinator.

Dr. David received her Ph.D. in Higher Education Administration from the University of Texas at Austin, M.Ed. Counseling from North Carolina State University and a B.A. Speech from Louisiana Tech University.

In addition, Dr. David has credentials and specialized training as follows:

National Certified Counselor, Distance Credentialed Counselor, Certified Strength's Quest Facilitator, Certified Personal Brand Strategist, Strength's Coach, Strategic Planning, Performance Management, Certified Career Management Coach, Certified Achieve Global Trainer Noel Levitz Customer Service Training and Leadership Advisory Boards. Her teaching and training experience includes both traditional and online delivery options.

Dr. Sarah David, Ph.D.
832-444-3734
sdavid@consultant.com
www.empoweredwomensinstitute.com

Bill Davis

"Everything in life, ... has to have balance."
Donna Karan

A Good Front End Decision...

..will usually prevent a rear end problem. Bill's journey into operating a successful home based business taught him a great deal and took some time. Now, looking back, it seems to have been written in the stars, the place where dreams are created.

After drifting through high school in the 60's and tenure of military service, Bill was highly motivated to gain an education. Working full time while attending college was a huge challenge but proved to be of benefit. He was hired before graduation by IBM and began his selling career which spanned over twenty five years of remarkable success in the technology sector. Working for major companies such as Digital Equipment, Xerox and Sun Microsystems, prepared him to develop methods in discovering the "real problem" and finding solutions in performance and priority management. Ownership in a real estate firm and a consulting company enriched his skills and furthered the journey to his destiny.

After achieving great financial success, at the young age of 48 he retired from the corporate grind to enjoy a two year sabbatical of self-discovery. With this re-firing of his purpose, he was excited about his future.

Married to the love of his life, Kelly, who operated an MLM dealership, the two complement each other's strengths and weaknesses. High energy, enthusiasm and strong work ethics with focused attention to details, systems procedures and controls make for a dynamic combination. However, as with most working women today, having too much to do and too little time, Kelly found it difficult to keep a narrow focus and a good balance of personal and profession time. But what was the real problem?

Bill discovered that time wasn't the problem; it was the managing of priorities. He formulated a solution but was unable to find a planning tool on the market to meet their needs. This opportunity was the foundation for his next venture.

My Daily Director was created to assist his wife and their team to become organized, focused and properly prioritized. This easy to understand, simple to use paper based planner has been a powerful addition to their life and to thousands of other business owners as well.

Have you also noticed that managing a business and your personal life by a mere schedule can quickly put you into overwhelm? When you design your life around your most important priorities, things just work better! If you have your priorities in order, you can become your best, resist urgencies and have control of your time to realize your dreams and destiny.

Finding balance in an unbalanced world is difficult but necessary. Becoming your best and keeping it all together is a daily challenge. Having a powerful tool in your arsenal can help you achieve your dreams, discover your purpose and fulfill your destiny.

The *My Daily Director* system is the planner of choice of champions who understand that the problem isn't in time control but the correct management of priorities. When things are put in order and done in order, you get predictable results and a sense of balance and control.

Since its creation, the Davis family has enjoyed more time together, produced more, helped others more, found better balance and dreamed more.

Bill Davis – Founder
www.mydailydirector.com

Bill Davis

Recipe for SUCCESS!

1. Know who you are. Your self-concept precedes all your behavior.

2. Dream big dreams. Don't think small, our lives are the manifestation of our thinking.

3. Define your goals. Goals are dreams with a when and a why. WRITE THEM DOWN.

4. Articulate your purpose. Define your life's purpose by what you do and don't do.

5. Set your strategies. Strategies are the broad plans that lead to your tasks and "to do" lists.

6. Assign your tactics. Tactics are the daily tasks that support strategies to achieve goals by fulfilling an ultimate purpose.

About Bill Davis

Bill Davis holds a B.A. degree with majors in business and psychology. He worked full time while completing his formal education, and he has served in the military. Immediately after graduation Bill began a sales career, which spans over 30 years, touting high-level positions with technology companies such as IBM, Xerox and Sun Microsystems. He has started and owned successful businesses in the services and real estate sectors. He continued his quest for knowledge and wisdom resulting in his exceeding his financial goals and career aspirations. During his career, Bill played a key role in approximately $100 million dollars of transactions. In addition to his financial success, he compiled many successful years of experience in coaching individuals and businesses.

In 1999 Bill "retired" from the corporate world at 48 years of age, highly successful but burned out. He invested two years seeking new meaning and purpose. After much soul-searching, he defined his ultimate mission: to directly help one million people find their God-given purpose. In 2001 he joined his wife in her EcoQuest home-based business and took the organization to whole new level.

As a result of helping others gain financial success and life direction, Bill created the My Daily DirectorTM system - an effective group of tools to assist those who want a balanced and meaningful life by their own design. This unique process focuses on the benefits of experiencing life through priority management.

Bill enjoys a significant life by following his own system, of putting and keeping his priorities in the proper order. He invests most of his productive hours coaching and consulting business owners, and managing his real estate portfolio. Performance cars capture his attention but long bike rides and pleasure boating with his wife and friends are his leisure activities.

Bill has traveled the world, yet has chosen to return to his roots and calls the Midwest "home." He is married to the love of his life, Kelly, and has one son, Stephen. He and his wife are also involved in ministry, having founded Glory to God Ministries, an organization designed to strengthen and equip Christian leaders through the principles of Living In Faith Every day.

Bill Davis
www.mydailydirector.com
Bill@mydailydirector.com

Kelly Davis

"The place where God calls you is where your deep gladness and the world's deep hunger intersect." Frederick Buechner

Follow Your Passion

Kelly started as a very young entrepreneur. At four years old she created her first business – manufacturing and distributing potholders in her neighborhood. Since it's pretty hard to turn down a four year old on a five cent item, the positive reinforcement for sales and entrepreneurial endeavors had a great start!

This was followed by neighborhood theatrical productions, a dog sitting business and lots of fund raising throughout her life. At the ripe age of 20, she started in her first network marketing business with gusto. While not earning the really big bucks, she developed enough retail profits to quit her job and live independently. She learned that growing her own business not only provided a living, it expanded her life.

Kelly's true passion has always been tied to ministry and for the next 20 plus years she dedicated herself to working with a religious group. To financially support the organization, Kelly was instrumental in helping the group develop several small businesses - everything from a small ski area, grade A goat dairy, an indoor flea market, voice mail answering service and a design and graphic company. All these different businesses were operated on a shoestring budget and yet all were profitable.

As an organization, the religious group she had been with for so long had "lost its way" and she felt a new burn to follow her dream of helping people fulfill their God given potential. She walked away from the group (with fear and trembling) but no hard feelings or cash! She did take with her a lot of experience and the belief that she could (by God's grace) build one more successful business.

So at 46 and single, Kelly started "Business Development Group" which was associated with a networking company that sold air purifiers and other healthy living technologies. By learning to follow a proven system, at the end of her first year, she was earning a six figure income, traveling, and driving a BMW! She also launched *Glory to God Ministries* and *Billboards for God* during that time. She was living the good life with one exception. Kelly had never been married and was still looking for the love of her life. At 48, while helping a team member call back leads, she met her soul mate and five months later was married and simply relocated her home based business. Together, she and her husband continued to expand their enterprises and have literally traveled the world enjoying the time, freedom and purpose driven work of helping others learn how to discover and follow their own God given dreams.

Kelly Davis
www.ecobusiness.com/kbdavis

Kelly Davis   *Recipe for* SUCCESS!

1. Have passion for your work and know your WHY

2. Expose your business (product or service) to a consistent number of people on a regular basis – this can be through paid advertising or sweat equity.

3. Be humble and coachable seeking out successful mentors and following their lead.

4. Follow a proven system and make yourself accountable to someone.

5. Be grateful at all times for everything; knowing that God will work it all for good if you allow Him to. People are attracted to this attribute like bees to honey!

Larry Davis

"Beware of the thief that's in the streets who seeks to steal your purse, but also beware of the thief that's in your mind who seeks your promise."

Jim Rohn

The Thumping that Heals

My emergence into entrepreneurship began with not much fanfare, some would refer to it as a nudge, others, had it happened to them may not have recognized it at all because as the quote goes "When the student is ready the teacher will appear." I refer to that moment as being "thumped!"

One of my most cherished mentors acquainted me with this theory by reintroducing to me the law of physics discovered by Sir Isaac Newton, while watching an apple fall from a tree. It's stated this way: "A body in motion continues in the same motion until acted upon by an outside force." Simply explained, I was the apple continuing on this same course of mediocrity and conformity until I was "thumped" via an invitation to come and listen to this brilliant young gentleman speak on the difference between profits and wages. "Wages will make you a living, but profits will make you a fortune!"

I was transformed by these new philosophies that were being introduced to me and the mentors and thought leaders that were being presented to me. At that moment I knew this was the void in my life which had been missing. I immediately began to immerse myself into countless numbers of books, audios and seminars relating to personal growth/personal development. I invested in personal coaching and, in the process, received my certification to become a life coach. Along the way I also began writing articles some of which were published in domestic and international magazines.

Finally, that "thump" has landed me in a position to impact many more lives than I would have ever dreamt, as an owner of an international coffee distributorship. I initially had no interest in this industry, mainly because I was not a coffee drinker and I was very pleased with other endeavors.

I was reminded of a famous quote. "A mind is like a parachute, it does you no good unless it's open," so I met with some of the executives of the company and learned amazing facts about the industry such as coffee being the second largest traded commodity in the world next to oil, coffee being the second most consumed liquid in the world, next to water and that 3 of 4 people drink coffee. The tipping point? This was no ordinary coffee. It was coffee with a healthy herb infused in it!

Coffee previously had been an industry reserved only for the elite or those who had been born into the business. Only those who fit into either of those groups could profit from it. Now, with all of the acidity levels and some of the health issues coffee would cause some people, I feel very blessed to be able offer a product to people that instead of impairing their health actually supports their wellness.

It is also gratifying to me that in this economic downturn for thousands of individuals, I'm able to introduce them to a business that is truly recession proof, because people drink coffee regardless of the economy. It also helps that this business has a franchise business model without the franchise price!

Speaking of franchises, here's a huge business clue, McDonald's, Burger King, Wendy's and Dunkin Donuts have shifted 70% of their advertising dollars toward coffee, featuring the McCafe, BK Joe, and America Runs on Dunkin. This is because they realized that coffee is the most consumable product in business history!

Just because I'm successful now don't be mistaken and think I didn't have challenges presented to me throughout my journey.

Having to be at the hospital or nursing home 3-4 days a week for three years while both my parents were, simultaneously bed ridden.

Conquering the inner enemy. In his book, As a Man Thinketh, James Allen shares that the greatest enemy is the "inner me," meaning the self-talk and the self-doubt that enables us all because we're travelling new roads.

The manner in which I was able to overcome both of these challenges were the same, through prayer to my creator, standing on the shoulders of giants who had experienced similar circumstances and my mastermind group which includes my wife.

Larry Davis
larry@sippinghealthycoffee.com
www.sippinghealthycoffee.com

Larry Davis'

Recipe for SUCCESS!

1. Hire a coach

2. Immerse yourself in personal growth material

3. Set specific measurable goals

4. Learn to discipline your disappointments

5. Dedicate time for mind/body/soul rejuvenation

6. Reward yourself for steps of achievements

7. Allow for infinite intelligence

About Larry Davis

Larry Davis resides in Houston, Texas. He is a sought after author, poet and speaker. Larry is a recognized leader in both the personal development and home based business industries, having trained and mentored numerous individuals, both domestically as well as abroad.

His primary passion for the past six years has been in the network marketing industry and he truly enjoys not only the income he is able to create but the joy it brings him in assisting others in being able to live the lifestyle of their dreams. Larry feels as long as we are committed to our dream and apply the action steps needed to make it happen that we can turn our dreams into reality despite the odds and the many challenges we may face. "What ever the mind of a man can conceive and believe he will achieve" Napoleon Hill

To find out more about Larry and the business he is currently building visit www.sippinghealthycoffee.com or contact him by email via larry@sippinghealthycoffee.com

Raven Blair-Davis

"I will do today what others won't, so that I can live my life tomorrow like others can't."
Jerry Rice

The Power of Inspiration

I personally know that the power of inspiration can change lives – it has totally transformed mine! My story is an example of how harnessing this power can help you achieve your goals and visions, way beyond your wildest dreams.

As a child, my parents wanted the best for me. However, my upbringing was very strict and having goals or dreams were not encouraged often. Little did I know that the strict ways in which I was brought up would later become the culprit for my life's obstacles, and the lack of positive support from my parents would later trigger a lot of self-doubt, low self-esteem, and little hope in accomplishing my dreams.   As I became an adult, I grew accustomed to settling for what I had in life. I began to believe that whatever I had was exactly what I deserved...and nothing more.

But somehow I often found myself wondering, Why not me? Why can't I have more? I began to read books like *Think and Grow Rich*, by Napoleon Hill, *The Game of Life and How to Play It*, by Florence Skoval Shin, and *Unstoppable* by Cynthia Kersey. I really enjoyed the inspirational stories Cynthia told of people who at one time had very little in life who, because of their strong will and determination, were now best-selling authors, extraordinary athletes, business owners, and some were even of the rich and famous. I begin to buy more books and soon had my own library. I added CDs and DVDs, all containing incredible stories that inspired me. I attended seminars to learn from famous luminaries from all over the world, and I began to hope again. I started dreaming again only this time I was having some very lofty dreams. It felt absolutely wonderful! But after about four years had passed, I noticed I had not seen much progress or change. I was still living day-to-day, and other than learning from some dynamic people, I had not seen much of a difference in our lives. Frustration and disappointment set in.

In my darkest hour, a light shined.....my journey begins!

In February 2006, my mother went into the hospital for surgery. We thought she would be home in a week or so, but it turned into six months. During the first three weeks, I sat and watched my mother lying helplessly in the Intensive Care Unit. I wondered if she had done what she wanted to do with her life and if she had any regrets.

Surprisingly, I came to realize that these were the very same questions I had about my own life. I realized I hadn't done what I wanted to do with my life, nor did I know my true passion. I had been so busy doing things for everyone else that I didn't have a clue about my own true purpose, passion, or vision. This was the day that God put on my heart that it was now my time to shine – my time to give to others, to make a difference, and to change lives.

A few weeks later, right there in the hospital waiting room, I started sketching out the format for a radio show created to inspire, empower and uplift women like myself. Women Power Talk Radio was created.

Now, this was not an easy task, and I had to overcome many obstacles. I had little time and few resources, and I had never tried claiming my own power before. I felt shaky and insecure about my abilities. But I knew this time I couldn't give up. I stayed focused even though it was extremely difficult. I set a launch date for my first show, got the tools I required, lined up my guest, and two months later Women Power Talk Radio aired! (http://www.womenpower-radio.com) What an unbelievable feeling that was – I did it!

Today I can truly say that I've never been happier or more fulfilled. My radio show has expanded into a network with three radio programs, and my career as a talk show personality continues moving in new and exciting directions.

Use Inspiration to Change Your Life: Five Essential Keys

1. Know that your dreams are worth the effort.

And you are worth your dreams! Do whatever it takes to turn your dreams into reality. Be true to your vision and claim your power.

Being on the radio was a dream I had in my early teens, but somehow along the way I had given up on it, mainly because of fear. I was afraid I would fail the FCC test that was required. Now, here I was at age fifty-five, and my long lost dream of being on the radio had not only surfaced but was a living reality. And there was no FCC license required to have an Internet radio show or podcast!

I made a wish list of all the people I had admired throughout the years who I'd love to interview on my show. I wanted my listeners to hear their stories, learn their success strategies and formulas, and how they overcame their challenges. I wanted to be a modern day Napoleon Hill! I immediately began to send out email requests and make phone calls, sharing my story and asking if they would be willing to share their knowledge in order to empower others. One by one, without ever asking me how many listeners I had, they accepted my invitation. Yes, some of my very favorite authors and speakers – like Cynthia Kersey, Lisa Kitter, and Rene Reid Yarnell – agreed to be guests on my show! I've also had the incredible opportunity to interview acclaimed actress Jayne Kennedy, as well as former President Clinton's diarist Janis F. Kearney and Claudette Robinson, the "First Lady of Motown."

2. Ask and you shall receive.

Make a list of what you require and who could assist you. Don't try to do it all yourself. Have the courage to ask others for their support. You'll be amazed at how many people will willingly share their time and talents.

In my case, I asked family members, friends, and complete strangers, "Who do you know that would be open to being a guest on my show?" I needed a professional looking Web site, and I had no extra money to invest so I bartered to get the necessary tools and resources.

One day I was sharing some of my challenges with my friend Lisa, and I asked for her assistance in getting the word out about Women Power (http://www.womenpower-radio.com). She agreed to put a little blurb about me in her newsletter that would attract advertisers. A couple of days after our conversation I acquired over a dozen advertisers for my show, and since then I've had no problem consistently bringing on new advertisers and sponsors.

3. Ask yourself, "*How badly do I want this?*"

What commitments and sacrifices are you willing to make so that you can accomplish your dreams? What inspires you that will keep you going during the tough times? Remember, if you are lacking inspiration right now, a vision of being of service to others in your own, unique way can totally inspire you. Find opportunities to assist other people, and watch your business grow in abundance.

I often wondered how was I going to keep my show going, but I knew deep inside that I had a taste of what accomplishing goals and dreams felt like, and I wanted it bad enough that I was willing to do whatever it took, even if it meant I had to get up three hours early and go to bed three hours late. I had a burning desire, and I knew I had to keep going.

4. Success is a combination of "inspiration" and "perspiration."

Developing a winning action plan is truly one of the big keys to success. When I start my day with a definite purpose, the outcome is fantastic! Each night I plan the next day's activities to insure that it will be a productive day. One of the things at the top of my list is to reach out to three personal contacts a day. I do that to build deeper relationships, joint ventures, and gain more referrals. My first choice is to pick up the phone and call them, but if I am pressed for time I will at least send them an email wishing them a very blessed and prosperous day.

5. "This too shall pass."

When life throws you a curve ball (and you will come up against some big challenges), remember that you are in control of your life. Circumstances can be hard, money can be scarce, and times can be tough, but it's how you handle these circumstances and your drive to overcome obstacles that will ultimately make the real difference. Trials and tribulations build character, so embrace them when they come and be confident and strong. Never lose faith, and never give up!

Sometimes just as you think you've seen the worst, something else happens that brings you to your knees, praying once again for strength and endurance. At one point, my husband and I were going through some difficult financial times, and we got a letter from our mortgage company saying we were fourteen days from foreclosure. That's when I begin to get really creative. I was determined that we were not going to lose our home.
I decided to launch my new broadcasting course sooner than I'd planned, and to get the money we needed I would pre-sell the course. I began to get ready for it mentally. I watched the movie *The Secret* twice a day; I listened to my favorite audios of teleseminar secrets by Alex Mandossian, I called my support team of friends and mentors, and we simply spoke it into existence.

One day the phone rang. It was a friend of mine who had just returned from a conference in another country. She mentioned that the speaker spoke about how beneficial it would be for the people in attendance who aspired to be speakers should strongly consider a radio show or podcast.

She said she immediately thought of me. Without even thinking, I told her she had perfect timing because I was launching a course designed to have her show up and running in six weeks. She was excited and told me she had met three other people who desired their own show too. All four of them signed up, and after that, others appeared. Another dream came true despite the curve ball I was thrown!

Always be true to your inspiration, call upon the unstoppable power within you, never give up, and be inspired by others who have achieved their dreams. The power of inspiration will transform your life!

Raven Blair Davis – "The Talk Show Maven"
Founder & Host www.WomenPower-Radio.com   www.careersfromthekitchentable.com
www.facebook.com/kitchentablecareers   www.twitter.com/workathomeradio

Read more about Raven on page 362

Raven Blair Davis'

Recipe for SUCCESS!

1. Start each morning by listening to messages that inspire or empowers you to go that extra mile...no matter what!

2. Set your intentions each day to stay committed and laser focus to reach your financial goals. Do not get distracted or quit.

3. Always think of what you can do differently than others in your industry and stand out above the crowd.

4. Use the power of your voice to grow your business faster (use the telephone to prospect, podcasting, create audio-books, teleseminars)

5. Develop a team to assist you and delegate. Free yourself up to work on your business not in your business. Do Not Try To Do It All Yourself!

6. Speak it, Claim it, Achieve it and be UNSTPOPPABLE in your pursuit.

7. Check emails twice daily and voice mail and stay in income producing mode 80% of the day.

More About the Compiling Author - Raven Blair Davis

America's Leading Authority on Leveraging the Power of Your Voice!

Raven Blair Davis, aka "The Talk Show Maven" is a women who, after many years of searching for her purpose, is fulfilling her lifelong dream. That dream, twenty years in the making, was realized April 23, 2006 when she broadcast her first radio show right from her own kitchen table.

Born and raised in Cleveland, Ohio Raven currently resides in Houston, Texas where she is not only fulfilling her own purpose in life, but she's on a mission to inspire others to do the same, by giving them the opportunity to shine in what they do.

As an award winning talk show host (named Universal 7 Radio Network's "Talk Show Host of the Year" award in 2008. Aired on 1320 WARL AM Radio), celebrity interviewer, columnist, speaker, author and executive producer of multiple radio shows, both live, on air and on the Internet, Raven has proven that the power of one's voice can pave the road to success.

She's a pro when it comes to interviewing thought leaders, celebrities, power business owners and ordinary people with extraordinary stories. Here are just some of the people Raven has had the pleasure of interviewing on her shows:

Hip-Hop & Business Mogul, Russell Simmons
Featured in the Popular Movie, *The Secret*, Lisa Nichols
Talk Show Host, Montel Williams
America's #1 Success Coach, Jack Canfield (co-founder of the Chicken Soup books)
Actress, Fran Dresher (You may know her better as "The Nanny")
International Motivational Speaker, Les Brown
Marketing Guru, Alex Mandossian
Cookie Man & Literacy Advocate, Wally Amos
Self-Made Multimillionaire, Ali Brown
The View's Sherri Shepherd
Actresses Lindsay Wagner, Victoria Rowell, Kim Fields, Tippi Hedrin and more!

Tracey Doctor

"The future belongs to those who believe in their dreams."
Eleanor Roosevelt

Shine Your Light

Tracey's entrepreneurial drive began out of a need and a desire to find a viable solution for her own hair challenges. She was determined to create a unique hair product to help achieve fuller longer, healthier hair within 30 days. From the initial idea she started her home based business. She began doing friends' and family's hair from home and soon became a successful salon owner who specialized in providing, healthy hair growth solutions for women with hair loss. She developed and created a unique concept where by women would now be able to get additional coverage without damaging their own hair. Her clients were excited and relied on Tracey for her knowledge of herbs and natural remedies. Her real passion and purpose, being of service to others, began to blossom and she added consulting.

One of her favorite quotes is this:

"Our deepest fear is not that we are inadequate. Our deepest fear is that we are powerful beyond measure. It is our light, not our darkness that most frightens us. We ask ourselves, who am I to be brilliant, gorgeous, talented, and fabulous? Actually, who are you not to be? You are a child of God. Your playing small does not serve the world. There is nothing enlightened about shrinking so that other people won't feel insecure around you. We are all meant to shine, as children do. We were born to make manifest the glory of God that is within us. It's not just in some of us; it's in everyone. And as we let our own light shine, we unconsciously give other people permission to do the same. As we are liberated from our own fear, our presence automatically liberates others." -Marianne Williamson

This explains very well Tracey's unique ability to help women find holistic solutions to their health concerns. While doing so she also encourages them to understand the healing powers of herbs as well as other holistic and alternative modalities.

Tracey has faced challenges along the way as have most in life. Her mother became very ill and had to undergo a life threatening surgery, but through the Grace of God she pulled through. There was a long recovery period once she was sent home and Tracey was determined to give her mother the care she needed and became her mother's full time caregiver. She was just as determined to not let that responsibility stop her dream of having a successful health and beauty consulting practice. In fact, she quickly realized that God had placed her in that position so she could truly understand the importance of what many of her clients had felt and expressed to her throughout her career, from the challenges of being healthier to the fears and emotional ups and downs that often come along with them.

Tracey's hunger for assisting her clients more authentically led her to willingly replace many hours of sleep for hours of research. The goal was to put together an effective coaching program that would be of benefit to her clients but more importantly, one that was heartfelt and unique.

Once Tracey began her action plan and things seemed as though they were finally coming together, she began to experience many adversities including financial setbacks. These hard times were not without lots of prayer. During this time, she learned how to become resourceful and resolved not to focus on what she did not have, but instead she focused on what resources she did have. She began to concentrate on the task at hand, staying laser focused on achieving her goal despite the odds & setbacks. Her motto became "If it's meant to be it's up to me!"

Being the resourceful woman she was, she bartered and traded services. Because of the intriguing and inspiring stories of life lessons that many of her clients shared with her, she began to realize that she too had the desire of bringing these amazing women to the forefront. That's when she shared the idea with her sister Raven, who immediately suggested that she take her Kitchen Table Radio Personal Broadcasting Course and create a show around her vision - interviewing the women who are making a difference and paying it forward.

A wonderful transition from her wellness coaching, where she was helping women make healthy lifestyle changes to hosting and producing a radio show where she was able to take her passion for helping women to a whole other level. Now she not only provides individual wellness coaching, but group coaching too. Her clients love the fact that she has a true passion for helping others and it definitely shows.

Tracey Doctor - Holistic Wellness & Lifestyle Coach Executive Producer & Host
www.amazingwoman-talkradio.com

Tracey Doctor's

Recipe for SUCCESS!

1. Start from where you are today.

2. Prioritize your long and short term goals.

3. Dream big, for the sky is the limit.

4. Always stay focused and committed.

5. Remember, everything that it takes to succeed is inside of you don't be afraid of success.

6. Start each day with gratitude and appreciation embracing your success.

7. Pay it forward, by sharing with others what you learned on your journey to success.

About Tracey Doctor

Tracey's Professional Journey started in the Health and Beauty Industry. She enjoys helping women make real lifestyle changes in the areas of health and wellness. While researching hair health through the years, and coaching her clients about taking control of their health, she's made the lives of countless women much better.

Channeling the Visionary from within Tracey created and launched the *Expressions Hair Enhancer System.* Her healthy hair care techniques have empowered thousands of women.

Tracey's strong beliefs have allowed her to conquer health challenges through prayer, research and great determination, opting to heal her body naturally.

Natural Health, Wellness and Healing, is her passion. Tracey is a Certified Holistic Health and Wellness Life Coach and she is totally committed to being of service to others. Tracey encourages women to turn their dreams into reality with her radio show.

Tracey truly believes that "Amazing" things happen when we share what's in our hearts by paying it forward.

Tracey Doctor
Phone 281-240-2885
www.amazingwoman-talkradio.com

Tyra Jones-Franklin

"Without light, there is darkness. Without change, there is chaos"
Tyra Jones-Franklin

Education is Key

In 2001, Tyra Franklin was hired as a GED Coordinator for a local Houston charter school. Despite frequent audits by Texas Education Agency (TEA), the superintendent asked Tyra to develop a GED curriculum with lesson plans for the entire school year of 2002.

Perplexed by the request, Tyra began conducting research and found that there were only prep books to refer to. During the drafting of the lesson plans, she realized that she could start her own GED program.

While serving as the GED Coordinator and Instructor, Tyra tracked her students' progress. In 2001, 63% of her students passed the GED examination. In 2002, 82% of her students passed the GED examination. Because of her students' success, Tyra received a $600 bonus, a $3,000 increase in her salary, and constant recognition of her professionalism in staff meetings. Before long, students who had been enrolled and not successful on the high school side of the school were transferring to her GED class. Her class became full to capacity and had to turn students away.

Five years later, with 10 years of teaching experience under her belt, Tyra began the process of putting this idea on paper, officially. She left the traditional classroom and began her journey of the vision that was given to her by God. She was careful and didn't make a step without His approval, even though at times she didn't move when He said "go."

As a third generation educator, Tyra recognizes the need for quality teachers in the classroom. Through her experience with at-risk students, she realized that the parents are sometimes not as resourceful because of their lack of the ability to work while successfully raising a family. We as parents sometimes need the outreach of the community to assist in the continued growth of the family unit. Educators can teach the child, but without the support of the parent, in most cases, some never graduate from high school, thereby repeating the family line.

Franklin Quest Education and Leadership Foundation, Inc.(FQELF's) mission is to provide the opportunity for students in diverse communities to receive training in the areas of adult basic education, entrepreneurship education, and moral and proper behavior in society and in business.

Tyra believes that if we turn employees into employers we will have significantly contributed to the economy of the greater Houston area. She also feels that the difference between an employee and an employer is education and mindset. "We have the power, through Jesus Christ, to create our own opportunity. Opportunities don't go away; they just simply pass us by. This means that they are always there if we are open. Open for change, open to be stretched by the challenge of operating within our life's purpose."

FQELF has spent the last 13 years working with at-risk children and adults. Now is the time to reach out to the community in expanding and formalizing the service to help even more people attain goals never dreamed possible. By educating the masses, they are ultimately lowering the crime rate, reducing the strain on the welfare and judicial system, and reducing the unemployment rate.

In 2010, FQELF, Inc. will initiate the extension of the educational and entrepreneurship component of a three year comprehensive plan that will include a "one stop" family life center and online learning community.

Join us as we become a part of the solution for change in the lives of this underserved population. Together we can make a bigger difference that will change the face of our community for the better.

Tyra Franklin, MBA/PA -Franklin Quest Education and Leadership Foundation, Inc.

"Your destiny is hidden among your fears."
http://franklinquest.pbworks.com

About Tyra Jones-Franklin

Tyra Jones-Franklin is President and CEO of Franklin Quest Education and Leadership Foundation, Inc. and its subsidiary Franklin Quest Consulting Group, LLC. The foundation was founded to serve underprivileged adults in the areas of Adult Basic Education and continued education through entrepreneurship, and corporate etiquette. The consulting group serves new business owners in developing their startup companies as well as established businesses' ability to run their firms with proper leadership structure. She is a regionally recognized successful educator and businesswoman with a solid background in sales/leadership and management. She left the corporate world of petroleum oil with several years of experience in research. She has served as acting President for Houston's Professional and Business Men and Women Club, member of the National Association of Professional Women, member of Texans for Lawsuit Reform, and Advisory Board Member of Westside Bible Fellowship. She delivers a step-by-step blueprint to small and large businesses on how to triumph over adversity and deliver results in a high performance environment through leadership development.

Her enthusiastic, dynamic delivery has earned her the recognition in several organizations as a Master Trainer and Mentor. She is a goal oriented business partner who brings a cohesive spirit to an organization. She is sought after in curriculum development and program implementation and has been featured in news articles and business publications identifying her leadership in several programs. This powerful educator and business developer creates a high energy level for her listener and offers practical tools for performance improvement in today's competitive and changing marketplace. She holds a MBA with a specialty in Public Administration and is currently working towards her Doctorate in Educational Leadership with a specialty in Education Technology.

Tyra Franklin, MBA/PA
http://franklinquest.pbworks.com

Tyra Franklin

Recipe for SUCCESS!

1. Take action in order to get results

2. Decide on your Niche

3. Narrow your Focus

4. Take the time to Write down your goals

5. Build your list both online and offline

6. Define your vision

7. Don't be afraid to Dream Big

Kellie Frazier

"The most inspiring thing to me is when you look inside your heart and like what you see."
Anonymous

Connecting To Your Tribe

In the early part of 2007, I lost 2 family members in two separate tragedies just months apart. Through the emotional turmoil and travel across country to assist family, I chose to close the doors to my successful investing company and wondered what to do with my life.

As the year came to an end life began to feel 'normal' again until I took a bad fall on black ice and landed directly on my head; injuring my brain and neck.   Seizures controlled my life for the next several months, pain and neurological problems were my closest enemies. Although my wonderful family and a few employees were there to help me, I consistently felt very alone. I knew I needed courage and a belief that I was not alone no matter how I felt.

There is Always Hope...I also believed that the creator of the universe had my healing under control. Not only did I believe it, but I felt it to my very core. My family did as well and would often remind me whenever they saw progress being made.

Six months later, in June of 2008, I awoke to bright sunlight in my room. I sat up in bed and realized there was no pain anywhere in my head or neck. I remember thinking "Is this really happening?" Everything in my mind seemed very clear.

The Possibilities Began... In my mind's eye I saw myself as an author, a speaker, and yes, even talking with Oprah Winfrey. To really appreciate this you need to understand - I despised writing and was certainly not a public speaker. And Oprah...?...she had never crossed my mind until that moment. I didn't see myself on her show, but in some relaxed atmosphere having a conversation with her.

I didn't know why I saw those things and I certainly didn't know how any of it was possible, I simply remained focused on being grateful every day, keeping up with my physical therapy, and literally putting one foot in front of the other toward my goals of success and healing. The seizures eventually disappeared and the healing process was in full swing.

I Educated My Way toward Success... Whenever I exercised, I chose to listen to successful people like Alex Mandossian on the MP3 player, on trips I listened to CDs of Jim Rohn and Les Brown and when I was home I read as many biographies as I could get my hands on to keep the neurotransmitters in my brain connecting and thinking success. I also spent quiet moments every day where I could reflect on that still small voice we all have inside and found a greater connection to my heart and my own desires, which enabled me to connect to others in a much deeper way.

Every day I began implementing the strategies these mentors talked about and every day I expressed my gratitude for the success I saw happening in my own life. My family and I to this day will discuss what 5 things we feel successful and grateful for at dinner time and I highly recommend it for everyone.

Who would have thought, that a little more than 1 year later, this brain injured gal would go on to help thousands of people better their lives, become a published author, a global world class presenter, an affiliate of other companies, founder of several companies and best of all, able to enjoy fabulous relationships with some of my mentors who unknowingly educated me. My heart of gratitude is never ending.

Tribes that Connect and Succeed... Bringing together the safety of tribes and teaching them to succeed through connecting is my gift and I now enjoy the income that comes with sharing my gift. The more I share and give, the more I receive. Anthropologist Margaret Mead discovered years ago that it takes a village to raise a happy child. If your business is like your child, then let me help you learn to build a tribe around it so that they can take you to the next level.

Kellie Frazier -Tribe Success Consultant and Presenter

www.kelliefrazier.com
http://www.tribecommunitynetwork.com

Kellie Frazier's

Recipe for SUCCESS!

1. Put *ego* behind you and with your whole *heart* lean forward.

2. Absorb your mind in positive education every single day.

3. Think big, play big but most of all B-E-L-I-E-V-E.

4. Build your systems to go from knowing to doing to winning.

5. Connect to a Tribe that empowers you toward success.

6. Be willing to take a risk – say yes to public opportunities to share your message.

7. Learn to be an excellent giver as well as an excellent receiver

About Kelli Frazier

Kellie Frazier is recognized as a leading expert interviewer and tribe connector for leaders in business. She is the founder of the U.S. division for Leaders Café 2020, a social networking enterprise expected to affect 20 million leaders by the year 2020. Kellie is also founder of Connecting LLC, where young leaders learn to connect from head to heart and the creator of the Tribe Power Hour. Kellie has taught thousands of people around the world how to be potent, successful leaders in business and in family life.

As an Author, Global World Class Presenter, and Tele-Seminarian, Kellie teaches the art of connecting to tribes for those who know they want to be relationally successful in the business world.

Kellie Frazier
http://www.kelliefrazier.com
http://www.leaderscafe.co.uk

Angela Gagauf

"Courage is not the absence of fear, but the mastery of it."
Franklin D. Roosevelt

Should Have, Could Have, What If?

Franklin D. Roosevelt said, "There is nothing to fear but fear itself." Intellectually Angela understood that quote, but emotionally, she just didn't get it. Her fear has driven her to constantly re-create herself, to learn new things, change careers, and to challenge herself. She prefers this FDR quote. "Courage is not the absence of fear, but the mastery of it."

So, what is her fear? The fear of being an old woman in a rocking chair and thinking, "I should have done that" or "I could have tried that", or even worse, asking herself "What If I had taken the chance?" and never knowing the answer to that question.

By the time Angela was 40, she had spent 20 years in the fashion industry. She had been a buyer for 14 years and for the last 6 years, a vice president of merchandising and design on the wholesale end. Both jobs were glamorous, full of world travel and gave her the opportunity to meet many interesting people. But there was also intense pressure every day. On her 40th birthday, she had to put her big celebration on hold because of a "fashion emergency" that had to be taken care of THAT day. Angela finally understood the term "burn-out". Unsure if it was the burn-out or her midlife crisis arriving right on schedule but the image of herself as an old woman in that rocking chair seemed very close indeed. And the thoughts, "should have, could have, what if?" conjured up more fear.

At that time, Angela's relaxation and passion was cooking. She thought to herself, could she possibly give up a six figure salary, world travel, perks and a 20 year career to follow her heart and passion? The image of herself as a bitter old woman flashed through her mind and the next thing she knew, she was enrolled in the French Culinary Institute. She was now earning zero dollars. Her fashion colleagues thought she was crazy to give up a successful career, and we won't even go into what her husband thought about the whole thing. Suffice it to say, that happily, their marriage did survive that period. She graduated at the top of her class and started a small, upscale catering company. And guess what? She didn't have to ask the question "what if?" any longer. She now knew that turning her love of cooking into a profession was a mistake. She hated it!

Now what? For many years Angela had an active interest in exercise and nutrition, not because she loved those two topics, but because she considered them necessary "evils" to maintaining a good quality of life. Her husband wisely suggested that she become a personal trainer. So she asked herself, "should I?" and she did. Again, Angela received the top certifications in the field and started an in-home personal training company called 40 Plus Fitness eleven years ago.

However, in 2008, a new opportunity presented itself to Angela. The realtor, who had quickly sold their last three properties, told her that she had a talent preparing homes for the real estate market and that she had an eye for decorating and she really believed Angela could be successful as a home stager and re-designer. Once again, she asked herself, "could I really do this?" And in her mind's eye, the old woman in the rocking chair smiled at her and nodded yes. Today, she is the proud owner of NJ Home Staging and Redesign. Angela HAD learned how to master her fear and venture into the unknown.

Angela Gagauf – Home Stager and Re-Designer
www.njhomestagingandredesign.com

Angela Gagauf's *Recipe for* SUCCESS!

1. Keep in mind who the prospective buyers will be and design the staging accordingly.

2. When working with real estate agents, keep them posted on your progress.

3. Get to know other stagers and don't be afraid to ask for help if you need it.

4. Always use a contract so everyone knows what to expect.

5. Get your name out there by networking, writing, and speaking.

6. Join real estate organizations as an affiliate member and participate.

7. And don't forget to take LOTS of before and after pictures of your work for your portfolio!

About Angela Gagauf

Angela Gagauf's 20-plus years of experience as a buyer, designer and merchandiser in the fashion industry helped her make a natural transition into home staging and redesign. Her many successes selling her own homes quickly and for top dollar, prompted her real estate agent to ask Angela for help in staging her current listings. And thus, NJ Home Staging and Redesign was born. "Angela has a very good eye and the homes she staged sold for more than asking or got multiple offers," said Natalie Wallach, a longtime New Jersey real estate agent.

Angela Gagauf
http://www.njhomestagingandredesign.com
Email: a@njhomestagingandredesign.com

Ellen Gaver

"Don't ask what the world needs. Ask what makes you come alive and go do it. Because what the world needs is people who have come alive."
Howard Thurman

Going Green

Ellen Gaver has had many careers. She has worked as a legal secretary, been involved with the motion picture and television industry, and has been employed in the non-profit arena...truly a "Jill of all Trades." When Ellen moved to the Central Coast of California in 1988, she found there was no demand for the skills she had to offer to the local economy. Almost as a last resort, she applied for and secured a job at the local grocery store – embarking on yet another career. In time, Ellen worked her way up the ladder and ultimately became the General Store Manager. It was around that same time that Ellen met her husband, Bob. They married and soon after welcomed their son, Danny, to the family.

When her son was eight weeks old, Ellen packed him off to full-time daycare and returned to working 60 hours/week at the grocery store. She worked (and cried) many Christmas mornings, Easter Sundays, nights and weekends as she left her family at home. She saw her son an average of two hours per day and the stress was unbearable. As time went on, Ellen decided that, whatever it took, her son needed her at home, and equally, she needed to be home with him! It was then that she left her career and began looking for ways to replace her income from home. As frightening as it was to give up her lucrative and stable income, it was the best decision she ever made.

Ellen never planned to be an entrepreneur. But as she stood at the precipice of a brand new life, not knowing whether to jump in or run back to the old and familiar, she made a decision that she would never allow someone else to control her time with her family. Thus began her search for an opportunity that would allow her to work from home on her own schedule, yet one that would not require a large investment or start-up.

One thing Ellen knew for sure was that any successful business would have to be one that included her passion for health, wellness, and environmental protection. During her search for a way to combine her passions with a viable business opportunity, she was introduced to a solid, progressive green manufacturing company that offers a risk-free opportunity for partnership and revenue sharing.

This customer referral business seemed like the perfect fit. And it was, but Ellen had never run a home-based business and didn't realize that without a mentor, learning to build this business would be a challenge. She knew in her heart that this business would work, so she set about finding the strategies that would create growth and success. With perseverance, her business grew slowly and steadily, and as she found success, she also found that her true calling was helping other moms and dads to find the balance she had craved and created in her own life.

The EcoMomTeam was formed as a way to mentor those who want to achieve their own success through our business model. Over the years, the EcoMomTeam has grown to be a diverse group of women and men who are all committed to creating financial stability, environmental wellness, and family balance. By teaching others to thrive within their business model, it strengthens the team, ensures its success and everyone wins.

Ellen Gaver – Entrepreneur
www.EcoMomTeam.com

Ellen Gaver's

Recipe for SUCCESS!

1. Follow your dreams. Every dream is achievable and your dreams are the roadmap to your future.

2. Think outside the box. Don't let others create your life for you – you are in charge of your destiny.

3. Don't reinvent the wheel – find a mentor. Follow the guidance of someone who is successful in the field you pursue. Benefit from their experience!

4. Manage your attitude. Attitude is a very small thing that can make a very big difference in your business and your life.

5. Enlist the support of your family. Paint the dream for them and help them visualize the long term benefits of your business.

6. Maintain a philosophy of abundance. Even teaming up with your competitors is often a great way to foster business growth. There's plenty of room for everyone to succeed – abundance abounds!

7. Never give up. If your vision is solid and your passion is pure, you WILL succeed. Success is a marathon, not a sprint. If you believe it, you can achieve it!

About Ellen Gaver

Ellen Gaver, founder of the EcoMomTeam, lives on the Central Coast of California with her husband, Bob, and their son, Danny. Ellen is a mission-driven entrepreneur whose life has been enriched beyond measure by those she has mentored along the way.

Ellen Gaver
http://www.EcoMomTeam.com
EcoMomTeam@charter.net
Phone: 805.474.8225

Elizabeth Gilmour

"A problem is a chance for you to do your best."
Duke Ellington

Excellence = Success

Elizabeth has a core belief in the entrepreneurial spirit and strives for excellence in everything she touches and never settles for anything less.

This has been rewarded with her Pilates studio being one of the fastest growing professional and personal services businesses in Houston, moving from a home based Pilates studio to a rented location and now into her own purpose built studio, having along the way increased revenues by 4 fold in 4 years. The business is built upon the foundations of her education in physiology and business management along with a Pilates certification from some of the pioneers in the industry and the path to success is guided by her laser like focus on providing excellence in all the services her company offers.

The path has not been without its challenges and some dark days when her resolve to continue along the entrepreneurial road were tested to the full. Elizabeth started her business as a single mum of 2 teenage boys and all the demands that come with that role. This is a tough role for anyone as they strive to provide and build a home, juggle the demands of the boys' school and out of school activities and to nurture a fledgling business. Add to that, a horrific high-school football accident to her older son which saw his leg crushed d and requiring constant care for months and more recently her younger son diagnosed with a life altering illness just as he prepares to head off to college. These are some of the personal hurdles seldom seen and even less understood that lie behind the business successes of Elizabeth and those like her. Just for good measure she also found time to get married and establish a new home!

Apart from the personal resolve, this success has taken considerable personal and financial investment to achieve and some tough decisions to continue with expansion plans even in the face of an impending recession. This required faith in her business offering, her skills to deliver and a deep understanding of market requirements for her services.

Nobody gets to know her clients better than Elizabeth. She strives to understand her clients and to work with them to set achievable health and fitness goals which will have a lifelong impact. Client retention is important to a business like Elizabeth's and she has a client base stretching back to the first days she opened the doors of her business. She brings a unique blend of exercise science, deep understanding in the Pilates method, artistry in how to utilize it to achieve success in overcoming clinical injuries and achieving fitness goals and delivered by extremely effective teaching methods. Oh, and just for good measure you get one of the best motivation coaches around!

Elizabeth always has a "can-do" attitude and life's barriers are there just to be hurdled. Elizabeth has lived in Louisiana, London (England) and Cape Town (South Africa) before settling in Houston, TX and brings a very wide perspective and global influence to her business. Elizabeth's business demands enormous amounts of her time but when she is free she loves to spend it with her family enjoying her own home or enjoying one of their family vacation road trips around the US.

Elizabeth Gilmour – Master Pilates Practitioner
www.PilatesofChampions.com

Elizabeth Gilmour

Recipe for SUCCESS!

1. Strive for excellence in whatever you do.

2. Identify your core business and keep reminding yourself what it is. Focus!

3. Understand your market and who your potential clients are, know who you want to reach and how to reach them.

4. Make it personal! If it is a professional/personal service then that is exactly what it has to be.

5. You can't do it all! Keep focus on what you do well and what you can do to build the business. Use contract and staff to fulfill the routine tasks.

6. Use focused marketing and advertising and sustain your campaigns. No point in being a well kept secret!

7. Set goals and devise a plan to achieve them. The path to the goals can change but success requires a strong sense of direction.

About Elizabeth Gilmour

Elizabeth Gilmour is Pilates Certified since 1987, has a Dance Background, Business Degree, and has travelled and lived in many parts of the world. She is an Exercise Physiologist with the American College of Sports Medicine; Principal Pilates Practitioner with the Studio of Dance; athletic trainer with the American Council on Exercise and a member of the American Associate for the Advancement of Science. Mrs. Gilmour trained under Isabelle Hill in England; Isabelle was a retired French Ballerina who taught Pilates in London, England. Sabelle Hill worked with Joseph Pilates before he moved away from Europe and kept in contact during this time in New York. After studying under Isabelle Hill, Mrs. Gilmour eventually moved back to the United States where she studied under Christie Brehm in Texas. Christie Brehm was trained by Rob Fletcher, and Ron Fletcher was trained by Joseph Pilates. The depth of knowledge and understanding of Pilates gained from this quality of training has been carried into the current generation by Mrs. Gilmour at Pilates of Champions where she has continued in the true spirit of Pilates neuromuscular clinical and classical exercise and added many innovative exercises across the full range of equipment. A few moments spent with Mrs. Gilmour will quickly reveal a wealth of knowledge, practical application and teaching experience in Pilates and exercise physiology. Her development and teaching of Pilates clinical and classical neuromuscular exercise are considered among the best in the world.

When Mrs. Gilmour moved back to the US in 1998, she started her "fully equipped" Pilates studio in her home located in Houston, Texas. She also worked as a Pilates teacher at the Gil Rome, Margo Marshall Dance Studio, "The Studio of Dance, Inc." Her Pilates of Champions, LLC has been growing exponentially year after year ever since she decided to move her home studio out of her home and into a commercial studio in 2006. Her words: "It's been the best business decision I've ever made embarked on for my clientele and for the growth of Pilates of Champions."

Elizabeth Gilmour
www.pilatesofchampions.com
www.asfpp.com
Phone 281-685-5711

Monica Hancock

"Success is be measured not so much by the position that one has reached in life as by the obstacles which he has overcome"
Booker T. Washington

Follow Your Passion!

Monica's path into entrepreneurship began while working in the oil and gas industry. After working relentless hour's day in and day out feeling exhausted and drained, Monica began to realize that this was not the path she wanted to take in life. Her true passion was the desire to be self-employed and be her own boss. While still employed she began her custom window treatment business on a part time basis in 1991 and worked like this for (8) years.

Despite her dedication of (18) years in the oil and gas industry, she felt the need to do something that really fulfilled her life that she was passionate about. Monica knew she had the drive to be successful as an entrepreneur so she decided to give her two week notice and pursue her dream on a full time basis. Without consulting anyone she made this decision on her own and knew that if she had the determination and faith in God she could get thru this. It was a scary decision at first because she was recently divorced, but she knew this was her calling in life because she had the ability to be creative as a seamstress designing custom window treatments. Everyone was very supportive of her decision, even though her mother was shocked at the idea of her walking away from a secure paying job. Despite Monica's decision, she has been there for her every step of the way.

Monica spent about (6) months wrestling with the idea of leaving her secure paying job and decided she need to at least follow her dream. She began sewing in school at the age of (12) by taking a Homemaking class and because of her interest as a seamstress her mother purchased a sewing machine for her to continue utilizing her sewing skills. While still being married she purchased a new home and began creating window treatments for her own home. Her family members and friends liked what she did so they started requesting window treatment designs for their own homes. She discussed with her husband about turning her hobby into a business, but he just laughed about it and thought it was a crazy idea. After doing hours of research on starting a business she decided to get her DBA and pursue her passion.

With the will and determination, Monica immersed herself with learning about the custom window treatment business so she could become an expert. Even though she was successful as a seamstress learning on her own, she decided to enroll in a custom drapery class on the weekends to learn the basics and polish up on her skills so she could perfect her designs. After attending about (2) semesters and constantly getting more business thru referrals she decided that she needed to spend more time on the weekends to go on appointments so she could increase her clientele.

Monica's business began to flourish while she was still employed full time so she had had developed a steady flow of clientele. With more and more requests for other interior decorating projects she started offering other products and services related to interior design to her customers. It was September of 1999 she made a decision to walk away from her full time job and pursue her dream as being self-employed full time. She knew she had to start marketing her business more so she could keep a steady flow of clientele to operate her business on a full time basis successfully. Within a month after starting her business full time she was approached with an opportunity to purchase another local blind business company that was going out of business to pursue other interests. She realized this would be a great opportunity to increase her clientele because she would be obtaining the referral and repeat business while continuing to increase her own clientele. After taking over the additional business along with her own clientele increasing, Monica quickly realized that she had to wear all the hats of being a sole-proprietor and it became a bit overwhelming. It just took some time to focus on developing some organizational skills so she could continue to operate her business and still be at the top of her game. She also learned that she had to enlist the services of other people to continue being proficient in operating her business as a sole proprietor. Even in times of adversity Monica never gave up because she was determined to make this business a success. Monica has had her share of challenges, but after (18) years of entrepreneurship she is still growing strong.

Monica Hancock
Window Fashions Designer
Email: mhancock@creationsbymonica.net
www.creationsbymonica.net

Monica Hancock's

Recipe for SUCCESS!

1. Do what you love and are passionate about

2. Start your business while you are still employed

3. Don't do it alone – you need a support system

4. Get clients or customers first – focus on networking and marketing

5. Write a business plan to avoid starting a business that will not succeed

6. Do the research – become an expert on your industry, products and services

7. Get professional help – you will not be an expert on everything you do

About the Author

Monica Hancock is recognized as a certified Window Fashions Professional and registered as a Priorty Dealer for Gulf Coast Window Coverings which is the largest manufacturer of Hunter Douglas products. She is the founder and owner of Custom Creations by Monica. Her custom window treatment design business was established in 1992 and she has been creating beautiful window treatment designs in the Houston and surrounding areas for over (18) years.

As a Window Fashions Designer, Monica has appeared on radio shows, in magazines, and in news articles sharing her secrets and success on building her custom window treatment business. It has always been her goal to create unique and innovative custom window treatment designs that were an expression of her client's personality and lifestyle. Known for her creative style, Monica is still creating window designs beyond your imagination.

Monica Hancock
Window Fashions Designer
www.creationsbymonica.net
mhancock@creationsbymonica.net
Phone: (281) 820-1977

Cathy Hansell

"Only those who see the invisible can do the impossible"
Dr. B. Lown, inventor of the defibrillator

Safety and Wellness

Both of my parents worked when I was growing up, so my grandmother and great aunt watched me each day, until I was old enough to go to kindergarten. They instilled in me a set of values, that some would say are "old fashioned." Not to me. They are the golden rules of being nice to others, working hard, never lying, not taking credit for the work of others; saying "please," "thank you" and "I'm sorry," appreciating nature and having great faith in God and Jesus Christ. Also at a very young age, my father instilled in me self-confidence. He told me that I am smart; I can do anything that I want to do and not to be influenced by other's negative comments.

I have carried these values and advice with me all my life, forming a drive within me to serve others and to provide a greater good. As I grew and attended college, the drive to serve and provide a greater good showed itself in my career goal of environmental protection. I earned a BS in environmental science and engineering from Cook College. As I worked in the environmental field, I obtained additional degrees in Toxicology from NYU Institute of Environmental Medical and a Law degree from Rutgers Law School. As the years went by, my career shifted to product safety, product stewardship and quality/six sigma.

My last career shift turned my attention to personal safety, where I found my purpose in life. Other previous work experiences provided support to this primary area of personal safety. I confirmed this to myself when I studied "A Purpose Driven Life." I have passionately worked in the occupational safety field for over twelve years, where I have found great joy and satisfaction in helping others to be safer and healthier.

Two years ago, I found myself at another decision point and my first significant personal challenge. I chose to leave the corporate world and form my own consulting business in safety and health. I founded "Breakthrough Results," a firm dedicated to helping people lead safer and healthier lives. I contacted friends and colleagues, openly asked for any advice and help, and implemented most recommendations to launch my new consulting business.

New work was coming slowly, and I wondered how to jump start my new business and to reach more people. This was the next challenge: how do I market myself-my skills, products, services and availability? I addressed this challenge in two ways.

First, I accepted every speaking invitation, and pursued key speaking engagements with professional safety organizations. I needed to be seen and heard. People, as potential clients, needed to meet me.

Second, I needed to market myself. I created a website and joined LinkedIn. I also saw an advertisement in Powerful You for Raven Blair Davis. Raven was a guest speaker, who would be describing how to start your own radio show. I said to myself...this is it! I can do this and reach many more people through radio podcasts. I listened to Raven, her story and her passion to help others start radio shows. I immediately signed up for her class and soon launched "Safety Breakthrough Talk Radio."

"Safety Breakthrough Talk Radio" has been a wonderful venue to meet new people, to get safety messages out to many people and to increase traffic to my website and business. I have been privileged to interview national and global experts in such fields as teen driving safety, pandemic planning and corporate social responsibility.

I don't believe in coincidences. I believe that I was meant to form my new safety firm, to find Raven and to launch "Safety Breakthrough Talk Radio." In the safety field, I'll never really know how many people I positively influence and possibly help to prevent an injury or illness. I don't need to. I do this because I love it.

Cathy Hansell - CCSR, M.S. J.D. President
www.breakthroughresults.org

Cathy Hansell's

Recipe for SUCCESS!

1. Develop an initial business plan: know your immediate and ultimate goals and timeline; define which products and services you will offer for free and which you will charge; set a level of work to be obtained and if you work alone, hire employees or contract out work to other consultants.

2. Develop and register your company and radio show domain name(s)

3. Develop a website; it need not be perfect to start out, just get it operational.

4. Protect yourself by copyrighting your work products and materials.

5. Organize your business: purchase a laptop computer and office equipment (fax, printer, and scanner); radio recording and editing software; contract for technical, accounting and legal support; set up 800 and conference numbers and Pay Pal account.

6. Get out and be seen! Attend and speak at meetings, even if you are not paid; aggressively network; set up professional accounts on LinkedIn and Twitter.

7. Maintain your integrity and stay true to your values, even if your clients would request or settle for less.

About Cathy Hansell

President, Breakthrough Results

Breakthrough Results is dedicated to helping people lead safer and healthier lives. How? By providing a "one-stop shop" for expert safety and health information and guidance. Whether for yourself, your family or your business, Breakthrough Results (BTR) and its president, Cathy Hansell, will help you.

For over 30 years, Cathy has held senior VP and Director positions in safety, health, environmental (SHE), product and manufacturing quality at several international corporations including AlliedSignal, Honeywell International, BASF, American Standard and Trane Company. She holds a BS in environmental science/wastewater engineering from Cook College: a MS in environmental toxicology from NYU Institute of Environmental Medicine and a JD in law from Rutgers University Law School. Cathy is a certified Malcolm Baldrige examiner; a Crosby, Deming and Juran Quality instructor; a Total Quality Master Facilitator, and a certified Six Sigma Green Belt. She received the ASSE Executive Safety Management Certification and the Centre for Sustainability and Excellence Practitioner Certification in Corporate Social Responsibility, approved by the UK International Environmental Management Association. Most recently, she was selected as the National Association of Professional Women 2010-2011 Woman of the Year in the Safety, Health and Wellness Field.

Cathy is a member of ORC Worldwide Consulting Group. She is also an affiliate with The Lawrence Bradford Group and the Centre for Sustainability and Excellence. She is currently a member of the NJ and American Bar Associations and the ASSE.

Cathy, through BTR, is working with manufacturing, chemical, energy and construction industries, military and academic clients. Projects include developing and implementing a safety strategy and culture; change management; educating and engaging leadership; integrating SHE into business processes; defining culture self-assessment tools and leading metrics; applying six sigma and lean tools to improve safety culture and performance; preparing for pandemic threats; wellness programs; and coaching SHE professionals to be skilled, motivating change agents. For each of these consulting service areas, products are available, including culture and safety assessment tools; a change model and checklist based on John Kotter 8-step model; leading metrics; training materials and tools; safety and culture programs, checklists and procedures.

Cathy Hansell
chansell@breakthroughresults.org
www.breakthroughresults.org
Phone 888-609-6723

Roberta Harris

"Look UP, be UP, warm UP, send UP, wake UP, climb UP, dream UP, show UP, make UP, love UP."
Roberta Harris

UP

Somewhere along the line I learned that one should always "look up" to art. The context relates to the hanging of art on a wall...a little higher is better than lower. In retrospect, throughout my career as an artist, I have been inspired to create images that move the observer up—physically, emotionally and spiritually.

Sometimes it feels like life serves us a ubiquitous diet of "DOWN". News is rarely news unless it is bad—a fire, a murder, a hurricane, a death. The market is down; another leader has fallen; a child is abducted; a plane crashes. Another terrorist attacks, another marriage breaks; another friend is diagnosed with cancer. When is gossip ever empowering?

I consider this preoccupation with "DOWN" a fundamental distortion of life. Certainly life presents its challenges. The stresses we feel are real. Our grief can be deep. But to me, being human means that we cultivate the ability to tap internal and external resources of power to bring light out of darkness, joy out of sorrow, order out of chaos, and life out of death. Metaphorically, while the climb may be steep and treacherous, nevertheless, we climb.

UP is fundamentally about hope.

Hope is not wishful thinking. Hope is rather the ability to stand amid what is broken and chaotic and envision a positive future story. Hope is based on an honest assessment of individual and community resources and the commitment to employ these in a personal and collaborative way to create an environment in which people can thrive. Hope is therefore the catalyst of power and the antithesis of victimization.

Throughout my career, through a variety of media, my mission as an artist has been to inspire hope and its corollaries—dialogue, joy, encouragement, strategy, peace, kindness, and imagination. This approach is not the least bit sentimental; given the challenges that we face, hope demands courage, commitment, endurance and renewal—the best expressions of the human spirit.

Throughout history and in every culture, women and men have symbolized hope through varieties of color and shape—birds, sticks, rectangles, checkerboards, rainbows and religious images, to name a few. Out of this tradition, my art employs these primitive and modern symbols to create a dialogue with the viewer (and among viewers) and ultimately to inspire actions that shape the future by bringing to life the voices, talents, achievements and aspirations of those who experience it.

My personal journey of coming to see and understand the world through art has followed what has been for me an interesting and integrated path. Exploring one idea or area of focus has consistently led me to the next. As a child drawing a ballerina on point, experiencing the feast of senses I discovered in the forest next to our home, spending many hours with my father in his workshop as he cut and fit glass and mirror into perfect rectangular shapes, or watching my mother carefully meld mosaic shapes into colorful designs—all these early experiences have influenced both what I have come to recognize as "familiar" in the world and what I have chosen as the symbols of hope in my work.

Roberta Harris, Artist
www.robertaharris.com

Roberta Harris'
Recipe for SUCCESS!

1. Follow your dreams.

2. Do what you do best and stay true to your own unique self. Play to your strengths.

3. Make a difference...with your family, friends, community and the universe.

4. Remember that when one door closes, another one opens. Pay attention!

5. Always keep learning.

6. Friendship comes first. Business second.

7. Love what you do. If you don't, you're doing the wrong thing.

About Roberta Harris

Roberta Harris was born in Passaic, New Jersey and grew up in Houston, Texas. She has lived in New York, Washington, D.C., and Santa Fe, New Mexico.

She was chosen for the Independent Study Program, Whitney Museum of American Art in New York. Harris studied at Parson's School of Design and Hunter College in New York. Her paintings and sculptures have been exhibited nationally and internationally and her work is included in numerous private and corporate collections including MTV Corporation, New York; Chase Manhattan Bank, New York; Frito-Lay Dallas, Texas; Dynegy, Houston, Texas; Compaq (Hewlett-Packard), Houston, Texas and Texas Heart Institute, Houston, Texas.

Harris has instructed at Glassell School of Art, Museum of Fine Arts, Houston; and the High School for the Performing and Visual Arts, Houston. She has been a visiting lecturer at the Kimbell Art Museum, Ft. Worth, Texas; Museum of Fine Arts, Santa Fe, New Mexico; Brookhaven College, Dallas, Texas; the University of Houston, Houston, Texas; the Menil Collection, Houston, Texas, and has served as an Advisory member of the Art and Architecture Panel, Texas Arts Commission; Houston Arts Festival; Cultural Arts Council of Houston and the Art League of Houston. Harris lives and makes art in Houston, Texas.

Roberta Harris
www.robertaharris.com

Victor Holman

"It is an immutable law in business that words are words, explanations are explanations, promises are promises but only performance is reality."
Harold S. Green

Filling a Need

Victor was just like most people who work a nine to five job every day. After all, it's what he was raised to believe was financial security and the "American Dream." While working for a top international consulting firm, it didn't take long for him to realize that he had a passion and gift for understanding business performance, best practices and applying creative techniques to solve client issues. However, as his skills blossomed, he began to feel unfulfilled and frustrated with the money he was generating for his company and the financial ceiling that goes along with working for somebody else. And so, he began to seek a way out.

His biggest challenge was to figure out how he could take his skills and build a business around them. For three years, he researched and interviewed top organizations in all kinds of industries, and documented what made them successful. He developed a much needed business model that applies successful techniques used by high performing organizations. His *Performance Mastery System*, which is a five phase, systematic, enterprise business approach that centers on 48 key business activities, includes an online business analysis tool that identifies organizational strengths, weaknesses, and cost savings opportunities, and produces a custom step-by-step roadmap for becoming a high performing organization. This resulted in his client's ability improve performance, cut cost and increase productivity at a fraction of the cost and time of his former consulting firm.

This was an exciting breakthrough for Victor. True to his nature, he wanted to take his expertise to an even higher level. He soon realized that many small business owners needed help in the most basic areas of planning.

This is when he developed the *Small Business Mastery System*. Using a proven, effective business model, Victor helps small business owners at every level develop high-performance, actionable business plans with a focus on mastering twelve core business areas such as marketing, sales, production, distribution, technology, etc.

After realizing the strong demand for his services and the enormous positive feedback from his clients, Victor knew he had to share this with others. He launched the *Business Performance Portal* and has never looked back.

Not only does his company help small business owners improve their core processes by utilizing the specialized tools he created, it also offers other services as well.

Victor offers corporate performance workshops where he teaches managers and teams how to apply the secrets of high performing organizations. He offers small business "boot camp" style seminars where small business owners learn to apply small business mastery techniques and the latest revenue and profit generating techniques. He has a member website that provides step-by-step processes and frameworks to overcome every business obstacle and offers a support system of other small and large business owners looking for advice and joint venture opportunities. He also offers business consulting and private one on one coaching packages where he walks you through every phase of transforming your business.

Victor Holman - Business Performance Coach
www.Lifecycle-Performance-Pros.com

Victor Holman's

Recipe for SUCCESS!

1. Do What You Love To Do – When you love your work you can overcome any shortcoming by the sheer passion you bring to your business.

2. Set Big Goals – Set goals that challenge your business and believe in your business more than anybody else.

3. Be Comfortable With Being Uncomfortable – Learn to excel in situations that take you out of your comfort zone.

4. Exceed Customer Expectations – There's a saying "there's no traffic in the extra mile."

5. Don't Be Afraid To Be Great – Sadly, people often mock and ridicule those who speak of greatness. Ignore all naysayers and strive to be the best.

6. Celebrate Your Victories – Business is full of highs and lows. Celebrate when you hit milestones and goals, and bounce back fast when you fail.

7. Don't Let Your Business Run Your Life.

About Victor Holman

Victor has authored several books including *The 120 Day Plan: A Step by Step Guide to Implementing a World Class Performance Solution, The Complete Guide to Decision Support Systems: 95 techniques for Mastering Decision Making, Business Best Practices: 36 Best Practices That Drive High Performance, The Complete Guide to Business Intelligence: What Every Business Should Know Before Buying a BI Tool,* and *The Book of Business Methodologies: 45 Business Frameworks To Overcome Any Challenge.* He has also written over a hundred articles for small businesses on various hot business topics. He offers business toolkits, manuals, templates, videos, audio books and DVDs to supplement his coaching and teachings.

Victor is a devoted Christian who enjoys helping others. He has been blessed with the gift of teaching and coaching and loves to share this gift with others. When not working, he enjoys sports, traveling and spending time with loved ones.

Victor Holman
Business Performance Coach
www.Lifecycle-Performance-Pros.com
Email: victor.holman@lifecycle-performance-pros.com
Phone: 202-415-5363

Dr. Renee Hornbuckle

"Success is knowing my purpose in life, growing to my maximum potential, and sowing seeds that benefit others."
John Maxwell

Trouble Doesn't Ever Come at a Convenient Time

Five years ago, Dr. Renee's life was challenged in ways unimaginable, as she found herself faced with the GREATEST CRISIS of her life. She NEVER (and I do mean NEVER) in a million years, would have imagined that her life as she knew it and every dream she had for others, her family and herself would be shattered. Renee NEVER would have envisioned that her life would fall apart and that there would be attacks of the magnitude that she experienced against her, her family and others personally caused her to almost lose everything!

But like most of us, Renee had became comfortable with her life and assumed that because she was blessed, that really she had nothing to worry about. In reality, like most do, because life was GREAT, she expected it to always BE GREAT! What she learned from this experience is that TROUBLE doesn't ever come at a convenient time. It actually tends to come at times of inconvenience - as an interruption; when we least expect it! So, the truth is that as much as we desire for things to be just "right" in life - there will be troubles. She likes to say it this way, "Life Happens and when it does, will we be ready?" So, in the midst of your life and your dreams coming to pass...and things being wonderful...LOOK OUT! Trouble may be lurking around the corner. Dr. Renee learned quickly that when you have mishaps in life, that's when you must KNOW WHAT TO DO!

Coping with any type of loss/crisis/tragedy, whether it involves personal possessions, a job or a family member, can be very stressful and quite painful. Dr. Renee will not try to sugarcoat, the stuff we go through hurts, YET, we can overcome if we know WHAT to do! In the world around us every day, we are seeing the collapse of major financial institutions, major corporations, national disasters and more; yet, we must know without a doubt that WE CAN still make it through these things. When faced with a loss, crisis or life-changing event, you are suddenly thrust into an unfamiliar world, one that can be frightening and unsettling. Knowing HOW to make it can help.

In the midst of her crisis, because she FOUND HOPE, KNEW WHAT TO DO, and followed THE PROCESS, she has been able to launch a home-based business and rebuild her life doing what she loves!

She learned early in life that SUCCESS is the completion of goals and objectives necessary to achieve a particular task realize a particular dream or satisfy a particular need or want, for a particular period of time. This definition of success implies that you always be in a state of constant motion because you must focus on and move toward "that thing" that you want so badly. Often those things that we want so badly seem impossible, or they seem difficult or out of reach. But, the real success is not in the attainment of the "thing" itself, but it is in the actual process you go through in order to get it.

It is the sweat that you put out and the long hours you put in.

It is in the decision you make that you will stay in the fight.

It is the lessons you learn as you strive to constantly reach higher levels.

This is the reason you can make bold statements about your success even in the absence of physical evidence because of the process. You become able to visualize yourself as strong and successful regardless of the environment you temporarily find yourself in. To be successful is to remain in motion in order to use all of your potential within. The SECRET of your future SUCCESS is hidden in your daily routine! Keep your daily routine in motion and you will find your success!

Dr. Renee Hornbuckle, Ph.D.
Coach, Author, Speaker

http://www.reneehornbuckle.com

Dr. Renee Hornbuckle's

Recipe for SUCCESS!

1. Focus: Focus on getting it completed! Focus on crossing the finish line!

2. Be Disciplined [Discipline – focused behavior for a future habit; habit – product of your focus]

3. Create the right atmosphere. The atmosphere you create around you determines what you produce.

4. Practice doing what you know to be right. Doing what's right is a very practical rule for success.

5. Make it your goal to think only on positive things. Don't foster negative thoughts. Simply refuse to recall unpleasant events or situations.

6. Make everything you do reflect, "I'm confident!" <u>Practice confidence boosters! To think confidently, act confidently! Think yourself to confidence!</u> Gain the courage to confidently walk in your purpose and become a successful producer!

7. Take Action! Action cures fear. Isolate your fear and then take constructive action. Inaction – doing nothing about a situation – strengthens fear and destroys confidence.

SUCCESS

About Dr. Renee Hornbuckle, Ph.D.

Life Coach - Author - Motivational Entrepreneur - TV Personality - Crisis Coach

Renee is **a woman of influence**, **a gifted motivational speaker**, **a life designer**. Known as one of the **premiere voices** that God is raising up to help others discover that God is truly the source of strength for life. Whether in the church or the marketplace, this woman excites and motivates those that she comes into contact with to live a more fulfilled life! Having overcome many challenges and trials that would have taken most out, Renee displays a passion and fire for God that says God is absolutely in control .Her testimony and life-changing messages delivered with grace, dignity and strength, in her own unusual style will point you to how to live a life of victory by applying God's Word. She believes that God's Word is the sustaining source that when applied empowers anyone to live a powerful life full of hope and purpose! She is a walking representation of the WORD at work and she makes it her business to equip others to lead a life of power! Her heart is to empower lives, heal hearts, and win souls for the Kingdom!

Renee currently **serves as a Life & Crisis Coach and as Senior Pastor** of Agape Christian Fellowship, in Arlington, Texas. She holds a Bachelors of Arts in Business Administration, a Masters of Biblical Studies and a Doctorate in Religious Philosophy.

Renee also hosts an internet show, "Real Living with Renee" - And Agape Live! Both on www.LifeStream.TV

Although Renee is in great demand as a conference speaker and bible teacher she believes that family comes first. Whether Renee is in the secular or the sacred environment, she ministers and presents a challenging word of change in a savvy style uniquely her own. Her desire is to see others on the right path fulfilling their destiny regardless of their background or past mistakes.

Connect with Dr. Renee on Websites, Twitter, Face book, and LinkedIn

www.mylifecompass.com/womenofinfluence || www.reneehornbuckle.com
www.facebook.com/reneehornbuckle || www.twitter.com/reneehornbuckle

Leah Humphries

"When you face what you fear - you become fearless."
Joyce Meyer

From Pain to Power

Leah's entrepreneurial journey certainly had its share of mountain sized roadblocks but this "go getter" is not afraid of hard work and persistence. After 13 years in the advertising industry with her former husband, Leah changed the course of her life by quitting her job and filing for divorce. *"Emotional abuse survivors understand it when I say; there is a pivotal moment when you know you've finally had enough."*

With no employment options on the horizon and a young son to support, Leah dove into what she knows best - creating award winning marketing and design for her new company, Apple Creative Group. With the guidance of The Small Business Development Center in her hometown, Leah plugged into an incredible array of resources and found she was quickly becoming successful.

During that first uncertain year in business Leah did the unthinkable... she lunched a 2nd company that took this small town girl to the national stage.

Inspired by her own personal story of illness and ileostomy surgery, Leah launched My Heart Ties™ - The World's most beautiful ostomy pouch covers." This niche web-based company is changing women's lives by helping them reclaim their dignity and self-esteem. In 2007 My Heart Ties™ received a patent as well as plenty of buzz from nationally acclaimed hospitals like the Cleveland Clinic, Hollister International and the United Ostomy Association of America. Statistics tell us that approximately 750,000 to one million individuals in North America have an ostomy and those numbers are growing.

Leah has won numerous design awards for her work with Apple Creative Group but was moved to tears when notified she would receive the coveted Pennsylvania's Best 50 Women In Business award in 2009, presented to her by Governor Edward Rendell in Harrisburg, PA.

Leah Humphries – Entrepreneur
www.Pain2PowerPrinciple.Com

Leah Humphries

Recipe for SUCCESS!

1. Design Your Life Around Your Priorities. If you want to be home for your kids, DO IT! (I work from home and I run 2 businesses.)

2. Tell that negative nasty inner voice to get lost. We all have nagging doubt on occasion the trick is to give it the boot (each and every time).

3. Network, Network, Network (that does not mean stand in the corner with coffee and a frown.)

4. Find a Mentor who will hold you accountable. (My mentor will kick my rear-end if she needs to and I'm ok with that.)

5. Read, Study, Listen then read some more. TV will not make you smart (unplug it).

6. ASK for what you want. It took me 40 years to finally get this one and it is BIG!

7. If it scares you… do it anyway. You only become bigger by stretching your boundaries

About Leah Humphries

Leah is an entrepreneur, creative innovator and advocate for women. She is president and CEO of two companies, Apple Creative Group, a full-service creative firm, and MY HEART TIES®, a niche web-based company that designs and manufactures ostomy pouch covers.
As many as one million men and women in North America have an ostomy and Leah is dedicated to helping the women in that group reclaim their femininity and sexuality.

Humphries' journey doesn't end there. She gradually realized that she could use the pain she's experienced in her life for an even more productive purpose: to help other women figure out how to reclaim the power within them so that they can move on to live fulfilling lives.

Today she's reaching out to women who are still stuck in a place of pain, whether from physical illness or abusive relationships, by speaking and writing about her experiences. Her website, Pain2PowerPrinciple (Pain2PowerPrinciple.com), is one part of her new mission.

Leah has received numerous ADDY awards for her work as a designer and the prestigious Pennsylvania's Best 50 Women In Business Award in 09'. This energetic wife and mother certainly sees life's difficulties as opportunities to succeed.

For more information or to contact Leah directly
http://www.myheartties.com
http://www.Pain2PowerPrinciple.com
http://www.AppleCreativeGroup.com

Rev. Criss Ittermann

"Because the ones who are crazy enough to think that they can change the world, are the ones who do."   Think Different ad campaign Apple Computer

Healing Magic

In her childhood, Criss wanted to be a teacher and a healer, but what career covers both? She abandoned the dream of teaching because children didn't want to be forced to learn, and abandoned the idea of energy healing once convinced that magic didn't exist. She shut the spirit world out.

In her 20's Criss led a dual-life as a part-time geek while volunteering at The New York Open Center. Her first business venture was selling wild crafted herbs and medicinal preparations. Then Criss was initiated into shamanism and opened up to her spirit connections. After becoming an Interfaith minister in 1997 and thus "Rev. Criss", she stumbled on Reiki and realized there was "healing magic" in the world after all.

Criss burned out many times, from limiting jobs and her pursuit of a psychology degree. She was increasingly dissatisfied with classical psychology and ached to explore Transpersonal and Humanistic psychology, but school was in the way.

In 2004, Criss started her second business in web design. Soon she became a go-to person for business advice, offering brainstorming sessions capitalizing on her amazing capacity to synthesize information and come to unique intuitive conclusions.

Then she met several life coaches, and Criss found her dream career. By 2008, Criss began coach training, yet while changing careers Criss was volunteering with 6 organizations, building websites, working an MLM business, networking, attending trade shows, training to become a coach and coaching clients, and dealing with her children. Everything came to a head: dreams collided with reality and Criss burned out again.

This time was different. Between a past shamanic vision of "Rock Bottom", side research for her target market, and her own frantic state, Criss' soul broke open during a meditation and the answer came directly from Source. As a result Criss crafted the SURRENDER™ system and became both the messenger and pilgrim of the keys for living in the 21st Century.

With SURRENDER™ to Passion, Criss helps stressed-out and overwhelmed people get around the obstacles that keep them prisoner and hold them back from achieving their dreams.

Criss Ittermann, Life & Small Business Coach
http://www.LiberatedLifeCoaching.com

Criss Ittermann's

Recipe for SUCCESS!

1. Make networking a game of playing matchmaker. It's a fun position of helping others rather than pushing a product. You'll never come off like a slimy salesperson. It all comes back to you.

2. Look for referral partners. One client is great, a person who can refer 10 clients is better. Referral partners are golden. Ask how you can promote them.

3. What did you want to be when you grow up? You may have given up on it for the wrong reasons. Why did you want to do that? What other career might be similar?

4. Put yourself in a position to speak in public often: join a Toastmasters chapter, go to business "Speed Networking" events, or join a weekly referral group (like Business Networking International). If you're really ambitious, do all three.

5. Take care of yourself. Healthy water, fresh local food, play, love, feed your eyes with art, feed your heart with music, and feed your soul with meditation or prayer.

6. Life is a game; enjoy it for everything it is. Marvel at the magic, laugh at the peculiarities, be dazzled by brilliance, and truly listen when others speak.

7. Set progressive fees. Stop worrying about whether anyone will be willing to pay "that much" — make sure that you're respecting yourself. You're worth it!

About Rev. Criss Ittermann

Rev. Criss Ittermann is a Life Coach, Interfaith minister, Shamanic practitioner, and Reiki Master.

As a shamanic life coach Rev. Criss lives in the world of intuition & spirit, tunes in to subtle clues and synthesizes the vastness of another person's life to see where the holes are and lead her client to uncovering their own answers. She teaches people how to become authentic, discover their true life's purpose, listen to their intuition, and ask themselves the right questions. Life Coaches are the ultimate healer of the modern disease of a lack of fulfillment and corporate and financial enslavement.

Criss is recognized for her brilliant intuition and uncanny insight into personal motivation and energy management. She is honored to have been gifted with the SURRENDER™ to Passion system from Source, and in addition to teaching the system directly, Criss has created book & audio packages to help people unlock their personal power.

As an active member of the community, Criss fundraises for her local CASA program, coordinates networking events, serves on the board of directors of Independent Living, Inc. (Newburgh, NY), and writes articles, books & poetry. At home Criss is mother of two teens and four cats, and she likes to crochet as a mindfulness meditation.

Criss Ittermann
Life & Small Business Coach
www.LiberatedLifeCoaching.com
email: info@liberatedlifecoaching.com
Phone: 866-993-8932

Martha Johnson

"Four steps to achievement: plan purposefully, prepare prayerfully, proceed positively, pursue persistently"
William A. Ward

Help2Grow Christian Life Coaching

Help2Grow Christian Life Coaching was birthed out of my life experience as well as a desire to help others overcome the rough places that we all face in life. Because of several unhealthy relationships and other areas in life wherein I found myself stuck I was pressed to find a way to work through these issues to a place of health and wholeness both mentally and emotionally. My journey along this path included counseling, therapy and support groups. These were major contributors to my emotional healing and the ability to begin to make healthy choices in my life. As a result I found myself using these experiences to help others also. This, along with specialized training in the area of counseling, life coaching, and support, has evolved into a practice designed to help others move from places of immobility and challenge in areas of their lives to empowerment enrichment and excellence. As a behavioral change agent I am dedicated to the overall growth and wholeness of those I am charged with coaching.

One of the challenges I faced when I decided to begin a formal practice of life coaching was to organize it in a business fashion. Because my desire to help others flowed so naturally, I found myself coaching whenever someone began to share their challenges. It became critical to the success of the business for me to resist the urge to coach others without appointment setting and fee commitment. Once this hurdle was overcome my business was off the ground. The next challenge was to consistently acquire clients. This challenge was met through the technology that the internet affords us. There are many ways to utilize this technology. For me it was trial and error. The main thing I learned from this was that advertising is always necessary. There may be times when word of mouth brings the best success, but other avenues should always be considered. Being willing and able to coach others to their next level organizing a business format and being dedicated to consistent advertising has created a practice that is both helpful to others and fulfilling to me.

Martha Johnson
helpingu2grow@gmail.com

Martha Johnson

Recipe for SUCCESS!

1. Work with ethics and authenticity

2. Keep your vision in front of your mind's eye

3. Keep a positive attitude

4. Avoid negative people and ignore doubters

5. Develop confidence

6. Be consistent

7. Take time to write down your goals, and review daily

About Martha Johnson

Martha Johnson is the founder and CEO of Help2Grow Christian Life Coaching, www.Help2GrowLifeCoaching.com, a strategic practice with Christ at its center. She is a Certified Counselor in Christ centered Counseling; A Member of the American Association of Christian Counselors; and An Ordained Minister & Founder of Seeds of Significance Women's Ministry, focusing on developing wholeness from the inside out. Martha is also the Executive Producer and Show Host of Help2Grow Talk Radio, www.help2grow.podomatic.com, a show brought to you by Help2Grow Christian Life Coaching and designed to help listeners discover how adversity is only a means to thrust one forward rather than hold one back. It is dedicated to helping women redefine the stuck places in their careers, relationships, and lifestyles, as it empowers them to become vibrant, effective, and growing in these areas of their lives. Our inspirational and educational topics as well as interviews with empowered women enhance, enrich, and energize the lives of our listeners.

Her accomplishments are birthed out of her twenty plus years' experience counseling, teaching, coaching and mentoring in the areas of self-esteem, healthy relationships and Christ centered living. As a life coach she is known for empowering people as a behavioral change manager and has developed and facilitated empowerment programs that help shape, mold and develop women into their God ordained purpose; she has been instrumental in bringing life changing improvements in relationships, family, self-esteem, personal development, and life skills and is results oriented in her strategic life coaching that propels individuals to their next level.

www.Help2GrowLifeCoaching.com
helpingu2grow@gmail.com
www.help2grow.podomatic.com

Kimber King

"I can do all things through Christ who strengthens me."
Phil. 4:13

Ordinary Stay at Home Mom Earns an Extraordinary Income Focusing on Others

In mid June 2002, I was a busy stay at home mom with three boys, ages 6, 4 and 2. I wasn't looking for a way to make money from home, but when I began using a line of nutritional cleansing products called Isagenix that dramatically impacted my health I couldn't help telling everyone I knew about it. The products were sold through a network marketing company and I actually had a very negative view of the industry. But the results I had with my own health far outweighed all the negative things I felt about the business. So I quickly signed up enough family and friends to reach the top rank level in my company in the first six weeks. Within 90 days, my monthly earnings matched the full time income I had previously been paid in the corporate world.

I soon began reaching beyond my immediate circle of contacts through social networking on the internet.

One night I stumbled upon a website that described itself as a business networking site. It was free and on the site you had the opportunity to create a profile page for yourself. This was long before the days of Facebook and Twitter. I dove right in and started connecting with a ton of people so I was "Social Networking when Social Networking wasn't cool." I did some things very naturally that literally launched my business on the internet. I began cultivating online relationships mostly focusing on other stay at home moms and focusing on their needs and goals and soon became a 6 figure income earner working part-time from home.

I credit much of my success from values and work ethics my parents instilled in me. I worked with a spirit of excellence in me and focusing on others. It's always about others and not me! What are my client's needs? What are my team members' goals? What are their strengths? I still never focus on the money but my client's needs and goals. If you focus on others, all the prosperity can't help but come!

Trusting God is also very central to my business approach. It's all about relationships first and then anything that flows out of it from there I leave up to God. I trust Him completely with my business and that He will also put those in front of me that I am supposed to serve. When people ask what I do to create success in my home business, I tell them two simple things: pray and take action. I pray for those who are looking for me and for those I can serve. Then I pick up that phone or connect with someone. "Faith without work is dead!" I have faith in my Heavenly Father to provide the way but I also know that I have to step out on that path in faith.

Kimber King - Entrepreneur
www.kimberking.com

Kimber King

Recipe for SUCCESS!

1. Focus on other's needs – If you help enough people get what they want you will get what you want.

2. Don't compare yourself to others – You are unique and have different gifts and skill sets and diversity of leadership is needed in this industry.

3. Keep it Simple – If you have to be the expert in your business and no one can do it without you, your business will never duplicate.

4. Follow Directions – If your leaders have a proven track record of success, don't let your ego be tempted to reinvent the wheel. Just follow in their footsteps.

5. Stay coachable – Even after I reached a 6 figure income, I still have a coach and mentor(s). Michael Jordan never fired his coach at the height of his game. You need to stay sharpened.

6. Difference of Goal setting vs. Why – Don't just focus on your big dream(s) or Why, you must set many smaller baby step goals that are realistic and achievable to get you to your BIG WHY!

7. Become a People Expert – Don't just become a "product expert." Learn all you can about your clients and team members. If focus on learning more about people than your product all the rest comes naturally. "People are your product."

About Kimber King

Kimber King has spent the last 8 years helping 100's of people achieve success both financially and physically.

Because of her passion to help others reach their own personal goals of health and wealth, Kimber and her husband Stewart have been able to create a high 6 figure income working part-time from their home, all while enjoying a balanced, rewarding, family and charity focused lifestyle.

Kimber is *dedicated to serving God, her husband and their three sons*. She enjoys spending time with friends and family, traveling, self discovery and improvement and is passionate about helping others break free from what holds them back so they can create success in their own lives as well.

Kimber King has been recognized by her company and industry:

- Top 50 & 100 Income Earning Awards
- Top Team Builder Award
- Outstanding Women of 2004 Award
- Recognized by a Multi-Millionaire Industry Trainer for her work and as an expert in Social Media Marketing
- Recognized in Success from Home Magazine
- Featured Story in "Making Money from Home" by Donna Partow
- Co-Host of Weekly Internet Show for Work at Home Moms, "The Real Wahms," www.TheRealWahms.com

Kimber King
Kimber_king@msn.com
www.kimberking.com
801-644-6997

Christine Konopko

"Change is the only thing that you can expect"
Jaymi Wiley

Following Your Heart

Had you asked Christine 10 years ago "would you ever run my own business" she would probably have laughed at the idea. But sometimes things just happen and events and circumstances force us to make choices and lead us in directions we never might have imagined.

Sometimes we simply raise our sails and the winds of chance control our direction. Then it's our choice if we sail with the prevailing wind or fight against it.

From a very young age Christine knew she wanted to be a nurse. Looking after others came very natural to her. Christine entered nursing and became an RN.

Christine was born and raised on a beautiful island on the south coast of England, called the Isle of Wight. But after entering nursing she became interested in travel and through nursing was able to live and work in several different locations in Britain.

She met and married her first husband and with him I moved to the Middle East and worked for 12 years in the military hospital in the Sultanate of Oman. Christine loved the people, the work and the country. Being in the Middle East was also a great opportunity to travel the world and we traveled to several continents.

Unfortunately her first marriage did not last but they did part as friends.

Christine decided to remain in the Middle East and a few years later met her second husband and through him I moved to America in 2000. Life was good for a while. Her new husband earned enough money that she didn't need to work. But looking back that was a mistake because she had always worked and being a housewife was just not stimulating enough. Unfortunately, her new husband was a very controlling person and eventually that marriage also ended.

Christine found herself broken hearted and thousands of miles away from family. Having not worked in 7 years and not a registered nurse in America, what would she do? She was a permanent resident but not a citizen and had no work history. Not even a credit card or bank account in her name. After 7 years of marriage Christine found she had very little self-confidence left.

After thinking long and hard about the options Christine realized she could not cope with going through both a divorce and moving country again. She decided to stay in America. At the same time Christine realized that the thought of returning to nursing made her feel exhausted and that her outlook about health had changed. You see, Christine no longer believed that drugs and medication were the whole answer to health and wellbeing.

Christine always had an interest in massage and certainly loved receiving massages. She realized that the thought of becoming a massage therapist was energizing. Six months later Christine had her Texas State License and became a Licensed Massage Therapist (LMT).

In March 2008 Christine leased an office space and started her own business with a determination to succeed.

Believing that one never stops learning, she went on to obtain her National License as well as her Massage Therapy Instructors license (MTI), and because of her nursing back ground Christine soon found herself teaching anatomy & physiology to massage students. Being able to inspire the next generation of therapists is something Christine is passionate about.

Despite the recession and a visit from Hurricane Katrina, through hard work and a solid belief in what she was doing, Christine continued to build her business and managed to do so debt free!

Learning how to market one's self efficiently is a big part of business and sometimes that is done through trial and error. Christine found that getting out and doing chair massage worked well and found that one thing leads to another. Referrals from satisfied clients are priceless. And of course she never leaves home without my business cards.

Christine found that one can make themselves more marketable by continuing to learn new skills and techniques to better serve her clients. She went on to learn Craniosacral Therapy, Lymphatic Drainage Therapy, Deep Tissue Massage, Hotstones Massage, Reflexology, Aromatherapy and Body Wraps.

For Christine failure is not an option and giving excellent customer service and being good at what she does is of paramount importance.

Life is a constant learning experience and running your own business is a continual reminder of that. Sometimes we all make mistakes with the choices we make with managing the business, but at the end of the day we only answer to ourselves.

For those of you who are thinking about running your own business do not imagine for one minute it is going to be easy, because it isn't. There are some weeks and months you may not get a day off and other times you may have very little work, which can be worrying.

What makes it worthwhile is having a passion for what you do and a belief in yourself. If you are following your heart then you really don't notice the hard work because you're enjoying yourself.

Christine Konopko
cakonopko@hotmail.com

Christine Konopko's *Recipe for* SUCCESS!

1. Believe in yourself and in what you do – follow your heart

2. Start small and work within a budget

3. Write an effective business plan and revisit regularly

4. Always carry your business cards and give out two at a time per person

5. Learn from your mistakes

6. Excel at providing the best in customer service

7. Don't compromise your ethics

About Christine Konopko

Christine has 20 years' experience as a Registered Nurse in England and worked 12 years in the Middle East as a nurse. But after moving to America she decided to change direction with the way to care for others and became a Licensed Massage Therapist.

Over the past 3 years Christine has successfully built her own thriving business and has done so debt free. She has a wide range of clients from teenagers to the elderly and tailors each massage to suit her client's needs

Christine has also become a Massage Therapy Instructor and teaches at the Phoenix School of Massage on a regular part time basis.

Christine enjoys everything about the field of massage and believes strongly in preventive therapies like massage to improve and maintain better health.

Christine Konopko
cakonopko@hotmail.com
281-636-7710

Diane Lampe

"Nothing is more powerful than a made-up mind."
Anonymous

Sick and Tired of Being Sick and Tired

In 2005, Diane found herself with a mortgage business in debt to the tune of $175,000. The failing real estate and mortgage markets at the time meant that Diane, and her business partner and husband Bill, had no alternative but to examine everything they had been doing and how they were doing it. Diane refused to be bowed by this enormous debt, but decided to set herself and her business on a new course. First, she had to acknowledge and accept her situation – to write a list of all her debt so she was clear on what needed to happen.

In facing financial ruin, Diane and Bill acknowledged that nothing less than massive and dramatic positive action would change circumstances. Frankly, Diane was sick and tired of being sick and tired. The ongoing debt weighed her down, making it difficult for her to see options rather than hardship. Hard as it was, Diane and Bill recognized that embracing change and transforming their life was imperative, even if neither of them knew exactly how the change would manifest.

Diane knew she and Bill had to do something momentous, because anything less would not relieve their financial burdens. Change, both personal and professional, is the key to reinvention and Diane focused on the benefits of change instead of lamenting the turmoil change would bring. Her attitudinal shift meant that she and Bill could actively, openly seek new opportunities -- the one they chose would take them from debt of $175,000 to earnings of $1.2 million within 18 months of launching the business.

So what really happened? As the quote above intimates, focusing on the negatives of life seems to bring on more negative. Diane recognized that focusing on their debts just appeared to bring more bills to the mail box. Things don't get better with hard work; they get worse, faster. In everyone's life there is a time to embrace new concepts because the old ones are no longer working. For Diane, her debts made it time to think about and imagine a different outcome – and this thought process has to occur each and every day. You can't continue to do the same things and expect a different outcome. Diane learned this valuable lesson in a hard way, but acknowledges that sometimes hardship is the best teacher.

Visualizing a positive outcome and focusing on personal and professional (written) goals led to profound positive changes for Diane (and Bill). She and Bill became affiliates of an organization that provides unlimited opportunities for her and her family – and could provide the same opportunities for the others she hoped to bring to it. She sleeps well each night knowing that they, and the people who follow them, are doing the right things for the right reasons, and that her business fits their goals and values.

As a business owner and mentor, Diane recognizes that to be truly successful she had to move away from doing the same old thing. By focusing on new outcomes and embracing change, she is able to mentor others who can duplicate her accomplishments and success – not in years or months, but in weeks.

Diane is a high-energy wife and mother who is incredibly creative. When she is not focused on creating simple systems for enhancing business productivity, she and her husband enjoy traveling to warm weather locations.

Diane Lampe - Entrepreneur and mentor, best-selling author
www.lampeteam.com

Diane Lampe's

Recipe for SUCCESS!

1. Never give up on yourself, even when others try to steal your dreams.

2. Be the copy worth duplicating... would you hire you?

3. If you don't hire an assistant, you are one.

4. Learn to be a finisher; that is where the BIG rewards are.

5. Be a Do-it First leader.

6. Find a mentor(s) and/or coach; be accountable to yourself and your mentor.

7. Make a plan and work that plan for what you focus on you move toward.

About Diane Lampe

In 2006, Diane Lampe co-founded a business that earned her and her husband over $1.2 million in their first full year of business and even more in following years. They protect families' financial assets and help secure their retirement and you can too!

For those interested in joining their business and being mentored by Diane, at no charge, set up a personal appointment and interview.

Diane is a best-selling author, national speaker, mentor, and has appeared on radio shows, sharing her secrets to success and how to create the life and income so many dream of.

Diane Lampe
Entrepreneur, Mentor, Best-Selling Author
www.lampeteam.com

Diamond Leone

"The greatest good you can do for another is not just to share your riches but to reveal to him his own." Benjamin Disraeli

Are You Stuck in a Rut?

Not really sure what you want the next chapter of your life to be? Maybe you have some good ideas but just need some help to overcome obstacles and turn one of your passions into a profitable business. This is Diamond's specialty.

Anyone who has had the pleasure of meeting Diamond will tell you that she is an amazing and unique person to learn from. Her mission in life is to make a difference in people's lives by helping them to discover and reach their own best potential.

Diamond's story is one of triumph over adversity. Having grown up in some of the poorest areas of DC and Maryland, and being raised by a single mother with 3 kids, often times Diamond and her family found themselves homeless and hungry. These defining moments in her early life coupled with her strong faith in God, gave her the tenacity and compassion to help others rise above their current circumstances and go after the life they dream of and deserve.

Her experience ranges from starting a successful IT business with her husband and selling it for millions of dollars, to becoming a successful real estate investor.

Although these successes were rewarding financially, they simply didn't fulfill her need for creative expression. She began a journey to find her real passion. She gave herself permission to explore acting, modeling, and various other creative outlets. Life was going great and then another major challenge surfaced.

Her marriage of 8 years ended leaving her to raise two kids as a single mom. Exploring these passions was fun, but it didn't pay the bills. It was on this journey that she realized how many other people were just like her... people searching to find their inner passions and yearning for a way to turn them into a profitable business.

Utilizing her years of research and artistic flare, she began coaching people one by one to discover their passions and create a profitable business model around them. It was at this time that DivasMakingaDifference.com (DMAD) was created.

Make no mistake; this is not your average coaching style business model. In addition to individual coaching, DMAD offers weekend retreats where clients follow an itinerary complete with spa treatments, business development workshops, meditation and group brainstorming sessions. In the near future, there will be a member site where divas from all over the world can unite to support each other by forming business alliances together.

Diamond's energy is infectious and her humorous, "kick in the butt" style of problem solving is like no other out there. Simply put, she delivers results. When she's not kicking butt for her clients and fellow divas, she enjoys spending quality time with her two children, traveling and biking.

Diamond Leone - Creative Coach
www.divasmakingadifference.com

Diamond Leone's

Recipe for SUCCESS!

1. Develop a mindset that's unstoppable - You become what you think about most of the time. Think only about your goals and what is the next step to achieving them is the key to success.

2. Always be true to yourself - If you know you would rather be a cook than a lawyer, don't ever let anyone convince you otherwise.

3. Know what your true values are in life - Once you know what your values are, every decision you make in your life should be centered around them.

4. Take the time to create a life map - This will save you years of your life. Most people don't do this and wake up when their life is half over and wonder why they are not happy. It's because they're not pursuing their passion!

5. Set Daily, weekly, monthly and annual goals for yourself - If you don't have your goals written down, you will go nowhere fast.

6. Get around like minded people - Every successful athlete or business person has a coach to help them get to the next level. It's not a cost to you, it's an INVESTMENT IN YOU!

7. Work harder than you ever have - Remember, if you want what you don't have right now, then you have to become someone that you aren't right now.

About Diamond Leone

Diamond is passionate about helping people find their inner passions and create a business doing what they love. She has written several books on the topics of goal setting, clarifying your values and creating a life map. Her coaching program is in such high demand that clients are only accepted after an application and interview process. As the creator of www.divasmakingadifference.com, her goal is to inspire as many women as possible by providing an online community where women from all over the world can login and share ideas and help one another.

She has been a successful real estate investor and business owner for many years. However, it's her creative background in the arts and her humorous personality that compliment her down to earth style of coaching, making her a unique and fun person to work with. Diamond is currently in the process of co-authoring a book with the legendary bestselling author Brian Tracy. Brian has helped over 4 million people from all over the world achieve their business, personal and financial goals. He is a sought after public speaker and Diamond is honored to be working with him on this project. Too often women settle for a boring life that doesn't fulfill their passion. Diamond helps women "get their Diva on" and live with passion, purpose and flare!

Diamond Leone
Creative Coach
www.divasmakingadifference.com
Email: diamondleone@gmail.com
Phone: 703-209-9012

Anne-Marie Lerch

"Only those who will risk going too far can possibly find out how far one can go."
T. S. Eliott

Transforming Adversity into Opportunity

Anne-Marie's journey on the path to success began ten years ago when she was dissatisfied with her life. Anne-Marie graduated from a top university with a bachelor of Mathematics and a double major in Business specializing in Systems Management. She had a love for business and strategy and with her mathematical mind she was an expert at solving problems.

Upon graduation, Anne-Marie landed her dream job for her choice company, one that she dreamed of for years, as did hundreds of other peers that graduated from her class. Her career was taking off but her personal life remained painful and unbearable. In hopes to solve her problems she turned to self-help, personal development, spirituality and manifestation. She became aware of the invisible world of possibility and learned that her thoughts could actually change her reality. She dared to dream of a better future and began to rely on her intuition and dreams to help guide her.

On New Year's Day of 2005, she made a list of the four things she wanted to accomplish most in her life.

1. She wanted to increase her salary by $30,000.
2. She wanted to move to Seattle and work for the best software company.
3. She wanted to meet a good man and be in a healthy relationship.
4. She wanted to become a speaker and teacher and eventually start her own business.

As she trusted her inner guide, she quit the job she once loved and took a leap of faith to achieve her goals. With only $1,000 to her name, she left her family and friends to drive cross-country in hopes of getting a position with her desired company.

The day before she arrived in Seattle, she got an email about a position for the company she dreamed of working for. Four short months after writing down her goals, Anne-Marie crossed two items off the list; she got the position at the company for the exact salary and the exact role she wrote down on New Year's Day.

She made the most of the opportunity to work for this globally-recognized corporation. Yet even though the work in computing and project management was challenging and the job seemed perfect for her, Anne-Marie could not escape the nagging sense that her inner gifts were still being left untapped and she was destined for even greater things. There was still more of the mountain to climb. That same year, she met a great man and was married soon after. Goal number three had been fulfilled as well.

After the birth of her first child, Anne-Marie was able to realize the fourth goal on her list, to become a professional speaker and have her own business helping others manifest their own dreams and access their higher self just as she's been able to do.

Her main professional and personal challenges have been to try to weather the storm of the current economic downturn, and continue to have faith and apply her principles throughout these troubling times. In the face of bankruptcy, Anne-Marie was able to turn her previous year's income into her monthly income.

It is all too tempting to think small when things turn difficult. Anne-Marie has transformed adversity into opportunity by deepening her studies and creating her *Manifestation Success System* using scientifically proven techniques.

Through using your mind and application of universal laws, which you can read more about at CoachMeNow.com, Anne-Marie has been able to help countless small business owners and professionals accelerate their own success by setting bigger goals and then consistently achieving them.

Anne-Marie's step-by-step program helps her clients get rid of their old ways of thinking that have been holding them back. Through her coaching, she enables her clients to go with the bountiful flow of the universe through relying on their intuition as their guide to their higher self.

Through creating her own business and manifestation system, Anne-Marie has found the ideal way to tap into her inner gifts, and support others as they travel on their own journey to success.

Anne-Marie Lerch - Business Strategist & Mindset Coach
www.CoachMeNow.com
Email: info@CoachMeNow.com

Anne-Marie Lerch's

Recipe for SUCCESS!

1. Dare to dream big. Small ambitions equal small achievements. Great ambitions equal even greater ones. Dream big and define your goals. Get a clear vision of what you want and hold it firmly in your mind.

2. Tell your subconscious. Access this powerful mind to help you in the process to success. Your results are a reflection of the beliefs you store in your subconscious.

3. Think it, before you live it. Whatever you are seeking is seeking you in return. Open yourself to new possibilities by first creating the thought. Everything is created twice, once in the mind and then in the real world.

4. Strengthen Intuition. We are all born with an inner guide, our intuition. Strengthen your inner guide by trusting intuition to lead you to the greatness you're capable of creating for yourself.

5. See with different eyes. Dr. Wayne Dyer says "If you change the way you look at things, the things you look at change". Shift your perspective, change your point of view and you have created a whole new world to live in.

6. Raise your vibration. Your rate of vibration attracts the circumstances in your life. If you want greater things, change the frequency and energy level that you operate at, and start living your life with more abundance and ease.

7. Access your Higher power. Why do it alone if you don't have to. Ask the Universe, God or Higher Power to work through you to accomplish things you never thought possible

About Anne-Marie Lerch

Anne-Marie Lerch is recognized as a leading technology consultant, Mindset Expert and Business Success Coach. She is an expert in thinking and how the subconscious mind works.

She is the founder and CEO of CoachMeNow.com, and also the creator of the Manifestation Success System. Through this system, she has helped countless clients in a variety of industries, from real estate to financial planning to small business and marketing to follow their intuition and attract more of what they want for their business using scientifically proven techniques. By identifying goals and awakening them to new ways of thinking, her clients have been able to identify and manifest their business and personal goals.

Anne-Marie is a licensed coach, a worldwide speaker and member of the National Association of Public Speakers. She has been a guest speaker at numerous success seminars, and is a popular presenter on how to manifest your personal vision. She is known for her natural ability to identify the thought patterns that hold people back from achieving what they want. As a mathematician she is easily able to solve problems with her thorough analysis. Her intuition and business background allows her to help entrepreneurs and professionals develop systems to grow their businesses strategically.

Anne-Marie Lerch
Business Strategist & Mindset Coach
www.CoachMeNow.com
Email: info@CoachMeNow.com
Phone: 1-877-83-SMILE (76453)

Laura Lopez

"Our chief want in life is somebody who shall make us do what we can."
Ralph Waldo Emerson

Do lessons from home translate to more effective business results?

Laura often says she has always been a late bloomer. At a ripe age of 45 she became a mother.

And with motherhood came the best lesson of all, how to become a more effective leader.

Before becoming a mom, Laura was dedicated to climbing the corporate ladder. She worked her way up to become a VP, Marketing at The Coca-Cola Company. However, it wasn't until she adopted her daughter Leila that she learned the true meaning of leadership and how to achieve better results through others.

Laura always knew that she wanted to make the jump from Corporate to becoming an entrepreneur, but it wasn't until she adopted her daughter that she knew the kind of business she wanted to build.

Inspired by the lessons she was learning from her daughter about leadership, she decided to write a leadership book that was like no other leadership book out there: "I took the leadership lessons I was gleaning from home and applied them back to business for outstanding results and impact." The result was her award-winning book, *The Connected and Committed Leader. Lessons from Home. Results at Work.*

Now Laura works with businesses of all sizes to build long-term results through more effective leadership. She develops customized workshops, individualized coaching and gives motivational speeches on the topic of leadership. Laura launched www.laura-lopez.com and www.lauralopezblog.com as a way to guide people to a new way of leading and growing their business.

Laura believes that most people have the wrong idea about leadership, especially women. She says that leadership is the exact opposite of what most people think it is. She is determined to redefine leadership for the 21st century, especially for women trying to find success in the business world.

The challenge of achieving "balance" between home and work life is a very real issue for many women. Whether you are a new mom trying to start a business, a business professional on the climb with conflicted feelings of wanting to start a family, a mom with grown kids reentering the workforce, or some other variation where balancing the demands of being a mom with your life at work can be a point of stress and guilt.

Laura's 7 essential leadership insights help people be more effective in life, both at home and at work. After all, Laura believes that people today are looking for work that works in their lives! Men and women alike, no longer want to sacrifice one part of their lives for another.

Laura Lopez, Author
www.Laura-Lopez.com

So can parenthood prepare you for building a successful business? You bet! These 7 ingredients will help you get the results you are looking for, both at home and at work.

Laura Lopez'

Recipe for SUCCESS!

1. Believe and let go. When you believe and let go you allow others to confront their own abilities or inabilities. By letting go, you give people the freedom to ask for help and receive guidance.

2. Be curious and see everyone. Leaders should never play favorites. You should be curious about everyone on the team, even if they are just warming the bench. This shows that you truly value people; and in doing so, you will unleash their potential to perform at their best.

3. Be receptive and yield. The real leader is the quiet one who listens and asks the questions, rather than the one driving and giving the answers. Why bother having people work with you if you aren't going to allow them to contribute their own ideas and talent?

4. Be real and serve. Being a great leader takes the courage to be real. People aren't going to be real with you unless you are real with them. They must know that you have the best interest of the team in mind at all times, and you are serving them and not just yourself.

5. Be humble and keep your ego in check. The most common reason leaders fail is because of arrogance. The reality is that many rising stars in large organizations don't experience any, or enough, humiliation in their lives, either at work or at home. This is unfortunate because humiliation can be one of our greatest teachers.

6. Be consistent and clear. Character and integrity are essential qualities of great leadership. Integrity is more than just telling the truth. It is about standing up for what you believe in and having the courage and conviction to do the right thing, regardless of social or political pressures.

7. Be vulnerable and give of yourself. It is only through the heart that you connect with and fully engage people. They don't care how much you know until they know how much you care. Passion can drive long-term success.

About Laura Lopez

Laura Lopez has been leading teams and achieving results for major Fortune 100 Companies since the early '80s. Most recently, Laura was a highly successful Vice President at The Coca-Cola Company

Today Laura helps businesses of all sizes and industries to achieve superior results through connected and committed leadership.

As a sought-after keynote speaker, award-winning author, consultant and executive coach, Laura Lopez is a performance strategist that helps clients build more sustainable personal and professional results to achieve greater levels of success. Laura believes that effective connections with employees, consumers and customers are what drive outstanding performance.

Laura holds an MBA from The American Graduate School of International Business and a Bachelors of Science degree from Bucknell University. As a contributing author, Laura Lopez's articles have been regularly featured in the acclaimed magazine Leadership Excellence, as well as in Personal Excellence, CW Bulletin, The Central Valley Business Times, and The Long Beach Business Journal.

Laura Lopez has also been interviewed or quoted as a leadership and branding expert on The Today Show, Fox News, Harvard Business Publishing, Success Magazine, The Houston Chronicle, and Latina Magazine.

Laura Lopez
www.laura-lopez.com
www.lauralopezblog.com

Deborah McNaughton

"One person's thunderstorm is another person's light rain"
Les Brown

The Road Less Traveled

Deb's life story can be summed up as "when there's a fork in the road, take the road less traveled." The path from her humble upbringing in the rural Midwest to her current role as founder of a successful national direct sales company has been twisty indeed.

As a first generation college student she chose the demanding field of mathematics. With her doctoral work just a faint memory, Deb worked first in the male dominated field of actuarial science and then switched careers to the slightly more family friendly field of biotech.

Although a rising star she was, Deb soon tired of the corporate grind. Sensing a need to once again make a major change in her life, Deb decided to take a completely different path. Combining her desire for a more balanced lifestyle and her love of jewelry resulted in the creation of her true passion, AZULI SKYE (www.azuliskye.com).

Now freed from the constraints of corporate life, Deb's passion to inspire and connect other woman is insatiable. As the founder of AZULI SKYE, Deb has the pleasure of helping hundreds of incredible woman every week achieve their dreams of balance as well.

Getting to this point has not been easy. **Many doubted her decision to start a business and called her "crazy" for leaving the so-called security and income of corporate life behind.** The biggest hurdle of all occurred right in the middle of starting AZULI SKYE.

Just months before the launch of her new company, Deb had a terrible accident and broke both her arms so severely that major surgery was required. Months of tedious recovery ensued, but this did not stop Deb from getting the company off the ground with a national launch.

In hindsight the timing couldn't have been worse. Little did Deb know that her planned company launch date (September 2008) would coincide with the start of the most serious recession this country has seen since the 1930s!

Despite the formidable odds, Deb's steadfast nature and unshakeable resolve has resulted in AZULI SKYE growing and thriving as a national direct sales jewelry company. As Deb always says *"One person's thunderstorm is another person's light rain. It's all how you look at things"*.

Debora McNaughton
www.azuliskye.com

Deborah McNaughton

Recipe for SUCCESS!

1. Work your business every day. It creates the magic of momentum. You must do something every day, no matter small; those small steps add up to miles.

2. Set a plan for what you want to accomplish each day. If you don't you'll soon wonder how time just slipped away. Hold yourself accountable and reward yourself for results. That's what being your own boss really means :)

3. Don't take rejection personally. You likely don't need hundreds of customers to have a great income. A handful of great customers often does the job.

4. Without leads you don't have a business. Marketing must be a key part of your business plan. There's no point in having a great product or service if you don't have any customers.

5. When your mouth is closed your business is closed. You can share without being perceived as pushy. Most of business is about relationships, not strictly abilities. People work with people they like.

6. Have a support network. You may be in business by yourself but you need the emotional support to get you through those tough days.

7. Rely on the expertise of others. If it's not your core business, find someone else who can do it better than you. Think of all the time you'll save, which you can use to earn money for what you really like to do.

About Deborah McNaughton

Deb McNaughton is the founder of a national direct sales jewelry company. Started on her kitchen table just two years ago, AZULI SKYE has grown to encompass hundreds of passionate independent sales representatives.

Deb is an expert at helping women dare a bigger dream for themselves. According to Deb, "Women today are so busy doing things for everyone else, they leave little time for themselves."

As a frequent radio personality Deb is known for her warmth, wit, and passion for helping woman live the life of their dreams. Deb's desire for helping others is so strong that she also created a free online resource for all Direct Sellers (www.TheDirectSellingUniversity.org).

As a believer in work/life balance, Deb's favorite activities involve her two children (Abigail Skye, 10 and Grant, 8), her super supportive husband Allan, and their family pet, Brodie.

Debora McNaughton
www.azuliskye.com

Marcia Merrill

Whether you think you can or think you can't…You're right!
Henry Ford

Change is good!

What do anxiety/panic attacks have to do with creating a home based business? Like most people I thought I'd retire and perhaps do something as a second career or nothing at all!

After a rather debilitating episode of anxiety/panic attacks I realized I was no longer going to be able to give my usual 110%. I spent eight months in careful reflection and decided to retired from a 15 year position in a University Career Center.

I spent that first summer learning I couldn't drive again due to a neurological balance challenge! So, I set up my business model and plan, set up my corporation and became a solopreneur. Who knew I'd work from home connected to my phone and the computer every day. I used what I learned in teaching teleclasses in Career/Life Transitions and I became certified as a Career Management/Life Transitions Coach.

Creating great programs to help others succeed is very rewarding! But one cannot do it alone! I personally found that as a solopreneur it's important to reach out and learn from others too!

Michael E. Gerber, author of "*The E-Myth*" and Jay Conrad Levinson, the *Father of Guerilla Marketing* opened my eyes to what was possible in this internet age where so many can be touched. I then moved on to one of my favorite books, *"Purple Cow,"* and the concept of *Permission Marketing* by Seth Godin.

As an entrepreneur, you must be responsible for your own professional Development! It is a worthwhile investment. Share a book by buying it together. I'm an audio learner so I have many MP3s I listen to while I'm working at my computer!

One of the best things I've done for my business is an early birthday present I gave to myself. I attended my first live event, full of gurus, experts and connections.

They were all great, but it was Andrea J. Lee who literally changed how I looked at my business. Andrea teaches *"Multiple Streams of Coaching Income"* and *"Money, Meaning and Beyond"* which helped me see that coaching is my passion but other multiple streams would allow me to do more of what I love!

Most of my clients come to me through word of mouth as well as my attending networking events. I learned early on that going to networking events and NOT taking the time to follow up with those you met, is like taking a shower with your coat on. You are wasting your time!

There is an 80/20 rule that states that the 20% of the Marketing that you do yields 80% of your business.

Networking really made a difference for me, as my neurological challenges took me "off the grid" for at least a year. It was during this time I realized that clients are not just a source of income; they can be here for you during hard times as well. Many that I met in networking groups emailed, called, and mentioned me in their prayers sending healing energy to me. It doesn't get any better than that.

Now that I'm holding networking events in and around Baltimore, I incorporate a donation for every non-profit we sponsor such as canned goods for the Food Bank, Coats for the Homeless, a donation for Red Cross and Haiti, etc. I try to give back and create positivity and abundance both for others and myself as well.

Are you a candidate to become a solopreneur or entrepreneur? Never before has it been so easy to find the tools needed to do so. Put your fears aside, like I did, and take the leap. With the right support and mentoring, you can have a successful at home business!

Marcia Merrill
The Transition Chick™
www.ecareercorner.com

Marcia Merrill's

Recipe for SUCCESS!

1. Be honest with yourself.
2. Risks can be fun!
3. Decide what you want to do and stick with it!
4. Keep learning.
5. Networking can "make" your business.
6. Find those who resonate with you and learn from them.
7. You must enjoy what you decide to do!

Marcia Merrill

I Listen For Deeper Meaning Because I Believe in Making A Positive Difference in Peoples' Lives!

Having literally reinvented her career (and redefined her goals and herself) many times over, Marcia Merrill has definitely earned the title of being known as the Transitions Chick!

Before she answered her true calling, namely coaching, she was a Staff Analyst for a consulting company; a Resource librarian; and taught English, Spanish composition, and English as a second language in all levels of schools, from elementary through to doing substitute teaching during her graduate schooling.

Her fervent desire to continually learn and explore different avenues led her to obtain two Masters degrees, the first in Bilingual/Bicultural Education and Instructional Systems Development from the University of Maryland, and the second in Counseling Psychology from Loyola College, Maryland.

Marcia draws upon not only her solid academic background and her 18+ years as a Career Counselor, but also her own personal transitions that she has weathered and emerged from victoriously. She definitely 'walks the walk and talks the talk' and her primary objective is to help women achieve the level of contentment and success they desire from their life and their career or business. Whether it's transitioning from an entry level position to an executive manager, changing jobs to realize their hopes and dreams, to learning how to cope with the setbacks that life in general sometimes throws at us, Marcia always applies her caring and creative problem-solving skills to her clients.

Her mission statement, "Fall in love with your LIFE & your work (and in that order!)" shows how Marcia prioritizes her life, and her clients easily achieve the same balance in their lives from her superb coaching skills.

Marcia Merrill – The Transition Chick™
www.ecareercorner.com
www.networkingcentral.biz

Ludolph L. Misher, III

"Life Won't Offer Many Guarantees; However, Preparation and Confidence Will Offer Favorable Results." Ludolph L. Misher, III

You Set the Bar

 Ludolph's background is one of many versified talents. Starting his entrepreneurial quest at the age of 12yrs old, Ludolph, "Leon" learned the value of being successful by approaching simple chores with precision and consistent perfection. This trait is the result of loving and responsible parents.

Ludolph learned to apply his perfectionist mentality to every endeavor in which he pursued, and those that know him will say he has always participated at the top of each endeavor.

His efforts have been rewarded by receiving numerous awards and recognitions throughout his life – starting at the age of 12, when he received the first of many "The Yard of the Month" award many times, which invoked many neighbors to request his services. From there he earned many recognitions and awards throughout his life, including his company in the US Navy's "Honor Man" award. From there the instability of the real estate industry prompted Ludolph to begin a career in catering. The catering business propelled him to one of the Northwest's most popular Caterers. More importantly, it allowed Ludolph the privilege to mentor young men between the ages of 14-21 as waiters for his company. Catering, as most things in life and business, did not come without challenges.

Ludolph talks about his business challenges while in the catering business:

"One of my first Business challenges happened during a major event my catering company provided for a large hospital's 150th anniversary in Seattle, Wa. The menu consisted of multiple ethnic foods which represented the men and women who helped to build this great hospital.

This challenge was set up buffet style to serve 700+ people. Now...this hospital was operated largely by Catholic Nuns, and their representative requested serving time for this event to be promptly at 1pm. Prior to serving time, there was a Church Mass which was to start at noon, after which time the 700 people would converge in the dining facility at 1pm sharp to begin the celebration.

Well…the Church services ended early and all of a sudden the doors of the dining area flung open at 12:15pm with people flowing from all directions with hunger in their eyes! By 12:30pm there were approximately 500 hungry people staring us down.

Catering services are one of the most stressful occupations there is, and mismanagement of time can be your biggest foe. As then and now, I have always practiced being prepared ahead of time for the unexpected, and throughout my life I've narrowly escaped total disasters on numerous occasions by being picky about being on time. This is truly one of my biggest pet peeves! Just ask anyone who knows me. Even though we were not completely ready at 12:30pm to serve, my staff and I worked with quickness and started to serve people with hand held platters of finger foods, coffee, tea, and punch.

Soon the buffets were up and fully working joined by the sounds of laughter, small talk, and smiling faces….at my crew! That was the proudest time of my food service career! My company received a formal letter expressing the appreciation of our quick response and service while under undisputed pressure.

The hospital offered my company a healthy gratuity, which I divided amongst the crew [not keeping any for myself]. The fact that we pulled if off was good enough for me!"

Another challenge Ludolph faced also came while working in the catering industry. After working very hard to build a reputation as a top catering company and landing an opportunity of a lifetime, his crew showed up at an event on time only to have the person who was to let them into the building, where they would prepare the food for the evening's Christmas party, two hours late.

He knew by the time the doors were finally opened that the job was compromised. Because his crew wasn't allowed access on time, it ended up causing the main event to start late. 45 minutes later than originally scheduled his team was finally serving, but it was not a success by any means in Ludolph's eyes.

"This was the first and only disaster of my career, thus, I was inclined to reimburse one half of the agreed contract amount back to the organization voluntarily."

My company's slogan of "Delectable Dining with Impeccable Service" was tarnished and devastating to me. I continued to serve with dignity and honor throughout my career, and because I did not give up on myself or the ability to bounce back, life has granted me opportunities to continue in my quest for excellence, honor and success!"

Now retired, Ludolph's ability to achieve whatever he set his mind to, has finally brought him full circle to his "perfect niche" as a writer. Inspired by a dear friend, Ludolph's first book/guide, "Cougar Women - From a Man's Perspective", entails true and accurate descriptions of his experience and knowledge as it relates to women who desire to date younger men. Ludolph's candid descriptions of the how to approach is illustrated throughout his book/guide. Because of his many life experiences, Ludolph will continue writing "how to books and guides" for those with a true and sincere desire to get accurate information "From A Man's Perspective."

Meet & Connect with Ludolph L. Misher, III on Facebook http://facebook.com/ludolphmisher Email: ludolph@maturecougarwomen.com

Ludolph Mishler's

Recipe for SUCCESS!

1. Start by setting aside designated times for an outlined and detailed work plan.

2. Compile information which will assist you in structuring a plan of proven success.

3. Avoid repetitive procrastination, this hazard can be the one thing which prevents a successful venture, after all, *"the Fortune is in the Follow-up."*

4. Seek assistance from those who are qualified in your area of interest and learn how it applies to your plan of attack.

5. Make the information that you provided for your potential clients easy to read, understand, and follow. Marketing literature should not be too busy or confusing at first glance.

6. Proof read every aspect of your Marketing Plan, and make the required adjustments until total efficiency is achieved = Positive Results.

7. Once your Plan is implemented, continue to monitor the progress, keep your goals fined tuned with enhancements where ever needed, and remain open to constructive criticism by making the appropriate corrections as needed.

Joelle Niedecken

"For I know the plans I have for you," declares the LORD, "plans to prosper you and not to harm you, plans to give you hope and a future."
Jeremiah 29:11

Research – Research - Research

Joelle Niedecken is a Sales Director/Trainer and small business developer in the home-based business industry. Joelle is passionate about her company's services and about helping others find and enjoy the same flexibility and freedom that being your own boss has allowed her to do for the last 4 years. Joelle has been mentored and trained by acclaimed industry leaders such as Dani Johnson, Jeffrey Combs, Diane Hochman, and Todd Falcone.

Joelle discovered some years ago, the importance of having a *PLAN B ... she* was already a stay-at-home mom by choice, but with that choice also came letting go of some things that she was accustomed to, and A LOT of self-discipline. Her husband's income wasn't much, so she had to learn to spend only on necessities for their family of 4. She knew, though, that even if she had worked out of the home, what she would be letting go of then... would be her children... time with them, loving on them, having them love on her... and teaching them these thing...just sharing their lives. She didn't want to settle for that. Joelle says, "I can remember thinking back to even when I was a teenager and hearing someone talk about sales, network marketing or some kind of entrepreneurial ship. So I already BELIEVED in the idea, I just needed to find out how to make it work for me. I believed there had to be a legitimate way to make money from home. What I DIDN'T KNOW was that there was a GREAT BIG WORLD out there of people already doing that exact thing... alas... the INDUSTRY OF NETWORK MARKETING!!"

If someone is serious, really serious about starting a home biz, do your research. Research is a great investment to put into yourself and your time, and it's a great skill to have. Just start with a few basics. First decide if you would rather work with a product or service-based company. What's your passion? Second, just start googling for different companies. Third, research them. If you find one, or more, that peaks your interest, research. Check them out with the BBB, with the US Chamber of Commerce, and/or different organizations. There's lots of information on the net, so try not to get discouraged while you're looking. Fourth, double check about start-up costs and any 'extras' that you'll need to be investing

Joelle also recommends working on your leadership and self-development/improvement skills at the SAME TIME you're doing your research looking for the company that's a right fit for you. This will be a great time-saver for you if you can master this multi-tasking skill. Search out the industry leaders that are already out there, listening to free teachings and recordings as you're surfing the net.

If you're coming in totally 'green' (and don't feel intimidated about it if you are... a lot of people in the industry) Joelle just recommends that you need to have the mindset of being in it for the long haul. No quitting for *at least* one year! Joelle stands by a quote that one of her National Vice President's is fond of saying, "Where will you be and what will you be doing a year or longer from now anyway?" Honestly, it's one of the things that brought her into the industry.

Speaking of being 'green', that was one of the obstacles, as mentioned before, that Joelle had to overcome. She was actually looking for a 'job' when she found the home business she's in. She knew none of the terms...like a very common and appropriate one for her... can you say, 'learning curve'?! Joelle says she definitely had a huge one to overcome! She didn't even know being in a home business made you a part of the network marketing industry! Hang in there and you too can have a successful home based business!

Joelle Niedecken
www.dreamsrock.com
www.affordabledentalandmedical.com
jniedecken@ameriplan.net

Joelle Niedecken's

Recipe for SUCCESS!

1. Pray and read your Bible ~ IT IS the #1 'way to SUCCESS' book out there. Give the first 10% thinking of your day to God. Any combination of praying and reading your Bible and seeking Him; God will honor it and lead you when you seek Him first.

2. I LOVE this quote by Jim Rohn. "The challenge of leadership is to be strong, but not rude; be kind, but not weak; be bold, but not a bully; be thoughtful, but not lazy; be humble, but not timid, be proud, but not arrogant; have humor, but without folly." Jim Rohn

3. Do your RESEARCH for whatever business or company you want to affiliate yourself with. When you finally talk with someone from the company, you are 'interviewing' them as much as they may be 'interviewing' you.

4. As you do in other parts of your life, seek out EXPERIENCE.

5. If 'free' resources are available for help, accept and use them.

6. Don't use people

7. You're not promised tomorrow, so keep your heart and motives constantly in check TODAY. Be positive and encouraging.

Sheila Pearl

"Many successful people have found opportunities in failure and adversity that they would not recognize in more favorable circumstances."
Napoleon Hill

Thank You For My Depression!

How crazy does it sound to say *"Thank you for my depression!"* or *"Thank you for firing me?"*

Coming from a perspective that every failure and adversity has within it the kernel of a gift and a blessing, Sheila Pearl has created her eighth career and an ever-evolving profession for herself which would never have been possible without the profound challenges she has experienced throughout her six decades of juicy living. It has been these very obstacles and her stories of triumph over them which have become her greatest opportunity for creating success in her life coaching and public speaking career.

Sheila has experienced one big dream after another morphing into something entirely different from what the original vision was; she has learned that for her, it is essential to trust the universe and just "go with the flow".

Early in her life, Sheila envisioned being a famous opera singer. That opera singer later became a cantor in the synagogue, using her voice in ways she had never imagined, singing music that was foreign to her.

As a young woman, Sheila dreamed of having lots of children and living in a big house. Instead, she helped her husband raise his two teenagers and became "mother" to hundreds of children in the synagogues in which she served as spiritual leader.

At an age when many people are retiring, Sheila opened her doors to her full-time life coaching practice. Having learned the value of networking during her previous careers, she applied her skills of relationship-building to the process of networking, acknowledging its value in building her practice.

In an area where very few people had ever heard of Life Coaching, Sheila had a challenge:

How could she attract clients and ask them to pay for her services when they didn't know anything about coaching? Also, how could she entice people to pay "cash" for her services, which were not covered by insurance?

By joining networking groups, including the local Chamber of Commerce, meeting new people, expanding on the relationships she had already established through her clergy presence in the community, she expanded her web and sphere of influence.

She began to offer classes and workshops on topics which were related to her expertise and life experiences. She offered introductory "complementary" sessions, so that her referral sources could experience her in action. She created discount "packages" as incentives, calling her fees "tuition" as an added distinction that coaching was education, not therapy. She placed small ads in the local newspaper, inviting people to her "FREE" workshops.

In her early 40's, Sheila was struggling to survive cancer. At that time, it would *never* have occurred to her that she would later see that experience as one of her "greatest blessings." She suggests "your life isn't just about *you!*" Whatever she learned about herself in the process of her illness became "grist for the mill" in Sheila's grasp of the human condition and her topics for workshops and speaking.

One of her "FREE INTRODUCTORY WORKSHOPS" was entitled *"Thank God I Had Cancer!"* That one workshop attracted over 50 participants, and from that group, five people became regular coaching clients. From those five, another ten individuals and/or families became clients within a year.

Following her article entitled *"Thank you for firing me!"* written for a local newspaper column, she received inquiries from dozens of people. The article expressed her gratitude to her congregation for NOT renewing her contract, and for essentially setting her free to open the doors to her coaching practice. Readers were inspired to have a conversation with this "wise woman".

For ten years, Sheila was a daily partner in her husband's struggle with dementia and Parkinson's disease. She navigated the denial, anger, fear, and then the surrender to *what is*. She wrote a book about it. She speaks about it. A core aspect of her coaching practice is the attitude known as "Loving What Is" (Byron Katie's work). Because she has lived it, she can teach it and coach it.

With each challenging circumstance, Sheila habitually looks for the gift. Whether healing from the loss of a loved one or coping with illness, adapting to shifting dreams or surrendering to a beloved's transition to death, Sheila seeks ways to view adversity as an opportunity. In her work, she seeks ways to bless all of life, and creates tools to teach others how to recognize the gift.

Sheila uses the gift of her singing and speaking voice to inspire and uplift clients and audiences. As a wisdom teacher, she mentors others to embrace each aspect of life as a gift that opens the heart and invites passionate living.

Sheila Pearl – Life Coach & Speaker
www.LifeCoachSheila.com
www.SheilaPearl.com

Sheila Pearl's

Recipe for SUCCESS!

1. Engage in EXTREME SELF CARE: Nurture your mind, body and spirit daily with healthy food, environments, sights and sounds. Be careful to protect every aspect of your most valuable source of success—You! You cannot take care of others unless you take care of YOU!

2. Seek to COLLABORATE and COOPERATE: create the ongoing intention to create strategic partnerships and alliances with people who are not only great referral sources, but also part of your team of experts in arenas which are not your strengths.

3. Create a BOARD OF ADVISORS: surround yourself with big thinkers and entrepreneurial mentors; invite feedback; create a "mastermind" think-tank with your advisers.

4. LISTEN WITH CURIOSITY, not judgment or an agenda – active listening with your referral sources, your business associates, customers and/or clients requires an open heart and the inner question *"how can I be of service to YOU?"* rather than *"what can you do for ME?"*

5. NETWORK NETWORK NETWORK: your most effective marketing vehicle is networking. Treat every networking opportunity and contact as your most powerful source of income. Don't forget that your networking creates your warm market.

6. FOLLOW-UP is key to creating viable relationships, generating new business opportunities and ongoing business, and essential for nurturing new contacts. Regardless of how charming you may be in any initial conversation, unless your follow-up efforts match your charm, it becomes an empty connection. Sending cards, making calls and even an email to acknowledge the meeting is critical.

7. STEP OUTSIDE YOUR COMFORT ZONE: go into arenas which are unpredictable for you; network with groups that are unfamiliar to you; place ads or articles in venues which would be an unlikely place to be. When we're outside our "comfort", we may be more alert to opportunities and may become more creative in seeing possibilities.

About Sheila Pearl

Sheila Pearl is recognized as a leading relationship coach, focusing on mentoring others in living life joyfully. She has been in private practice as family therapist for over 30 years, has been a full-time life coach for a decade, and has been on the platform as keynote speaker and seminar leader for over two decades. She is the founder and director of Mind-Body-Spirit Connections. She has been a staff coach for the Conversations with God Foundation since 2005.

As an author, international speaker and life coach, Sheila has appeared on television, radio shows, in magazines and in feature and news articles sharing easy tips and "golden nuggets" of wisdom for living life with less pain and more joy. She is co-author with 49 coaches worldwide in *"WAKE UP WOMEN BE Happy, Healthy & Wealthy—A Guidebook"*; co-author of *"The Winning Connection"* with a Foreword written by Bob Proctor; and author of *"STILL LIFE: A Spiritual Guidebook for Life Transitions"* with a Foreword written by Neale Donald Walsch. Her forthcoming book, *"Looking for the Gift: Wisdom Conversations on Being in Love with Your Life"* is also forwarded by Mr. Walsch.

Having been a spiritual leader and busy public speaker in the New York metropolitan area for over 25 years, Sheila has earned a reputation for her ability to inspire and motivate her audiences, bringing them to emotional crescendos ranging from loud laughter to tender tears. Whether she is working with her private clients, facilitating a teleseminar, giving a seminar or the keynote address of the day, Sheila shares her earthy humor and elegant grace with individuals and large audiences alike. Sheila's unique style of delivering her practical wisdom has been changing the quality of people's lives for decades.

A widow and grandmother, Sheila is often spending her free time enjoying her five grandchildren.

Sheila Pearl
Life Coach & Speaker
www.LifeCoachSheila.com
www.SheilaPearl.com
email: info@LifeCoachSheila.com
Phone: 201-303-5990

Mark Perkett

"If you change the way you look at things. The things you look at change."
Dr. Wayne W. Dyer

Online Business Success

Mark didn't realize he was going to be helping people reach their dreams of replacing a 9-5 job they desperately wanted out of and help them start over fresh with a business opportunity that let people stay at home and be with their family. Being successful at the same time was the cherry on top.

In 1984 Mark was honorably discharged from the U.S. Marine Corps 1ST Marine Division. His expertise at the time was rebuilding turbo diesel engines, what he was trained for in the Corps. In 1987, Mark found a copy of Napoleon Hill's Think and Grow Rich. That's when the ball was starting to roll towards a sales/entrepreneur mind set. His first real challenge was how to make ends meet on $7.00 dollars an hour and after six months be on straight commission. That's the first sales position he held.

"I remember making 100-150 phone calls a day just to get five people to listen to me." After five years of hard work, Mark was bringing substantial value to the aftermarket car parts industry. Hard work and his bull dog persistence were paying off.

In 2009, after twenty two years with the same firm, they closed their doors. "Poof! I saw it coming but couldn't conceive a profitable company like ours was gone, doors closed, locks on the doors."

Mark had the foresight to dabble in internet marking a few years before. "I signed up with a juice company first and ended up with endless bottles of inventory in my garage. Started marketing for a travel company after that and THE LIGHT BULB WENT ON! I was seeing these reps pulling down 40-100k per month. It was crazy money in my eyes."

That's when Mark really got serious and started learning multiple ways to advertise a business online.

"It's really simple, you find the sites that mirror your business platform and advertise on the ones that have the highest ranking. Genius and simplicity all created by alexa.com. I just started marketing for Numis Network three months ago and this company is the real deal. Silver and Gold coins, what a concept. Not only are you collecting beautiful MS70 rated coins, you can market them and help others achieve financial freedom. 'Coins are cool' that's the motto. If you started with Numis today and wanted nothing to do with internet marketing... in twenty years you would have a garage full of collectable coins for your retirement. That's the power of the business."

Mark can be found in Dana Point, CA enjoying the best weather in the world. When he's not at Mammoth Mountain in winter skiing the perfect conditions with family and friends, he'll be working on his golf game at Bella Colina golf club in San Clemente, CA.

Mark Perkett
Advertising and Sales, Numis Network
markperk@cox.net
http://www.perksprofits.com

Mark Perkett's

Recipe for SUCCESS!

1. Work harder on yourself than your business. If you don't feel 100% you won't give 110%.

2. Fish in a pond with the right bait. Always advertise to people looking for what you have to offer.

3. Find a mentor. Look for the most successful person in your field and mirror what they do.

4. Be Passionate. If you don't love what you're doing. Figure out what you love to do and never give up making it happen.

5. Stay on course. Most internet businesses worth their salt are not get rich quick schemes. Most people quit after a few month's seeing no success. In most cases it could takes years.

6. Stay on budget. If all you have is $50.00 dollars a month for advertising. Don't worry. There are well over a thousand web sites that offer free advertising. You'll just have to spend more time doing it.

7. Last but never least, set your goals high. If your rudder is out of the water you'll just go in circles.

Angelika Putintseva

"The teacher is one who makes two ideas grow where only one grew before."
Elbert Hubbard

Knowledge is Contagious

When Angelika Putintseva came to United States in January of 2000 all she had was her son (an 11 month old little baby with a big name – Max). She won a green card in a lottery and relocated to Los Angeles for a new life and new opportunities.

She had a dream for her son to speak many different languages and having a Master's Degree in Teaching Foreign Languages, Angelika decided to open a new business – Language School for Babies.

Every entrepreneur goes through hardships at the beginning of her way, but try opening a business in a foreign country, in a city unknown to you, in an unfamiliar culture and in a language you hardly speak... That is what one can call a challenge! Add to it a baby and the picture of the challenge is complete.

Angelika's first group had 3 little boys including her own son. Little baby students met in her one bedroom apartment twice a week. A young and charming French teacher from Paris played with them and taught them how to speak French. Angelika trained her and wrote the lesson plans for each of her lessons.

6 months later the group became too big for an apartment and they relocated into the local park – thanks to warm Californian weather. A few short months later, Angelika trained a Spanish teacher and opened a Spanish group for babies. This meant they really needed a better arrangement than the park.

The solution came unexpectedly. Strolling with 2-year-old Max through the mall, Angelika saw a recital going on in a children's music studio. She offered to sublease the space for the hours they had available in between their music classes. That is how WorldSpeak got their very first location!

Things became much more interesting after that. A few months went by and Angelika got her first 3 students for yet another group. This time it was Russian. Not long after that it was time to find teachers for and add more groups. First it was an Italian group, followed by Hebrew,

Chinese (it wasn't easy finding a teacher for the Chinese group but she eventually did), Japanese, Korean, Arabic, Farsi, Romanian, Hindi, and Gujarati. For those who don't know, Hindi and Gujarati are languages of India. These groups were all added within just a few years.

In just over 10 years, WorldSpeak has taught more than 2,000 students to speak more than 12 different languages. WorldSpeak has had contracts with more than 30 private and public schools in Los Angeles where the organization teaches after school and extra-curricular language, art and science. It is still – even 10 years later – the only professional language institute in Los Angeles that offers language classes to babies starting as young as 10 months old.

Today WorldSpeak has a fully-immersed preschool program where all instruction is done strictly in a second language. Children from 2 to 5 years of age interact with a French teacher who speaks to them only in French, a Spanish teacher who only speaks in Spanish and a Chinese teacher who sings songs, does art projects, serves lunch, and goes through all daily activities speaking only Chinese. These children learn 2, 3, 4 (some 5) languages at the same time. The children have a great time playing with play-dough, painting, doing dramatic play, dress up and more.

Angelika has traveled the world and with her love for children and languages has been able to welcome a world of cultures into her own life and the lives of her many little students. She is a believer of the many different cultures of the world. She sees that world as big, beautiful and worth sharing.

Looking forward, Angelika hopes to share her success and teaching methods with others. She envisions the future of WorldSpeak as a franchise opportunity with more schools opening with the help of many talented and enthusiastic partners by her side.

Angelika Putintseva
Director and Founder
WorldSpeak Language Preschools and In-Home Child Care System
www.WorldSpeakSchool.com

Angelica Putintseva

Recipe for SUCCESS!

1. Find your passion and act on it!

2. Believe in yourself every moment.

3. Surround yourself with supportive friends, colleagues, and customers. The spirit, the whole atmosphere around you must radiate happiness and support! Make them excited about your goals too. Find those who share the same passion and feed off each other's supportive energy.

4. Build your team. Love your team. Inspire and support your people. Say thank you for the little and big things they do. Celebrate more!

5. Pay attention to what gives you energy, excitement and happiness. Do those things more often. Know your sources of power and inspiration refill them each day and always keep them full.

6. Keep your business in momentum. Look around for innovative new ideas, learn all the time, change and improve your business often.

7. Find meaningful paths and have your passion lead the way. Be a giver. Live a legacy.

About Angelika Putintseva

Angelika Putintseva is the founder of Worldspeak Language School and Preschools. She is originally from Russia and moved to Los Angeles in year 2000. She has two Master of Art degrees: MA in teaching foreign languages and MA in journalism. She's been teaching languages to adults for more than 8 years. Among her students were journalists from The New York Times, CBS, Los Angeles Times, Reader's Digest, Boston Globe. In 2000 after the birth to her son Max she decided to devote herself to teaching children. With a special training in early children development, Angelika created a school for her son and other kids to use the amazing 'window of opportunity' to get a jump-start in life and learn how to speak 3 and 4 languages from yearly years.

Angelika Putintseva
Director and Founder of WorldSpeak Language Preschools and In-Home Child Care System
www.WorldSpeakSchool.com
email:info@WorldSpeakSchool.com
Phone: 310-441-5222

Helen Racz

"Be the change you want to see in the world."
Mahatma Gandhi

Energy Begets Energy

The last time Helen Racz had a home-based business helping others, her clients were all less than 5 feet. When they came to see her, drivers dropped them off and picked them up.

They weren't short millionaires. They were school age kids whose parents entrusted Helen with their care until Mom or Dad came home from work.

Now that her own children are old enough to care for themselves, Helen's home-based business looks a lot more grown up. But it's just as focused on helping others.

An energy healer by proclivity and choice, Helen helps nurture others toward financial freedom with her own program to align clients' motivation, energy and confidence with the new-generation, multi-level marketing company CieAura.

Her path to doing the work she loves was anything but straight. Twists and turns along the way led down dead ends and even threatened to leave her too ill to function.

At age 26, a car crash left her with a spinal injury. It wasn't long into her recovery that she discovered her dream of college would remain just that. Chronic pain, worsened by the simple activities of reading and writing, forced her to withdraw from school.

Marriage and children helped her discover an affinity for professional childcare and home-based entrepreneurship. After the business lived out its natural lifespan, Helen remained eager to put her family on the path to fiscal security. She became a voracious reader of books about how to achieve financial independence.

Putting her new knowledge into action, Helen drew up a plan that included real estate investment. She spent a year putting together real estate deals. It fed her family's bank account and advanced her plan. But it also left her hungry for work she found more emotionally satisfying.

Continuing with her plan, Helen set about opening a small business. There were no good gyms in her part of town, so she opened her own. Business was good.

Then without warning two national chains opened fitness clubs nearby, using deep pockets to offer prices she could not match. Delivering the second blow of a one-two punch, banks began to fail across the country, triggering an economic downturn that prompted her customers to pare nonessential expenses like gym memberships.

The day Helen closed the gym was a low point in her financial journey. But she took comfort in the fact that scores of customers had remained fiercely loyal to the end.

The seeds that would lead Helen to find a business that fit her like a glove were sown during her days as a gym owner. When certain clients came in, Helen noticed she felt a pain in various parts of her body. This went on for months before she made the connection that she was experiencing physical empathy.

Those who feel the pain or distress of others around them are considered to be physical empaths. The discovery of this trait motivated Helen to learn all she could about the phenomenon, including its relationship with physical energy.

Since then, Helen has developed her skills as an energy healer, building a practice that lets her help others align their energy with business success. Her partnership with CieAura came naturally, with the company's energy-centered products, plans for rapid growth, and commitment to outstanding support for retailers.

She has come full circle, once again running a home-based business that lets her use her natural abilities to nurture others in their quest for success.

Helen Racz - Expert in Energy Healing
http://www.helenracz.com

Helen Racz's

Recipe for SUCCESS!

1. Gratitude! Right now! Start with appreciating what you have to be in a very high vibration.

2. Spend time finding clarity of what you want and WHY you want it, this makes Faith easier!

3. Support FAITH by feeding your mind a steady diet of success stories through people, books, and audios.

4. Keep learning and seeking information on everything to do with success and your passion.

5. Always have a coach or mentor and friends that live in integrity and walk their talk.

6. Keep your word! Most especially to yourself first and then all others.

7. Only speak of what you want, never tell your "victimized" stories more than 3 times- EVER!

About Helen Racz

Fast-Tracking Financial Success With an Opportunity to Promote Healthful Energy

In looking at the future, Helen Racz didn't count on the car accident that would injure her spine, leaving her with chronic pain. Nor did she predict that Western medicine's limitations would send her on a rocky, 15-year journey into the unfamiliar world of complementary healing therapies.

More than 20 years later, she is pain-free, a recognized expert in energy healing, and a successful entrepreneur who helps others use CieAura to achieve financial freedom. The crisis that initially limited Helen's life transformed into an opportunity to discover her gifts as an energy healer and her ability to help others understand the power of metaphysical forces to bring about success.

Before teaming up with CieAura and its line of energy-balancing holographic chips, Helen's desire to assist others through energy healing led her to learn and teach Emotional Freedom Techniques, which uses tapping to stimulate the body's energy meridians. Seeking to bring better mind-body health to as many people as possible, Helen and a partner established www.thehealingshow.info, a place for people all over the English-speaking the world to learn and access a broad range of non-traditional healing techniques.

Helen's energy-healing practice centers on a program to link and support entrepreneurs all over the United States with CieAura, a new-generation, multi-level marketing company with energy-centered products and practices. Through a series of private and group sessions involving energetic tools and vibrational law, she helps entrepreneurs gain the clarity and confidence they need to expand into financial success as they make a positive difference in the lives of others.

Helen Racz
www.HelenRacz.com
Email: helenracz@comcast.net
Phone: 281-578-7949

Caterina Rando

"Action is the antidote to despair."
Joan Baez

Listen to the Messages and Say Yes to Opportunities and Ideas

In my twenties I owned a café and catering business. I loved owning a neighborhood business that allowed me to get to know so many people and I enjoyed making people happy with our mouth-watering sandwiches and fresh salads. Still, after a while I got tired of wearing tomato sauce every day and I felt like making cappuccinos and ordering plastic forks and paper cups was not my purpose on the planet. I had so many interests though I could not decide which way to go.

Then one sunny day a tall well-dressed woman approached me on the sidewalk outside my café, she was coming to see me. She told me her name and proceeded to thank me for the advice I had given her a few months earlier about how to make her business more successful. Honestly I did not even remember the earlier conversation. This conversation however I will never forget. As I looked at her big smile of appreciation, her gratitude literally touched my heart; I felt a strong pang of pride and joy at the same time. I took a deep breath in and noticed how much I was impacted by this moment.

When she walked away from our brief encounter I remained, and in an instant I decided to change my whole life. She made everything clear. I knew then that nothing would ever bring me more joy then uplifting the lives of women, their families and their communities by advising them on how to succeed in their own businesses.

After that day I started the process of getting certified as a coach, finished my master's degree in Life Transitions Counseling Psychology, sold my café and catering business and started to study with my business mentors more successful than myself. The advice and business guidance I had given away at every turn soon became what people paid me for as a speaker, trainer and business coach.

I have a few principles I let guide me. The first is to say yes to any opportunity that you think will advance your business even if you do not know how to do it. Early in my new career, I was asked to write an article for the Bay Area Businesswoman's newspaper. I said yes immediately even though I had never written anything before. It took me a week to write a mere 500 words and I hired a professional copyeditor before turning the article in to the paper's editor. That first article turned into a regular column and those articles eventually, caught the eye of a London publisher who gave me my first book contract for *Learn to Power Think.*

Saying yes to any opportunity no matter how big or small can lead to many more exciting things. I always do my best to be a yes to anyone's request. This has brought me many speaking engagements, many clients, lots of bright ideas and now many book projects.

In my Business Breakthrough Program I emphasize with my clients the value of positioning themselves as experts in their fields and they recognize that nothing says expert more than your name on the cover of a book.
One day I was chatting on the phone with a client who was telling me she was not finding any time to write her book, and she was the third client is as many days who had sung from the same song book. When I hung up the phone the idea came to me, I could help my clients write a book together and we did.
Our first multi-author book *Image Power* was comprised of twenty chapters by twenty different experts. That is the way the publishing division of my business got started. Today, just two years later, we are on our ninth book project.
Listening to what people say about you, saying yes to opportunities and your own ideas is the way to have a fulfilling life and a thriving business. What is it time for you to say yes to?
Caterina Rando, MA, MCC
Business strategist, master coach, speaker & publisher
http://www.attractclientswithease.com   http://www.powerdynamicspub.com
http://www.caterinaspeaks.com

Caterina Rando's Recipe for SUCCESS!

1. Establish yourself as an expert.

2. Create a value-based website and marketing plan.

3. Grow a huge list.

4. Cultivate Strategic Alliance Partners

5. Add new revenue streams.

6. Build an effective team around you to get things done.

7. Work on your business not just in your business.

About Caterina Rando

Caterina Rando, MA, MCC show entrepreneurs how to make their businesses thrive by establishing themselves as experts in their fields. She is an award winning professional speaker, business strategist, master certified coach, publisher and author of the national best-seller Learn To Power Think. Caterina is the founder of PowerDynamics Publishing a company that creates multi-author books to get the word out about emerging experts to the marketplace. To find out how you can get your message in a book visit http://www.powerdynamicspub.com

Caterina Rando, MA, MCC
Business strategist, master coach, speaker & publisher
Author of Learn to Power Think
http://www.attractclientswithease.com
http://www.powerdynamicspub.com
http://www.caterinaspeaks.com
Phone: 415 668-4535
Email: cat@attractclientswithease.com

Kimberly Rhodes

"Man must cease attributing his problems to his environment, and learn again
to exercise his will - his personal responsibility"
Albert Schweitzer

Health Happy and Living Life on My Terms

Kimberly always new she was an entrrepnuer. However having been raised by a single mom, she was taught to go to school and get a good job. As an obideient child she did just that and worked for some of the most prestigious fortune 500 companies in America. Family and friends thought she had it all. High income, company car, expense account and home office. However, she was not happy at all. Kimberly knew there was more and wanted her American Dream: Business Ownership.

It wasn't always easy. Well meaning people tried to 'protect' her by telling her all the reasons she should not go into business. They would say the econmy is bad, it's too risky or you need a lot of money to start. Some even laughed about how silly she was to want to leave the security of her great job. But it did not matter. She was clear about what she wanted her life to look like and committed to making it happen. Nevertheless, she realized that that there were some things that would have to change if she was going to transition from Corporate America to business ownership.

Then the unthinkable happened. She began to develop a chronic body ache. One day the pain became so unbearable she could hardly walk. A true daughter of the information age, she raced to Google and diagnosed herself. Then she went to see my physician, Dr. Levin.

After a series of tests she was called into his office and told that she had lupus. Her world came to a screeching halt. The doctor next began to ask a series of questions that did not seem medically related. It was as if he was reading her heart and mind with a crystal ball.

"How's your job?"

"If you could do anything you wanted, what would it be?"

"Are you using your God-given gifts?"

"Do you feel like you're making a contribution to the world with what you do?"

"What type of work makes you feel most happy?"

The last question hit her like a sledge hammer. She had been dabbling in Network Marketing for years now, with some level of success. These little MLM venture s had always brought her an oddly guilty satisfaction. She instantly realized that she was most at peace in that environment. Working with people she cared about and promoting products and services that she believed in made her happier than any of her high-brow corporate assignments. Her heart was clear. She was a true entrepreneur.

Now she just needed to overcome a few challenges to transition into full-time business ownership:

Create an exit plan. Kim was lucky because she was already having success with her home based business. However, if she wanted to leave a fulltime job she needed to make sure that she put a plan in place to do so. One of the first things she did was talk to people she knew that had successfully made the change and had the type of lifestyle she wanted. She did not just consider money. She realized she had always made great money but what she truly valued was time freedom and that she would not just trade time for money. If it did not fit 'her definition' of a successful entrepreneur then it was still for her.

Develop a support team. While Kimberly was frustrated with Corporate America because she hated working within a job description she now realized that she also could not do everything by herself. As a result she started to invest in herself taking workshops and seminars as well as got coaching from leaders in her industry. She knew this was the key to cutting her learning curve. Later some of these mentors became business partners.

It turned out that she did not have Lupus at all. She simply was unhappy. And her body was trying to tell her something. When she listened to her body and followed her heart everything turned around.

The result Kimberly has built a successful business that has worked on her terms. She now has multiple streams of income in different niches. When asked what advice would you give others she said there are 3 big lessons.

Invest in yourself. As Jim Rohn says, "Formal education will make you a living; self education will give you a life."

Success comes to those who work for it. Make a plan, implement it and then make changes as needed. If you don't take control of your life someone else will. Be sure that you are the captain of your ship.

Kimberly Rhodes
www.MyIncomeInsurance.com

Kimberly Rhodes

Recipe for SUCCESS!

1. Build your business around your life not your life around your business.

2. Be 100% responsible for your success in life.

3. Make sure you put systems in place that allow your business to work without you.

4. Remember leverage is the key to your ideal lifestyle.

5. Find solutions to your customer's problems and you guarantee your success.

6. Brand you and your business so that you stand out of the crowd.

7. Develop at least one stream of passive residual income.

About Kimberly Rhodes

Kimberly Rhodes is a leading authority on marketing in the Home Based Business industry. She is the creator of www.MLMSecretsForWomen.com   and a free 7 day e-course www.MyIncomeInsurance.com that walks you through how to start discovering If you are looking for a plan B she is a master at showing you how to take your skills and talents and develop a passive income stream from them.

With her unique blend of personal power, business acumen and nurturing as she walks you through step by step thought journey of your mind and discover your purpose, innermost desires and hidden talents. Then she teaches you the principles and gives you specific tools that you can put into use immediately to create the entrepreneurial lifestyle you desire.

Kimberly co-authored "How to Build a Championship Sales Team" with Rich Dad, Poor Dad Advisor Blair Singer, who is also the author of "Sales Dogs." She was also a contributing author to "It's Time for Network Marketing" alongside the likes of Robert Kiyosaki, Robert Allen, Kim Klaver, Mark Yarnell, Art Jonak and John Milton Fogg. Most recently, she became a contributing author for "Chicken Soup for the Network Marketing Soup" with internationally acclaimed success gurus Jack Canfield and Mark Victor Hanson.

Kimberly Rhodes
Email: Kimberly@MLMSecretsForWomen.com or
Kimberly@MyIncomeInsurance.com

Dawn Rickabaugh

"And the day came that the pain of remaining tight in a bud was greater than the risk it took to open."

Anais Nin

A Midlife Transformation

My journey of transformation started out with a raging, all-out midlife crisis at 39-and-a-half.

At some point, whether by internal pressures or external forces, we all get to come to that point where we decide whose voice we're going to follow.

The tectonic plates of our lives start shifting, our false constructs start collapsing, and we get to dig through the rubble to salvage buried gifts. We get to accept or reject the invitation to explore and follow our deepest calling.

My journey started out when I began studying the discounted note business. It fascinated and intrigued me. I bought many courses, attended many seminars, spent too much money, and fell flat on my face for a long time.

Because of the laws in California around dealing in notes, I went on to get my real estate broker's license, and cut my teeth in the real estate business as an agent and as an investor.

In the course of chasing properties to rehab and flip, I made lots of cold calls to people who owned investment properties, and I started to notice a pattern. Even if they were tired of managing and wanted to sell, many wouldn't because they:

- didn't want to pay capital gains (and didn't want to exchange)
- needed the income for retirement
- wanted to leave a good inheritance

This is where the note business and the real estate business started to merge for me. These sellers obviously didn't know about the Installment Sale (carrying back a note), because it addressed each of these concerns, plus it gave them liquidity (the ability to raise lump sums of cash by selling all or part of their note).

When I could address their concerns, I was able to put transactions together that otherwise wouldn't have occurred.

With the state of affairs these days, when banks aren't making loans and we can't trust governments, corporations or financial institutions to protect and take care of us, there are fewer perceived illusions of safety and security to tempt us away from following our own true path in our real estate dealings, or in anything else in our lives.

What I have become committed to at this point in my life is liberating people and showing them options they never knew existed when it comes to real estate, money and notes. I love helping people get what they want legally, ethically and intelligently.

I want people to understand that they are free and that they don't have to wait on anyone or anything to 'save' them:

Sellers can sell for top dollar, even in this market – and seller financing DOES NOT mean the seller can't walk away with cash.

Buyers can buy with bad credit or no credit.

Investors can avoid life-throttling capital gains with or without a 1031 exchange.

Private money & creative techniques can be used to put almost any type of real estate transaction together.

Hedge funds are making commercial and business loans that banks can't touch.

"When the banks say no, I say yes!" More than an owner financing coach, consultant, note buyer and real estate broker, I consider myself a real estate "transitionary." I seem to be gifted at helping people move through challenges with their real estate holdings in a way that allows them to discover what they really want, and how to get it in a way that allows them to move gracefully into the next chapter of their lives.

On a personal note... I have a life partner of 15 years, and together we have raised 4 children who are now amazing teenagers that inspire and delight us. We are into health, 'going green,' developing a sustainable lifestyle, and 2 out of our 3 cars run on waste veggie oil. I spend as much time as I can at a cabin where I don't have internet or cell phone reception.

Dawn Rickabaugh - Note Queen - Owner Financing Coach - Real Estate Transitionary
www.NoteQueen.com

Dawn Rickabaugh's

Recipe for SUCCESS!

1. Meditate at least 15 minutes every day.

2. Figure out what makes life fun for you.

3. Make a list of everything you're grateful for.

4. Create a vision board.

5. Get a little sunshine every day.

6. Exercise.

7. Walk barefoot in the grass.

About Dawn Rickabaugh

Dawn Rickabaugh is a CA Real Estate Broker specializing in legal, ethical and intelligent alternative financing. She regularly puts and keeps real estate transactions together without the need for new bank financing using a combination of owner financing strategies, private money and commercial hedge funds.

She is a writer, educator, coach and author of *"Seller Financing on Steroids: Pumping Paper for Power, Peace and Profits."* She has been interviewed and quoted by influential publications such as Investor's Business Daily, and the WSJ's MarketWatch.

Because she regularly buys and brokers notes secured by real estate (and businesses) she is powerfully poised to help sellers and their agents understand how to carry paper safely. Dawn originally graduated from Brigham Young University in 1987 with a Bachelor of Science in Nursing, and worked for several years in the ICU and ER at Huntington Memorial Hospital. She now pursues her passion for helping people through traditional and innovative real estate transactions. She has four amazing teenagers, and loves her life in Temple City.

Dawn Rickabaugh
http://www.notequeen.com

Mary Rives

"Every object, every creature, every man, woman and child has a soul and it is the destiny of all, to see as God sees, to know as God knows, to feel as God feels, to Be as God Is." ~
Meister Eckhart

What's in Your Garden?

Mary's journey into the health and wellness industry has been a path of self emergence. Her two children were both diagnosed at a young age as autistic. Her daughter was not only diagnosed as autistic, but with another rare disorder, Moebius Syndrome. Mary's love for her children and her determination to give them the life they deserve to live is her driving force. She believes that her children are here to help her to recognize and define who she came here to be....her life's purpose.

When Mary's life shifted and she became a single mom, she knew that many of the doors she had always been familiar with would close. This transformational process became a path of intense personal and spiritual growth.

She had not worked outside of the home for over 10 years while enjoying the opportunity to be a "stay at home mom" and raise her children. Mary clearly saw the challenges in front of her to create a successful business that would meet the needs of her children, herself and allow her to enjoy life. She had many qualifications for employment, but just having a "job" felt like settling and that was not an option for Mary. She made a commitment to herself.   No matter what, she was going to follow her heart and be happy building her new life.

Mary has always wanted to help and teach people. She felt that she had a lot to give and wanted to share that with others. She had been helping friends and neighbors for quite some time to find alternative solutions to health issues. In addition, she continued to work with her children implementing new concepts of energy medicine, creating pathways to health for them.

One day, Mary realized that what she was doing truly was having an impact on those around her. She could really help people. Her practice of meditation helped her to realize that this was her calling. Her daily affirmation became **"Infinite Spirit, open the way for the Divine Design of my life to manifest; let the genius within me now be released; let me see clearly the perfect plan."** *Florence Scovel Shinn*

Mary became focused on her goals, helping people to recognize that our lifestyle choices affect all areas of our lives. She now helps people who are ready to commit to making a change in their lives, allowing them to meet their goals.

Mary has furthered her knowledge and accomplished skills by completing the 12 month health coaching course offered by Hilton Johnson, becoming a quantum-touch® instructor/practitioner, graduating from the Touch of Healing School, completing courses from Doreen Virtue as an Angel Therapy Practitioner and Spiritual Teacher and other innovative methodologies. Along her journey Mary has discovered and developed her innate abilities of clairvoyance, claircognizance, clairaudience and clairsentients. She uses these wonderful abilities to help her clients in many different ways. She unites all of her skills in her practice as a health and wellness coach.

Today, seven years later, Mary has created a garden of business. Energetics of Health and Wellness is growing and blossoming. Many of the seeds she planted have come to fruition. Many didn't sprout. She will continue to maintain her garden. Keeping what thrives and making room to plant new seeds to grow.

Mary Rives, Energetics of Health and Wellness
www.energeticsofhealthandwellness.com

Mary Rives' Recipe for SUCCESS!

1. Define your direction and destination. Know that along the way the plan will change. Accept change as growth and expansion of what can be.

2. Know that you are not a rock. You need support, guidance and love from those around you.

3. Commit to constantly living and acting in accordance with your core values. Our core values bring us joy and happiness in life. When we stray from this knowingness within ourselves life can become more difficult than need be.

4. Success has no boundaries. We are all entitled to a joyful life of abundance. Let go of any preconceived ideas of limitations. The truth is we live in a world of unlimited abundance.

5. Because something has not been done before......does not mean it can't be done.

6. When you seek the truth, follow your heart. Your heart will lead you to what you truly seek to find.

7. Just when you think you don't have enough to give to make it happen....know that you do! Give yourself a break. Find something fun and fulfilling to do and then get back on task.

Eva Rosenberg

*Someone asked Dear Abby. Should I go to law school? I am 30 years old. I'll be 36 by the time I graduate. **Dear Abby replied. "How old will you be six years from now if you don't go to law school?"***

Giving up my dreams – made my fantasies come true!

My mother just called. She is over 80 years old and reflecting back on her life. It wasn't the life she expected as a girl, with the world ahead of her. Nazis took her mother and her future. But her mother prepared her for adversity. She made sure her daughters became consummate seamstresses. "With a skill like this, you will never have to be maids in anyone's home." Such prophetically sage advice! Those skills got us into America – and supported us.

As a girl, I learned to sew and help out. My mother discouraged me from becoming a seamstress. She said, "This is hard, demeaning work. You spend much of it kneeling at the hems of rich women. You have a brain. Use it for something better."

Until this moment, I'd forgotten that conversation when I was 10 years old.

I also made a practical career choice, giving up my dreams of being a writer and world traveler. Getting married young, I had to find a way to make a solid living at home . I chose to study Accounting – unquestionably, the most boring sounding major in the world, isn't it?

The career wasn't boring. He was. We divorced. I built a career more wonderful than anything I ever imagined.

My original situation is probably something like yours. You're stuck at home with children you adore. They make it impossible to join the career world and make the big bucks. You're depressed and money is tight.

Perhaps you had an amazing career and made a fortune. The economy went bust. You'll never get a job making that kind of money again. You feel emasculated and humiliated. You're depressed and money is tight.

Or you're retired? You have enough to live on. Without panache. You're bored out of your mind. You want to do something stimulating, fulfilling, getting paid what you're worth. You're depressed.

I hated my job, so...

I returned to college. At night. For 10 years. Graduating with a BA in Accounting and a Master's in International Business, I worked in national CPA firms. It wasn't for me. I hated the way they treated their smaller clients. Staff was treated poorly, overworked, not given time to study for the CPA exam, and until they passed, they were paid poorly.

I firmly believe you should always love your work and your life. So I left. In accounting, my degrees meant nothing; I wasn't a CPA.

How do you make a great living, with or without a degree, and earn respect?

An option surfaced that I had never heard of in ten years of college - become an Enrolled Agent – an EA!

This career is the best-kept secret in the tax industry. How many people would spend four years and tens of thousands of dollars on a college degree, pick up a ton of student loan debt then spend another two years as indentured servant in a CPA firm – if they knew you could become an EA without a degree?

Of course, you have to pass three of the toughest exams you'll ever face.

But once you pass those exams - you can work anywhere in the United States - or the world, preparing tax returns and helping people resolve their tax problems. Earnings range from $25 - $250 per hour – or more, as you become an expert in your field. It's a recession-proof career. Congress is always passing new tax laws. Tax laws are too confusing for anyone to understand – so they will need your help to fix their errors.

Eva Rosenberg, TaxMama
http://taxmama.com

Eva Rosenberg's

Recipe for SUCCESS!

1. Invest the time in yourself to become the consummate tax professional.

2. Decide what kind of clients and people you want in your life – go after them. Treat them well.

3. Become a tax expert in your chosen niche – stay up to date – always!

4. Even in the beginning of your career, it's OK to reject clients you don't like. In fact, it's profitable.

5. You don't have competitors – you have colleagues with whom you can brainstorm and share.

6. Never be too busy for your clients. If you are, it's time to hire out the grunt work so you can spend time with your clients when they need you.

7. New clients are easy to come by – treat your clients well, look after their interests, they will rave about you to everyone they know.

About Eva Rosenberg

Eva Rosenberg, MBA, EA, the Internet's TaxMama®, is recognized as a leading expert on U.S. taxation. She is the founder and dean of TaxMama's EA Exam Review Course and the www.TaxMama.com website.

 As a nationally syndicated Dow Jones columnist, McGraw-Hill author, popular podcaster, TaxMama® has made taxes understandable and accessible – and even fun! TaxMama® has appeared on television, radio shows, in magazines and in news articles providing tax advice, helping people cut their taxes, and training people how to pass the IRS' Special Enrollment Examination – which is often called the EA Exam.

Eva doesn't just teach people about taxes, she mentors her EA Exam students. Besides learning to pass the Exam, TaxMama's®, students learn how to care for their clients, to make the best tax planning decisions, to research tax laws and understand them - and how to build a million-dollar tax practice. Eva regularly refers new clients to Team TaxMama® – her graduates and colleagues.

Eva Rosenberg, TaxMama
http://taxmama.com
Email: info@irsexams.com
Phone: 800-594-9829 or 818-993-1565

Robert and Vikki Taylor Rosenkranz

"Constancy is the complement of all other human virtues"
Giuseppe Mazzini

Integrity: An Integral Part of Success

Robert and Vikki's business came about after a chronic problem with pain. Robert had searched for years for a solution to his hip and back pain caused from wearing a gun belt in the Sheriff's department. Nothing seemed to bring lasting results. In the spring of 2009, Vikki met a lady at a luncheon that introduced her to Nikken's magnetic technology. Not long after, another team member lent Robert a product that gave amazing results and from that moment on they were hooked.

"Prior to Nikken, we were looking for a business that suited our love of people and freedom to travel. We were also searching for a "green" product that would fit the concept of our company, Earth Patriot Technologies" said Vikki.

Robert has been a police officer for all of his adult life and he felt being a part of a reputable company was an absolute must. "A lot of times we would get excited about something only to find that the product or company lacked integrity. So we took our time with Nikken, only to find out that the more we dove into it, the more we liked it." Robert added.

"It has incredible stability - 34 years in the business and debt free. With their goal of being international, Nikken is already in 38 countries. There is longevity with its distributors and its training is considered by the industry as World Class. The really big decision maker was that we actually saw people deriving an excellent income while they improved the lives of others." explained Vikki .

Vikki had been laid off after many years full-time in the TV and Radio industry and was searching for a positive place for self-development. Nikken offered her the philosophy of the Five Pillars and it gave her the opportunity to help others become their best at whatever their goals and desires were in life. Since Nikken, she has been inspired to become a full time Energy Wellness Consultant. She still enjoys part-time assignments at a local Houston TV station.

Robert and Vikki "Taylor" Rosenkranz
www.EarthPatriot.net

The Rosenkranz's

Recipe for SUCCESS!

1. Be passionate. Whatever it is you do or the company you decide to work for, passion is the key. Passion brings energy and energy attracts. People will join because of YOU

2. Be a good listener. Ask questions and listen for how you can help. Don't miss the opportunity because you don't really hear what it is that that they are looking for. Assist them to finding a fit based on their personality, capabilities, etc.

3. Be flexible. It is ultimately "their" opportunity. They either see the vision or they don't. Find those that do.

4. Be patient. Work with the ones that are ready now. Keep the door open in a gentle way for everyone else. Build the relationship. (See step 3)

5. Be a good student. Never stop working on yourself. In business and life, WHO you are as a person is important.

6. Be a good coach. There are many great products and companies out there and endless ways to attain success, but a dynamic team and coach is critical; over and above the product. You may have an outstanding product but if you lack the support and knowledge on how to work and promote the business, it will be far more challenging to derive an income that brings you freedom.

7. Start each day with clear intentions on what it is that you desire to accomplish. Read aloud your "Vision" or "Dream" board. (If you do not have one, attend Nikken's world famous two-day Humans Being More Class.)

About Robert and Vikki Rosenkranz

Robert and Vikki's business came about after a crisis in their lives.

Robert's ability to fully enjoy life was limited by hip and back pain, from wearing a gun belt for his many years of service with the Sheriff's department. In the spring of 2009, Vikki was blessed to meet a lady at a luncheon that introduced her to a whole new way of life. It was not long before Robert was having amazing results - from that moment on they were hooked.

We quickly discovered that there was tremendous opportunity in the distribution of these life-changing technologies. "We were looking for a business that suited our love of people and freedom to travel. We were also searching for a 'green' product that would fit the concept of our company, Earth Patriot Technologies" said Vikki.

Robert has been a police officer for all of his adult life so being a part of a reputable company was an absolute must. "A lot of times we would get excited about something only to find that the product or company lacked integrity. So we took our time investigating Nikken, only to find out that the more we looked into it, the more solid it became"   Robert added.

"It has incredible stability - 35 years in the business and debt free. With our goal of having an international business, Nikken is already in 38 countries. There is longevity with its distributors and its training is considered by the industry to be World Class. The best part of the decision was that we actually saw people deriving an excellent income while they improved the lives of others." explained Vikki

Vikki had been laid off after many years full-time in the TV and Radio industry and was searching for a positive place for self-development. Nikken offered her the philosophy of the Five Pillars and it gave her the opportunity to help others become their best at whatever their goals and desires were in life. Since Nikken, she has been inspired to become a full time Energy Wellness Consultant. She still enjoys part-time assignments at a local Houston TV station.

Robert "Rosie" and Vikki "Taylor" Rosenkranz
www.EarthPatriot.Net
www.EarthPatriot.Info
Rosenkranz@EarthPatriot.net
713.298.5808 281.770.7092
Facebook: http://www.facebook.com/pages/Earth-Patriot/373323356902?ref=ts

Lea Rutherford-Williams

"Awakenings are epiphanies of evolution. Being open to them inevitably avails one to growth"
Lea Rutherford-Williams

The Journey From There to Here

Experience is a good teacher and so was Lea Rutherford-Williams until she decided to spread her wings and enter the wonderful world of Entrepreneurship, business ownership and self-employment. With so many gifts and talents, Lea found herself seeking avenues to express herself and to share her experiences with others. In 2007, after landing a sought-after leadership position in the Houston Independent School District where she began her teaching career in 1995, Lea decided to leave the public sector and take the road less trod. Now three years later she is a testament of the philosophy, "what you think about you bring about." As singer, poet and author as well as the founder of LeaSpeaks International, Education Today Enterprises, Young Entrepreneur Society Int'l., and co-founder of Aunt K's Place, Inc., and LeChar LLC, Lea is dedicated to heightening self-awareness and empowering the global community with relentless possibility. In addition, she has authored three works that are ready for publication and written several songs that are prepared for recording.

Her biggest hurdle was and often still is overcoming the fear of failure and rejection. Because entrepreneurs do not flow in the mainstream, they seem to often work in a vacuum of visions and dreams that they bounce off of their own subconscious and gut feelings. To bring those dreams to fruition, one must take a chance, confidently knowing that they are the designated canal through which their specific vision must traverse and be birthed. Whether one has a midwife or not, the dream must still come to life. It is at that point that one has to look fear in the face and know beyond reasoning and apprehension that you will be successful. Then you push...and the dream is born. If you do not believe in yourself no one else will. Arthur Andrews said it like this, "Fear knocked. Faith opened the door. No one was there."

One of the ways Lea overcomes fear is through the power of affirmations and positive thinking. She began to use and teach others the *I AM* process that turns negative thinking around and shifts powerful paradigms to ones that produce massive positive results. For example, when a negative thought is present, Lea begins an affirmation with *I AM* and ends it with the opposite of the negative thought, turning that thought into a positive statement. For example:

Thought #1: *"This is a bad day and it has not even started yet."*

I AM Affirmation: *"I AM successful and this day is another opportunity to impact someone's life positively. Customers desire my products. The people that I seek to bring my vision to life are seeking me too.*

Thought #2: *"I am fat and unattractive. Look at my _____ [(undesirable body part(s)]."*

I AM Affirmation: *"I AM beautiful and desirable. God made me in his image. I am fearfully and wonderfully made. My _____ [undesirable body part(s)] is/are strong and capable of doing their job."*

Removing oneself from the comfort of family and friends in order to think clearly and concisely was another one of the hardest things Lea had to do on the path of success. It is not possible to birth vision in a crowd, while relaxing with friends, during conversations with colleagues or even while partnering with the closest loved ones. The fear to be alone with one's self may be the biggest hindrance to the delivery of your vision. Ingenious creativity and innate intra-personal discovery are rarely a group effort. Lea discovered that some of her major setbacks in life came because she was not fulfilling her pre-designated purpose. After depositing effort, energy, time and money into the manifestation of your set purpose for being delivered to the cosmos on the location of earth at this space in geologic time, you will find that your horizons will take on a much more colorful sunset.

Relocating to Houston Texas in 1995 after being born and raised in Altadena, California, afforded Lea many opportunities to understand the power of alone time. Although being away from family has its drawbacks and periodic lonely moments, the separation's outcome is positively evident. Lea is an example to her family that has roots in California and Arkansas as well as numerous individuals who have decided to take "the leap of faith" as a result of her tutelage, leadership and successes. All of the businesses that Lea has founded were incubated in her alone-time. Alone-time synthesizes the fuel of creativity. You are encouraged to take the journey and enjoy the landscape.

Lea Rutherford-Williams
www.AuntKsPlace.org
www.AuntKsPlace.com
www.etenterprises.us
www.LeaSpeaks.com

Lea Rutherford-
William's

Recipe for SUCCESS!

1. Affirm yourself daily either verbally or in writing using the *I AM* process.

2. Spend time journaling that which you are grateful for instead of that which you are hateful for.

3. Keep your visions to yourself. Write them down and develop them until they are ready for the birthing process. Everyone that you share your wonderful idea with does not necessarily have your best interest at heart.

4. Invest in yourself. Spend quality time in the company of those that are where you are trying to go. You cannot soar with eagles if you hang around with pigeons. If you are the smartest person in the group, it is time to find a new group.

5. Networking is the most powerful tool of business development. Always keep networking tools with you.

6. Brand your product/services. Be consistent in the presentation of your product so that others can identify with your brand via logos, mottos, colors, signature services, etc.

7. Don't be afraid to be alone with your own thinking. Thoughts lead to revelations that can be life changing for those that will be impacted by your story and your success. Someone is waiting on you.

About Lea Rutherford-Williams

Phenomenal. Prolific. Profound. Passionate. Provocative.

Lea Rutherford-Williams is a native of Altadena, California. Attending Spelman College in Atlanta, Georgia in 1990, she began an incessant journey that now positions her as an authority in the fields of leadership, education, empowerment, as well as personal and professional development. Her resilient nature and innate optimism creates a riveting delivery that will shake you to your soul and inspire your whole person to pro-activate and obtain the inheritance that we were created to enjoy – Abundance in every area of our lives.

As founder of LeaSpeaks, International, Education Today Enterprises, Young Entrepreneur Society Int'l., and co-founder of Aunt K's Place, Inc., and LeChar LLC, Lea is dedicated to heightening self-awareness and empowering the global community with relentless possibility. Her prolific message of hope, integrity and receivership transcends racial, gender, age, and status barriers. Her profound knowledge generates a platform that will catapult the paradigm and shift the atmosphere of any corporation, educational, personal or professional sector. Lea was born in Hollywood, California. She attended Meher Montessori School, Pasadena Christian School, Altadena Elementary, Altadena Christian Academy and John Muir High School. In 1990, she went on to further her education at Spelman College in Atlanta, GA. She began her teaching career in Houston, TX, in 1995 in partnership with Teach for America. Her leadership qualities were immediately identified and she initiated her quest for personal and professional development. Thirteen years later she is living her dream: transparently sharing her life, instilling wisdom and igniting people to growth and change.

She infectiously engages the heart and mind of the listener providing practical and easily applicable tools for next level readiness.

Topics:
Demobilized for Repositioning – How to move from where you are now to where you want to be.
Choices for Change – Tools for catalyzing change in your life, your home, your environment.
Sync In – Getting connected with your true purpose
Parent's Guide to Kidpreneurship – What does it mean to raise up a child in the way they should go?

Christina Scheiner

"Once you make a decision, the universe conspires to make it happen."
Ralph Waldo Emerson

My Life of Overwhelm & Sacrifice

I spent over 25 years in the Wall Street community. I worked on large mergers & acquisitions and as a stock analyst during the heydays of the 1980s & early 90s. I was working literally 80+ hour weeks and crisscrossed the country several times a month. I lost two husbands, didn't stop to have children (even though I wanted them) and had no personal life at all. I was so fed up that in 1995 I formed my own boutique research & small cap IPO consulting firm. I started my business so that I could get some control over my life and have some freedom. My little firm took off right away and was very successful. I consulted with literally 100s of companies to accomplish their goals. But, more than ever, I was working 90+ hour weeks, had no weekends and was travelling extensively (not the fun type of traveling, either). Yes, I bought my 5200 sf. dream house and furnished it beautifully. BUT I could not enjoy it because I was stuck in my office 24/7.

Disaster Strikes

After September 11, my little firm was OVER. To this day, the small cap companies I worked with have still not regained favor on Wall Street. It's all big companies now, not the small entrepreneurial companies that I loved.

I closed my firm in January, 2002, sold my house and took a few years off. I got married again ... this one will work.

A Brand New World Opens Up Before My Eyes

Then I discovered the Internet business coaching and training world. My eyes were opened to what's possible in this NEW environment. There is truly a paradigm shift taking place today. There are so many resources for the ambitious entrepreneur. There is no reason to give up your personal life, free time and suffer for the sake of a successful business. The technology, virtual teams and practically free marketing available today is unprecedented for business owners, creating a new kind of entrepreneur for our New Information Economy.

I formed Rapid Business Building to help the conscious expert create a successful business and avoid mistakes so many entrepreneurs make, including MY COLOSSAL MISTAKES. I decided to attract only the ambitious entrepreneur who wants to create a high 6 and 7 figure business because, frankly, that is what it takes to have true lifestyle freedom and the resources to effectively serve THEIR clients and customers. I help clients get their gifts out into the world in a big way. I enable them to have a great lifestyle with free time for everything they love, without stress or overwhelm. This is a huge priority because I lived the opposite life for many, many years.

My Life's Purpose

My purpose is to help my clients change the world for the better. When my clients change the world, I helped in that change. I contribute my Wall Street experience to conscious experts who want to participate in the explosion of NEW entrepreneurship. I help clients take advantage of what's available and create an outrageously successful, coaching, mentoring and information marketing business.

I continue to get EXTENSIVE training from experts in information marketing and coaching. I share the best ideas with my students. With my own business experience, I distill these skills; tools and knowledge so that my clients will stay out of overwhelm and create a successful business.

My clients get the tools to generate MORE INCOME FAST. Their business runs automatically so they are not a slave to their business. My clients are free to perfect the work they love. As I said, I know about being a slave to work. Now, my business works for me, not the other way around. AND I want my clients to be the MASTER of their business, not the slave!

Christina Scheiner, the Massive Income Mentor

www.RapidBusinessBuilding.com

Tina Scheiner's

Recipe for SUCCESS!

1. Create a Plan for your business with your "life" style & "working" style in mind. So you're happy when it's created.

2. Decide on your "Ideal Client" that you love to work with, and offer products or services THEY WANT. If they buy, THEN create the product. If they don't buy, create a different offer.

3. Create _automatic_ systems that give you: 1) lead generation, 2) sales conversion, 3) client retention, 4) profit multipliers.

4. Build your team, employ automatic technologies and put them in place so that you are not involved in the day-to-day. Check on your systems once a week. Focus your time on high-pay-off activities.

5. Set up your marketing systems so clients are flocking to you, instead of you going after clients.

6. Develop clear communication skills that make your offerings irresistible to your Ideal Client.

7. Be very clear in your integrity, and _always_, _always_ be of VALUABLE SERVICE to your Ideal Client.

About Christina Scheiner

Christina Scheiner, known as the Massive Income Mentor, is the founder of RapidBusinessBuilding.com. RBB is the go-to place for ambitious entrepreneurs, coaches and experts. They learn how to create a highly lucrative business using their unique expertise in any field through writing, speaking, seminars, workshops, coaching and online programs.

Christina helps her clients generate predictable income FAST. She teaches experts how to get all the rights parts of their business working automatically and in sync so they are free to work in their passion. RBB focuses on: 1) Mindset, the inner game of the true Entrepreneur; 2) Model, <u>what</u> to provide and <u>how</u> to provide it; 3) Magic Systems, <u>what</u> to do & <u>how</u> to do it.

Christina understands business building and income generation inside and out. She worked in the Wall Street community for over 25 years in mergers & acquisitions and as a stock analyst. She had her own very successful boutique research firm for 7 years where she helped small companies prepare for their IPOs. She has helped literally hundreds of companies reach their goals. She is now using her corporate finance expertise to help the solopreneur and conscious expert make their dream business REAL.

Christina is known for communicating seemingly complicated business concepts so they are simple and easily understood & implemented by entrepreneurs at any level of business experience. She is passionate about making massive income generation and profitability FUN & SIMPLE for her clients.

Christina Scheiner
http://www.rapidbusinessbuilding.com

Kathleen B. Schulweis

"Courage is not the absence of fear, but rather the judgment that something else is more important than fear." Ambrose Redmoon

Surrender to What IS: A Story of Recovery

Kathleen never dreamed of becoming an entrepreneur. She viewed herself as an academic dedicated to an intellectual pursuit of knowledge that would define the world around her and enable her to inspire others to greatness.

In graduate school, however, she began to see herself as a fence sitter. While she enjoyed the rigors of academia, the rigidity of its structure made her desire a greater sense of creative autonomy. She felt stuck, unable to commit to either path.

Her first post-graduate position was university administrator, where she worked in an intrapreneurial atmosphere, (an environment where entrepreneurship is accepted within a structured organization). It was the perfect match for Kathleen, a place where her love of research and her ability to think outside the box were both encouraged and appreciated.

Lured by the promise of expanded opportunities, she then took a position at an established scientific institution where she encountered an entirely different approach. By contrast, it was a small organization, highly bureaucratized and 'slow as molasses.' Although she was given the responsibility of making changes within the organization, the resistance she encountered prohibited her from doing so, to the extent that she was continuously harassed, threatened and bullied. After years of bucking the tide, of believing in the struggle, and in the face of deteriorating health and self-esteem, Kathleen finally surrendered. Recognizing that she alone did not have the power to change the situation she quite literally began to pray. Every morning she recited the following: *"I go forward in my career with a light heart, an open mind and the confidence to be fully present each day. May God be my inspiration, my integrity and my mentor!"* With her Spirit restored, she then went on to address the remaining aspects of her life, including her next career move.

First she hired a professional coach who helped her discover her unique and hidden talents. Then she set about learning everything she could about entrepreneurship. With a burgeoning expertise she quickly became a much sought-after advisor to women and men seeking venture capital investments in the hopes of launching new technology companies. Exploring the needs of would-be entrepreneurs became a tool for learning and expanded her skill set. People embraced her calm, confident approach. She shared with them her philosophy of surrendering to what is, and then working towards the possibilities, and this eventually aligned within her the dream of having her own business.

But, ultimately, while satisfying, teaching people the art of entrepreneurship and empowering them with the ability to raise money for their companies, simply was not enough. **Most of the people who came to Kathleen brought deeper issues to the table** – they were seeking help in recovering from deeply challenging work or life situations, including bullying and abuse. She was being called back to her original vision of helping others move to greatness.

From all her years of teaching and training, Kathleen saw that she now clearly understood how to build confidence in others. She had tools to share that would teach them to communicate with power and authority; to set boundaries, to plan their own futures. And she could assist them in achieving their goals by helping them face injustice, to stand up to bullies, and to distinguish between the bullies and those who were just plain poor communicators.

Today Kathleen helps individuals and organizations create outstanding successes by establishing communication and team building best practices using psychology, sociology and business theory. Many who seek her guidance dream of developing their own companies, and find their confidence elevated by Kathleen's gentle, insightful, motivational, and quantitative coaching style.

Kathleen B. Schulweis - Professional Coach
http://www.confidenceconnections.com

Kathleen Schulweis'

Recipe for SUCCESS!

1. Align your unique talents with your career choices.

2. Don't stay in situations that drain your confidence and self-esteem.

3. There are endless grand opportunities available to you.

4. Hire a coach who understands your big dream *and* your work style.

5. Be prepared to create your business dream and then re-create it. As you evolve, so too will your goals.

6. Work every day of the week but take time to recreate (or re-create) every weekend.

7. Challenge your limits by taking on goals you never dreamed were possible.

About Kathleen Schulweis

Kathleen is dedicated to the empowerment of women and men facing workplace and relationship conflicts including bullying and harassment. As such, she empowers her clients to create and put into action specific paths that both end conflict *and* transform it into harmony.

Kathleen's shrewd and compassionate approach is based upon her research, expertise and hard won experience. Her experience includes 1) Handling thousands of cases involving interpersonal and team conflicts at the University of California, Los Angeles (UCLA); University of Southern California (USC); and California Institute of Technology (CalTech) and 2) A decade of private practice working with executives, entrepreneurs, business professionals and academics.

Her expertise and solutions derive from her training and knowledge as a Masters Certified coach and a Sociologist with research interests in workplace bullying, assertiveness, and communication best practices. As such, she understands both the personal and interpersonal complexities inherent in workplace conflict.

Kathleen's strategic understanding of workplace bullying is also recognized within the professional community, as evidenced by her presentation at the 7th International Conference on Workplace Bullying in Wales, June 2010.

Kathleen Schulweis, CPhil, CPCC, PCC
Professional Coach
Confidence Connections Coaching & Consulting
http://www.confidenceconnections.com

Tuck Self

"If you obey all the rules, you miss all the fun."
K. Hepburn

Radiate "YES" and Share Your Story with the World!

I do not own a rags-to-riches story, a story about being destitute, homeless, diseased, addicted, or alone. I never thought about "my story," the story about why I have a fabulously abundant life and business today. (And yes, folks, it *is* fabulously abundant.)

I used to think that because I did not go broke, or was not miserable trying to pull myself out of some state of desperation or pain, I did not have a "real" story to tell. I thought that what I *did* have to share with my clients and the world could not measure up to more dramatic stories or be powerful enough to serve, teach and mentor others.

Over the years, as I have pondered and allowed this belief to keep me from sharing my voice, I have discovered that, although my story may not be a rags-to-riches one, it is *my* story.

So, what is my story? It is my own personal journey—my perspective on the life experiences I have faced, embraced and learned from. It is the tale of what made me the coach, mentor, speaker and radio talk show host I have become, the one I am *finally* ready to share with the world.

I am the child of an alcoholic and a child of divorce. I was raised by a single mom and an absentee dad. I experienced their unconditional love and, of course, their problems. I have been rich, and I have been poor; I have been loved by my "girl friends" and totally ostracized by my "girl friends." I have played team sports and solo sports, I have been married and divorced, I have been a single mom, and I have been an empty nester. I have been a Christian, a Jesus freak and a child of the Universe. I have been overweight, and I have been anorexic. I have experienced infidelity, and I have experienced soul mate love. I have successfully worked in the corporate world and out of my home. I have been an accountant, a personal trainer, a network marketer and, finally, a solo business owner and life coach. I have experienced the loves and the deaths of a best friend, a boyfriend and my parents. I am a sister, a proud mom, and finally...

I am a spiritual being having a fabulous human experience, living full-out: transforming my fears, looking for what is right, laughing along the way, learning step-by-step who I am and what blows up my skirt! (That is Southern slang for "rockin' my world.")

That's my story and I'm stickin' to it! It's my truth and voice to boldly own and express to the world, proclaiming and radiating: "Yes, yes, yes, and YES!"

Folks, I believe *each and every one* of us has a story to tell... a unique set of experiences and perspectives to bring to our work and share with others, a truth to own, a "yes" to radiate to life.

Will this life be a challenge at times? Yes. I have certainly been challenged along the way, but all of my trials have been opportunities to stretch, grow and learn. We naturally have what it takes to embrace uncertainty, face and maneuver obstacles, and move forward *while* celebrating life—squeezing as much juice and joy as we can from the journey itself.

How do we navigate the ups and downs of life while "squeezing the juice?" For this purpose, I created *The Road to Freedom*—a seven-step guide to finding bold self-expression, sharing your voice and living full-out and on your terms! Want to unleash your entrepreneurial spirit and take these steps with me?

Tuck@therebelbelle.com

Tuck Self's

Recipe for SUCCESS!

1. Celebrate your uniqueness. Learn to put yourself first. Freely celebrate your uniqueness. Share your experiences, and serve the world with your singularity.

2. Overcome your fears. Facing your issues *can* be fun. Allow your fears to be your greatest ally as you grow. Trust yourself—there is no boogie man in the closet!

3. Discover who you are. Find your passion and purpose. Follow your heart. Discover who you are beyond the rules and roles of others, and "work" your dream.

4. Step Four: Trust your intuition. Feel your way into alignment with your soul. Tap into your juicy source and serve your purpose from a place of intuitive authenticity. Feel it, feel it, feel it

5. Embrace uncertainty. Move fearlessly in the direction of your dreams. Affirm your "fabulousness." Boldly express your voice to the world, doing work you love.

6. When the student is ready……. Mentor with masterful models and teachers who will encourage your direction and inspire with their leadership. Remember… you are forever a student of life

7. Lighten up! Enjoy the ride. Celebrate, laugh a lot and remember to play

You are an amazing story. It is time to radiate "YES" and share your voice with the world!

About Tuck Self

Tuck Self, The Rebel Belle ~ A Southern Voice for Bold Self-Expression

Raised to be a "perfect li'l southern belle," Tuck was "appropriate" at the expense of her own happiness. Her journey has been one of finding and reclaiming her voice. A self-proclaimed personal growth enthusiast, Tuck is a coach, writer, speaker, and radio talk show host who inspires clients to trust their power and live with bold self-expression. She is a Life Development Coach; Quantum-Self Certified Success Coach; Financial Coach; Certified Hypnotist; Certified Natural Law Coach; Fitness & Intuitive Eating Coach; and Human Design Specialist. (www.therebelbelle.com)

Tuck Self, The Rebel Belle
Coaching, Workshops, Classes & Tele-classes
(803)736-9240
www.therebelbelle.com
Tuck@TheRebelBelle.com

Lori Snyder

"And the day came when the risk to remain tight in a bud was more painful than the risk it took to blossom."
Anais Nin

Life Altering Decisions

After twelve years of marriage, and two beautiful children, two wonderful people, Lori and her ex-spouse decided it was time to dissolve their union.

Although not what people who join together ever foresee happening, nor do they want this ending to happen, sometimes after all avenues have been searched, and exhausted together, this seems to be the best solution.

When something reaches a point of being unworkable, even after the two bring in the help of a third person to help facilitate change, when change does not occur, and the two people involved are unhappy, and the two are just not on the same page, and know in their hearts they never will be again, as sad as it is, the break-up is the only way to help each of them rebuild their lives, and empower themselves to create the life they were meant to live. The life that everyone is meant to live, and that is a life of unstoppable happiness, success and total well-being and fulfillment for themselves and their families.

This is the situation Lori found herself in, and she was able to come through stronger, wiser, and with accolades of happiness. And it is this gift Lori loves to share, as well as to help empower the people whose lives she touches. It is the power of a positive transition, along with the use of the correct tools to help create and implement a successful life plan for you that works. Lori loves working with people to help them to discover their happiness. Lori was able to focus and move her life in a direction of positive career change and self-growth, with the reward of achieving everything, and continuing to achieve everything she strives for.

The Road Was Not Always Easy

Once the transition was made and Lori's divorce final, there were roadblocks that seemed to creep up. Things that were not expected, like alterations of the original divorce agreements, the adjustments of leaving a home everyone was so comfortable in. The matter of budgeting to the penny, when this was never an issue before, for any family member. The adjustment of the children's well-being and giving them the love, strength and realization that they still have two parents who love them dearly. All of these things, and more had to be dealt with on a daily basis.

Lori watched as her savings just seemed to flow out of her bank account, with nothing going in, as she began rebuilding the life of herself and her family, with tons of faith. She never just settled for the sake of settling, and always strived for what she felt would truly make her happy.

With a degree in Sociology, and years of experience working in people oriented fields, such as mental health, finance and real estate, Lori wanted to bring to people all the skills she accumulated through the years to help empower them to create and establish a powerful life plan to help them step into a future of extreme happiness, success and well-being. Her dream is to help them to follow through with an excellent plan towards moving forward and rebuilding their lives to create an extraordinary one!

And The Road Leads to a Rainbow

Lori now helps many to re-discover, re-define and re-create their life; she helps them to focus on a plan that accepts nothing less than their full potential and involvement in creating, implementing and establishing their extraordinary life plan which leads to their true happiness and success.

Lori is a Certified Coach, who specializes in helping people to develop their inner essence, so that their outer happiness and success shines through. She is also an Accredited Energy Leadership Coach. Lori has been published in several magazines offline, as well as being published online. She had an on-going column with "The Long Island Professional Women's Organization", and was also on the advisory board of Newday's Wellness magazine, acting as their Personal Development Coach. Lori has also been featured in More magazine, and just recently on Life Coach TV.

Lori Snyder
www.CoachLoriSnyder.com

About Lori Snyder

Lori Snyder partners with people who are ready to begin moving their lives in an upward forward direction. I believe that each person hold within them powerful inner strength, that when tapped into, can help them to create positive results towards making their lives an extraordinary one.

Lori has a degree in Sociology, and is a Certified Executive/Empowerment Coach; she is also an Accredited Energy Leadership Coach. Lori received this certification from IPEC School of Coaching. She is also a successful speaker, writer, workshop facilitator and entrepreneur.

Lori was a columnist for The Long Island Center for Business & Professional Women. And she also was on the advisory board for Newsday s Wellness Magazine; she acted as their Personal Development Coach, and also enjoyed doing a 6 month feature with the magazine, she was also featured in More magazine, and Generations magazine, and was just recently on Life Coach TV. Lori can be reached at info@lori-snyder.com

Lori Snyder
info@lorisnyder.com
www.coachlorisnyder.com
info@lori-snyder.com

Shaun Stephenson

"The Future belongs to those who believe in the beauty of their Dreams."
Eleanor Roosevelt

The Circle of Ten

Shaun's dream since childhood became a reality when she arrived in America on September 3, 1993. She began her journey working as a waitress and nanny in the New Jersey suburbs, while seeking to legalize her immigrant status in the U.S. Within a few years she was able to acquire legal residency and from that point on she was unencumbered in seeking her American dream.

Shaun's faith and determination saw her through seven miscarriages, a near-death ectopic pregnancy, the lengthy process of becoming a U.S. citizen, financial hardships, and the jobs she initially endured, including her time as a live-in housekeeper where she escaped rape, and her stint as a live-in maid and nanny to five young children where she was worked nearly to death. This type of work was especially demeaning having come from jobs in banking, hotel management and library science in her native country.

Shaun went back to school, and shortly after landed a job as a bank teller. Her goals, however, were beyond a teller's counter, and began at the entry level at what would become a ten year career with a large insurance company. Her rise to Senior Client Service Consultant can only be described as meteoric. While working at the health insurance giant, she discovered entrepreneurship and it became her passion. She eventually began realizing her dreams but not without facing bankruptcy and other challenges first.

She stepped out on faith leaving Corporate America to pursue living her purpose. This journey took some interesting turns. She became certified as an Identity Theft Risk Management Specialist; however after many challenges that venture was no longer fulfilling or profiting. Shaun began to dig deep within herself for answers. Books on personal-development become her lifeline as she began to learn about the *Power of Intention* and realized thoughts are things.

Her daily walk was a one of faith. She learned about meditation and affirmations and *the Law of Attraction.* Her biggest challenge was getting out of her own way. Loving herself and embracing her authenticity opened doors of opportunities for amazing relationships in business, professionally and personally.

Her passion and desire to help others led to her vision for "The Circle of Ten"- A Movement to Inspire and empower others and to ignite divine love, peace and harmony at all levels of society. Shaun became a Spiritual Life coach and began impacting lives, supporting women so they can begin to dream again and believe in themselves. Shaun is inspired when others shine and rise above their limitations to achieve and live their dreams.

Shaun Stephenson - Spiritual Life Coach
www.shaunstephenson.com

Shaun Stephenson's
Recipe for SUCCESS!

1. **Move past your Fear** I'm sorry to tell you I haven't found a magic pill for this. It has to come from inside you. Nobody can do it for you. And it all starts with your vision.

2. **Create a Strong Vision You** need a vision that is so strong you can't possibly walk away from it. Once you have a strong compelling vision that's based on your passion and purpose in life, how could you let anything stop you?

3. **Stop Projecting Future Catastrophe** Are you aware that 95% of the things you spend your time worrying about never happen? So, isn't worrying about the outcome of things you haven't done yet ridiculous? Don't let your fears delay the inevitable.

4. **Get out of your way The** only courage you need to go for your dreams is the courage to get out of your own way. Just take a deep breath and move aside.

5. **Stay Focused no Matter What!** It's like the movies- Lights-Camera-Action. To fulfill your Dreams it's Vision-Focus-Action.

6. **Develop Self-Control and Flexibility.** This is key along with Focus and are the Pillars for Success

7. **You've always had it Dorothy!** The good news is you don't have to worry about how you'll develop the courage to go for your dreams. You already have it.

About Shaun Stephenson

Shaun Stephenson is known for her gift of inspiration, communication and bringing people together.   She is the Founder of Myanda Solutions -a Company that fosters opportunity for personal growth, self discovery and community wealth building, she is also the Visionary for "The Circle of Ten."

Shaun is an Author, Inspirational Speaker and Spiritual Life Coach, feature in the local newspapers, and graced the cover of Wealth Creation Magazine, co- hosted "The American Dream" with Stanley El and is a frequent guest on the show. The 2nd edition of her book Faith vs. Fate is being released on April 30, 2010.   She will be donating a portion of the proceeds to the Local Red Cross and Eden Place.   Eden Place is near and dear to her heart, it is a faith-based non-profit organization that helps single homeless, displaced veteran women integrated back to civilian life.   Honoring and supporting these women who fought for our country is a gift we all can give.

Faith is a major source of Shaun's inspiration, her success, and her work to now help empower others in business and life through coaching, workshops and an upcoming internet radio show she'll be hosting including topics such as, "Stepping Out on Faith;" and "Do you believe the Impossible? Miracles of Healing" and Embracing your transformation.   She is known as "Your Transformation Expert—helping others to ignite their inner power and live their life's purpose.

Shaun Stephenson
Spiritual Life Coach
www.shaunstephenson.com
Email: shaun@shaunstephenson.com
Phone 609-560-8370

Kalin Thomas

"Travel is fatal to prejudice, bigotry and narrow-mindedness."
Mark Twain

"My Travels to Entrepreneurship"

Owning her own business wasn't something that Kalin originally set out to do. She'd known she wanted to work in broadcasting ever since high school. After getting her Broadcast Journalism degree from Howard University, she was hired by Cable News Network (CNN) to start in their entry level position as a video journalist. After running studio camera, the teleprompter, and floor directing for various news programs, she moved into other positions at the company, and finally landed in her dream job as a producer/correspondent for CNN's weekly travel show, *CNN TravelNow.*

During her stint at CNN she won numerous awards for her work and traveled to six continents – including Antarctica. Kalin helped broaden the program's audience with shows about African American travel trends, gay travel trends, and travel for the physically-challenged. She says that CNN made her the journalist she is today – one who can meet tight deadlines with quality work.

But after 17 years at CNN, Kalin was hit by major layoffs when the parent company, Time Warner, merged with AOL. While searching for new opportunities in broadcasting, she started to do freelance writing and TV production. Then the horror of September 11th happened, and it seemed almost impossible to find work in the industry with TV stations cutting budgets for lifestyle programming. A few months after that, Kalin turned 40 and decided that she didn't want to go back to the high-stress of hard news, so she pursued freelancing full-time. With the help of a career coach, she began to learn how to be successful at entrepreneurship.

Travel and lifestyle stories and programming have remained Kalin's passion, so she named her multimedia company, *See the World Productions.* Kalin is grateful to Thomas Dorsey, Publisher & CEO of SoulOfAmerica.com who was the first to hire her regularly as a freelance travel writer/photographer. She has also done writing, TV production, media consulting and voiceover work for various organizations and media outlets, including: PBS, Essence magazine,

MARTA (Metro Atlanta Rapid Transit Authority), and Morehouse School of Medicine. She also co-produced and wrote an original lifestyle program, *Living Well*, which aired on CWAtlanta.

Kalin also enjoys public speaking and has spoken on many panels for organizations like the Public Relations Society of America, Travel Professionals of Color, and the National Association of Black Journalists. And her freelance travel writing has landed her positions as travel and leisure editor for www.WomenAtForty.com and as a senior writer/photographer for www.SoulOfAmerica.com. Though freelancing has its periods of "feast or famine," Kalin says she loves the flexibility of her time, as well as meeting and working with new people on every project. Her essay "Travel: The Ultimate Education" is featured in the book *Embracing the Real World: The Black Woman's Guide to Life After College*.

Kalin is currently writing her own book about her travels, *How Did I Get Here?*, and hopes it will inspire women and people of color to get out of their comfort zone and see the world. Kalin lives by her favorite Mark Twain quote listed above, and wants to be a part of helping to bring peace around the world through tourism and cultural exchange.

Kalin Thomas – Multicultural Travel Expert, Multimedia Producer/Writer
www.seetheworldproductions.com

Kalin Thomas' Recipe for SUCCESS!

1. Do what you love – even if you can only do it part-time.

2. Try to help others through your passion.

3. Join professional organizations in your field.

4. When you get knocked down, get back up – over and over!

5. Be persistent – It works!

6. Congratulate yourself for even the smallest of baby steps.

7. Form a cheering squad of friends and colleagues – but if you don't have that, be your own cheerleader!

About Kalin Thomas

Kalin Thomas is a freelance travel and lifestyle producer, reporter, writer, still photographer and speaker with more than 20 years media experience. Her work includes original programming, educational and promotional videos, documentaries, writing and photography for print and online publications, voiceover narration for videos, public speaking and media consulting. Before starting her multimedia company, See the World Productions, she spent 17 years with CNN where she won several awards for her work as a producer/correspondent for the weekly travel program, CNN Travel Now. She also helped broaden the program's appeal to a multicultural audience with stories that included: African American travel trends, gay travel trends, and travel laws & trends for the physically challenged. Her travels have taken her to six continents – including Antarctica.

Kalin is currently travel & leisure editor for *www.WomenatForty.com*, and is a senior writer/photojournalist for *www.SoulOfAmerica.com*, the leading Website for African American travelers. She's a member of the National Association of Black Journalists, The Atlanta Business League, The Atlanta Writer's Club, and sits on the advisory board of the International Association of Black Travel Writers. She is currently writing a book about her travels, How Did I Get Here? For more information, visit *www.seetheworldproductions.com*.

Kalin Thomas
www.seetheworldproductions.com

Devin Tindall

"It is not because things are difficult that we dare not, it is because we do not dare that they are difficult."

Seneca

Life After Divorce

Devan's life as a solo practitioner in the field of hypnotherapy and life coaching is a study in how to create a fulfilling life "post divorce" and post fifty.

Devan, after ending an almost 20 year marriage, had to choose a direction that would allow her to take care of herself. She realized that she could find work in office management since she had managed her husband's office for the duration of their marriage. However, she knew that she wanted to do something that would be more gratifying and was anxious to use the skills that she had been developing over the past 10-15 years of her life. Her training in Neuro Linguistic Programming, certifications in Hypnosis, the Enneagram, plus being a master teacher of Reike gave her the unique ability to direct people toward creating changes that would meet challenging life issues.

As her vision of what she wanted to create for a business became clearer she slowly, over the next 10 years, built a practice that incorporated all of these unique and powerful tools facilitating change and motivating clients in times of transition and growth in their lives.

Devan is a positive woman who continues to enjoy learning about human growth potential, speaking to and working with groups and with individuals in their personal journey. She enjoys spending personal time with her friends and family. She loves traveling, theater, good movies and simple things like a good book.

Devan Tindall, Hypnosis and Life Coach
www.simplefocushypnosis.com

Devan Tindall's

Recipe for SUCCESS!

1. Discover what brings joy or passion to your life.

2. Always know that it is NEVER too late to do what you love.

3. Have a daily practice of visualizing what it is that you want: See it. Hear it. Feel it. Feel what it would be like if it were already here. . now.

4. Each week find one small step that you can take to move you toward goal.

5. Create a gratitude list. . . . and really BE grateful.

6. Be willing to step out of your comfort zone. Change is not created by doing the same old thing. It is created by doing something different and sometimes very uncomfortable.

7. Find people you can trust to be real support in your effort to create change.

About Devan Tindall

Devan Tindall is a leader in the dynamic field of hypnosis and inner growth. As a solo practitioner and owner of Simple Focus Hypnosis Center she has created programs and cd's to help people stop smoking, lose weight and to feel more confident about themselves.

Devan has been on television, radio shows and in magazine articles. She has clients in all of the continental United States and in Canada. Her ability to inform in a way that breaks down resistance to taking that fist bold step toward creating change makes her sought after in the area of higher growth dynamics.

She is highly valued for her inspiring and compassionate approach toward helping clients eliminate undesirable habits and behaviors and the ability to shift their lives in a positive exciting direction. Devan guides people toward a life of healthier choices that have a positive impact on them and on the people around them.

Devan Tindall
Hypnosis and Life Coach
www.simplefocushypnosis.com
Email: devan132@hotmail.com

Karen Tompkins

"So often we live our lives in chains, and we never know we have the key."
Jack Tempchin/The Eagles – "Already Gone"

She Became an Expert in a Field That Was Cloaked in Cultural Prejudice, No one Had Ever Heard of, and No One Could Pronounce

Sixteen years ago, at age 50, Karen found her passion and has never looked back. She knew she could change lives with her work and persevered in an obscure and difficult science with no access to education or training in a field few had heard of or could pronounce. Karen had discovered Feng Shui (pronounced *Fung Schway*).

In 1994 years ago she watched an Oprah interview with an Emmy award winning actor, who attributed a change in the course of her life to having her apartment Feng Shuied. Karen was captivated, literally stopped what she was doing, and began taking notes. She had heard about Feng Shui, but never dreamed something like changing your environment could change the course of someone's life.

A believer in fate, not coincidence, Karen received a call the next day from a friend who was going to a Feng Shui class that night. The friend never showed up, Karen did, and she was hooked. Interestingly, she thought the teacher talked in circles, and gave no real information, but that did not affect her fascination. She left the class still knowing nothing, but was determined that if this teacher could find information on Feng Shui, she could too.

Her biggest challenge was finding information. At that time (pre Google) she could only find 4 books on Feng Shui, and she devoured them. She began to teach classes and build a practice. Every time a new book came out she absorbed the new information, staying only a book or two ahead of her students.

Karen practiced a popular form of Feng Shui called Black Hat Sect, a superficial, cookie cutter version that relied heavily on symbols and intention. Her clients were happy, and saw changes; nevertheless, as she began to study with the authors of the books she had been studying, she realized there were major limitations to her craft. She was not able to diagnose a problem and solve it. The system she was working with was optimistic, but not realistic or comprehensive. She had no tools to help with breast cancer, marital affairs, arguing, fighting and legal problems, computer crashes, nor could she explain why one person thrived in a house, and another suffered.

She knew there was another version of Feng Shui out there, Classical Feng Shui, and she knew it was based on using mathematical formulas, and the only way to study was with Chinese Masters. Her former career was a high school English teacher, and her worst subject and greatest insecurity was with math. It took every bit of courage she had to jump into Classical Feng Shui, and bring her fears to her passion.

She learned that Feng Shui Grand Master, Yap Cheng Hai, an old- school, patriarchal teacher, was teaching his first class in the United States. She flew to Los Angeles for the class, was given a workbook of round directional charts divided into 24 sections in Chinese.

The first words out of the Master's mouth were. "Don't speak, don't look, don't ask questions, don't think, just write as I speak." He pointed out the place to start, and said to write clockwise. Then in rapid-fire succession he rambled off numbers like an auctioneer – "+90, -60, +70, +80, -90, -09, -80", etc. Before the second of the twelve charts was complete, she put her pen down, and tears welled up in her eyes. She did not have a clue what going on, and she was the oldest person in the class, easily by 10 – 15 years.

That was Karen's introduction into Classical Feng Shui. She was never the fastest, sharpest person in the class, but she never gave up, and persevered where others fell by the wayside. She kept going back, and back for years because she knew she had found a secret that few knew, and she knew she could change her life and others around her with this comprehensive science, and that is exactly what she has done.

Karen took a risk. She studied an obscure science few had heard of, and many were afraid of. She never gave up, continued to study, and is now considered an expert in her field, and a trusted business advisor to individuals and multimillion dollar corporations. Her dedication to her craft has resulted in hundreds of changed and enriched lives.

Karen Tompkins – Classical Feng Shui Consultant

www.FengShuiBeyondtheMyth.com

Karen Tompkins

Recipe for SUCCESS!

1. Understand that effort is not the only factor in your success.

2. Be clear that **it is impossible for you to be successful without an environment that creates and supports your success.** Formulas for success are **always found** in homes of the wealthiest people in the world.

3. Be in the **strongest positions and locations possible**, especially your bedroom and bed location, and your office and desk location. You will attract into your life the influence you sleep on, or where you spend time.

4. Work with time – cures and positioning. It allows you to safely navigate land mines and capitalize on opportunity. **Time is your secret weapon**

5. Avoid dangerous locations – rooms, positioning, and doors.

6. Place personal cures that bring you opportunity, clients, business, and money.

7. Use **personal business strategies revealed** in the blue print of your living and work space.

About Karen Tompkins

Karen consults with clients nationwide using the transforming science of Classical Feng Shui. Her clients range from casinos in Law Vegas, to movie studios, medical facilities and large corporations. She is on monthly retainer with a number of corporations, businesses and entrepreneurs advising them not only on the physical influences of home and business spaces, but also on strategic planning personally and in business. Karen lectures nationwide and has been featured on television, radio and print media.

Classical Feng Shui does not resemble most populist Feng Shui myths. It is precise, mathematical, diagnostic in nature, and is personal to the person and the property. This is the form of Feng Shui used by world leaders, congressmen, and many of the wealthiest and most powerful in the world because it works, giving individuals a leading edge in business, and more ease in life.

Karen Tompkins – Classical Feng Shui Consultant

www.FengShuiBeyondtheMyth.com

Terry Tribble

"You are always only one choice away from changing your life."
Marcy Blochowiak

Persistence

Terry's journey into entrepreneurship is empowering and quite unique. After many years of working in the Oil & Gas industry and becoming a successful Consultant, she felt there was more to life than working in Corporate America.

Terry spent more than 3 years juggling a full-time 6-figure career and her part-time passion, of helping women reclaim a positive self-image after breast cancer. She worked countless hours at her fulltime job; which was stressful, unappreciated by management and she didn't have moral support from her marriage. Terry's corporate job offered their employees every other Friday off and she utilized those days marketing and networking in the medical community. She was determined to educate the community on the benefits her products and services offered women undergoing cancer treatment.

During her lunch breaks, she would make numerous calls to local hospitals and clinics explaining her services and how women would benefit from them. Success was not instant; Terry went to seminars and conferences on Breast Cancer. Wanting and needing a deeper understanding of how a woman felt once she no longer had breast or hair. Very few businesses specialize in Breast Areola MicroPigmentation tattooing for cancer patients.

Two (2) years of research and $50,000 later, Terry knew this was her calling. She's now a Certified Mastectomy Fitter with a MBA and has a Wellness Center dedicated to Women wanting to reclaim their self-image. You see after a woman is diagnosed with cancer, she is striped of her identity as she knows it. Terry's goal is to help every woman feel whole and in love with her new image without deformities.

Still working her corporate job; one Wednesday evening, Terry was called into the management office and was told the company was reducing its workforce. Surprised no... relieved yes. This was a tremendous relief for Terry, now she was able to pursue her passion of helping women diagnosed with Breast Cancer and Alopecia.

Terry's road hasn't been easy. Her filing for divorce after 22 years of marriage and starting all over has been a challenge. But on a lighter note, she has 2 pending contracts with local hospitals for her services. Terry, says "Persistence, helped me to achieve my goal. **At times you may feel it is impossible to reach your goal, but trust me—it can be done.**"

Terry Tribble, MBA, CMF - Woman's Wellness Center
www.HoustonLaceBrows.com

Terry Tribble's

Recipe for SUCCESS!

1. Meditation is Healthy for the Soul and your Success

2. Build a business based on your Passion

3. Stay Focused and aligned on your Vision

4. Get help. Hire a Business Coach to assist you along the way

5. Everyone is not a good client for your business – Know your market

6. Market and Network your business at all times…Word of Mouth is so POWERFUL

7. Don't overdo it. Get some rest. Without Rest you won't Survive

About Terry Tribble

Terry Tribble received her Masters of Business Administration (MBA) with a specialty in Marketing from Regis University, Denver, Colorado, in 2007. She graduated Magna Cum Laude from LeTourneau University, Houston, Texas with a Bachelor in Business Administration. Terry has a passion for women dealing with cancer, alopecia and medical hair loss, her mission is to help women reclaim a positive self-image.

Terry has devoted her professional life to the field of beauty and health, she is known locally and nationally for her work as a certified personal trainer. Her professional knowledge of health and beauty allows her to counsel women on the physical aspect of beauty. Helping women reclaim a positive self-image drives her daily. Terry is a member of the Society of Permanent Cosmetic Professionals and is beauty and permanent make-up specialist.

Houston Lace Eyebrows and Lashes was established in 2007 by Terry to offer women suffering from the effects of cancer, alopecia and other medical conditions and treatments a place to recover their beauty. Specializing in permanent cosmetic makeup and mastectomy areola Micro Pigmentation as a tool to help women reclaim a positive self-image. Houston Lace Eyebrows and Lashes is a beckon and constant reminder that women can look their best even if they are living with a medical condition.

Terry is a supporter of the National Alopecia Areata Foundation and a sponsor for the American Cancer Society working together to increase awareness for cancer and alopecia. She is an esteemed professional with many awards and great reviews for her work in the community with women dealing with cancer, alopecia and low self-esteem.

Terry Tribble, MBA, CMF
Woman's Wellness Center
www.HoustonLaceBrows.com
Email: info@houstonlacebrow.com
Phone: 713.522.PINK (7465)

Ken and Gretchen Umbdenstock

"All our dreams can come true, if we have the courage to pursue them"
Walt Disney

A Business that Helps Family & Friends

Ken and Gretchen's journey into entrepreneurship was an interesting one. Her first dabble into a home based business was when her children were young and was looking for something flexible, in the evening but could work majority of her business from home. Her business was quite a success but something was missing. Her business was a luxury item and that troubled her to get her friends, family and acquaintances to find money already in their tight budget to spend money on something they did not need. Her Husband Ken has been an entrepreneur with his families electrical contracting business his entire life. His father started the business 30+ years ago in the basement of his home. In the recent years Ken's father has retired and Ken has since taken over the business. Doing everything from home, commercial to service calls. But then the light bulb literally turned on for both of them.

Gretchen's first exposure to Ambit Energy found the truly most refreshing concepts out there and could meet all of her needs over her first home based business. Her business allows her the flexibility she craves but also a business she could become partners with her husband Ken. He is also still in the electrical business but their goal is to turn their Ambit business into their college fund for their kids and their retirement beach money. Could we truly find a company and build an amazing business from simple helping our friends, family and neighbors to save money on something pay for, month after month, year after year??? You bet!! With Ken and Gretchen's strong work ethic combined with the amazing support from Ambit's home office you will be on your way to becoming your own successful business.

Ken and Gretchen Umbdenstock
Marketing Consultants
www.Umby.energy526.com
www.Umby.joinambit.com

Ken & Gretchen's

Recipe for SUCCESS!

1. Find a business that can drive your passion.

2. Always work with integrity.

3. Make short and long term goals.

4. Set deadlines to attain those goals.

5. Surround yourself with positive and motivated people. Negativity will just drag you and your business down.

6. Work to live not live to work.

7. Never stop educating yourself.

About Ken and Gretchen Umbdenstock

Ken and Gretchen have been married for 10 years and are blessed with 3 children- Melanie 9 years, Emma 7 years and Kenny Wayne 5 years old. Both have grown up in Northern Lake County Illinois. Ken's outside hobbies include woodworking and playing his guitar. Gretchen enjoys gardening and stained glass. When they are not busy running around sharing Ambit's amazing opportunity they are living the simple life with their 3 children and loving it.

Ken and Gretchen Umbdenstock
Marketing Consultants
www.Umby.energy526.com
www.Umby.joinambit.com
email: gretchenumbdenstock@yahoo.com
Phone: 847-546-0778

Dr. Taffy Wagner

"Through wisdom a house is built, and by understanding it is established."
Proverbs 24:3 (NKJV)

From Survival Mode to Money Management Mindset

Being raised by a single parent, Taffy Wagner knew all about survival mode when it came to money. Knowing how to stretch money and also getting those staple foods when times were tough. Recognizing during her junior year in high school that the job market in her hometown was limited to professions she was not interested in, she decided to enlist in the United States Military during her senior year in high school.

Serving in the United States Military for eight years was one of her proudest accomplishments which she continued on the path of financial survival. Financial survival to her meant she had money coming in, paid the bills but not reconciling any bank statements, nor did she have long-term financial goals. Once she became a civilian, the school of life as it pertains to money really started.

Taffy successfully secured a job prior to getting out of the military; yet she was not thoroughly prepared for the financial transition that took place. The difference in pay, ensuring there were medical benefits with the civilian job and more were foreign territory because she had been accustomed to the discipline and structure in the military. Within eighteen months of being separated from the military, Taffy found herself homeless for a period of time from a lack of money management skills and knowledge.

It was during this period of time, she met her future husband. She began working for him in counseling youth and parents regarding obtaining a college education and career goals, despite the financial mistakes she had made as a young adult. Taffy validated what her soon to be husband had been sharing through seminars regarding obtaining a college education (Bachelor's degree) in less than four years because she had obtained three in 3 and ½ years. She found working with youth and families fulfilling because she could share firsthand tips and resources for obtaining a college education without breaking the bank.

She and her husband both entered their marriage with debt despite their different backgrounds. Remember, debt is equal opportunity and does not discriminate. Regardless of the financial mistakes she had made, they decided it was best that she manage the money for their marriage. Together they established a five year debt removal plan which they accomplished in two and a half years without filing bankruptcy or buying and selling real estate.

Taffy has always helped and encouraged people from the time she was in high school throughout her military career and even till this day. She counseled youth and parents with Youth Quest, Inc. for several years on career and college planning which also delved into planning financial aid and scholarships. She later returned to college to get her Doctorate of Ministry in Biblical Counseling.

Dr. T. as her close friends call her, shares her story in the Amazon.com Bestseller, Debt Dilemma which opened more doors for her to counsel individuals, couples and single parents. She worked with Warren Village organization in Denver, Colorado providing classes to single parents regarding money management, time management and relationships. She's conducted seminars for various Work at Home Mom organizations and Christian Women's groups on finances – personal and business.

Over the last fifteen years, she has continuously taught and provided counsel to individuals, single parents and even couples regarding money management and solutions.

Taffy is a much sought after personal finances educator, being tapped to write for Armywifemagazine.com on money and marriage, Breatheagainmagazine.com on money and marriage as well as Bizymoms.com.

Taffy has spent a lot of time writing about money and marriage for various wedding websites and conducted several seminars for brides and grooms. Based on her own experience with debt and knowing how hard it is to ask for help, she began conducting seminars. Dealing with a continuous low turn-out, she sat down one day and thought about all the different groups that she has conducted seminars for throughout the last five years. She discovered that they were wives that manage the money, they were online and turnout was high. Therefore, she now spends a great deal of her time developing newly released, Wife CFO community (www.wifecfo.com) for wives that are money managers in their marriage that need guidance, answers and encouragement.

 When she is not teaching engaged couples and working with wives, she is homeschooling their twins and assisting her husband with his business.

Taffy Wagner, D.Min, Certified Educator in Personal Finances and Consultant
http://www.moneytalkmatters.com

Dr. Taffy Wagner's

Recipe for SUCCESS!

1. Have a mindset for success and not self-defeat. Whether this is your first time or not starting a business, believe in yourself and do not focus on others saying you cannot do this or think about a previous business that was not successful.

2. Define and know who your target market is. Everyone is not your target market. You must be specific when it comes to age, spending habits, sex, income level and more. This will keep you from wasting marketing dollars in the long run.

3. Make sure you have a support team in place for your business (graphics designer, accountant, virtual assistant if necessary, mentor, etc).

4. Establish realistic and achievable business goals that also include financial goals for your business. You must have a blueprint for your business so that you know where you are going and what it takes to get there.

5. Manage business finances for success knowing how much you have allocated for marketing, promotions, supplies and more.

6. Being able to separate business from family is important. Establishing those healthy boundaries is always important when it comes to being a home-based business owner and having family time where you are focused on the family.

7. Remain focused on the vision of your business and do not get off track by this offer and that offer. Solidify your main vision and then brainstorm other ways your business can generate income.

About Dr. Taffy Wagner

Taffy Wagner is a nationally recognized expert on Money and Marriage. She is the founder and CEO of Money Talk Matters, LLC and also the creator of Wife CFO©. She has taught hundreds of individual, single parents and couples about money management, credit cleanup and reducing debt.

As a Best-selling Author, Personal Finances Expert and Speaker, she has appeared on national radio shows, television, magazines and in news articles sharing her tips on how to manage money before and after saying "I Do".

Known for her no-holds barred transparent communication style, Taffy consistently provides unbiased and non-threatening solutions to money and marriage issues as a means to reduce the number of divorces caused by money.

Taffy Wagner, D.Min, Certified Educator in Personal Finances and Consultant
http://www.moneytalkmatters.com
Email: drtaffy@wifecfo.com
Phone: 303-576-0670

Rita Wiltz

"Be thankful for what you have; you'll end up having more. If you concentrate on what you don't have, you will never, ever have enough"
OprahWinfrey

A simple book is worth so much!

Rita has always been a volunteer at-heart, even as a child. It all started with her grandmother who was a mid-wife and her mother as a community volunteer for the 4-H Club. This small town native Texan country girl knew what it meant when it came to sharing to help others.

She received a nudge from a church friend to start a non-profit business. That is when she met her mentor, the owner of one of the largest minority owned non-profit organization in Houston, Texas, and his lovely wife.

Rita's background was medicine, she provided life insurance exam physicals just before she decided to stay home and raise her children, the company she had worked for reached number one; that goal was met. After being a stay at home mom for six years, or should we say, stay at home *volunteer* mom, this wife and mother, helped her sisters take care of their senior parents, and became the ultimate soccer mom. The lists of charities and community groups the Rita volunteered her time are very long. Add community activist too as she worked for the survival of the community she grew up in that was being swallowed by surrounding subdivisions. Rita made sure 60 families received their food every month which she delivered with her truck and trailer, that was donated by a church food pantry Rita was a little busy...and still is to this day.

Because, Rita has always loved children, she spent a lot of time reading to them and donating books to at risk children in underdeveloped rural and urban cities. Thus, the dream, Children's Books on Wheels community based mobile literacy non-profit 501 (c) (3) was born, where she is the Founder and Executive Director of daily operations.

Children's Books on Wheels is a mobile literacy organization that was founded in 2004. It provides an unconventional opportunity for reading, education, health promotion, human health services application assistance for youth, teens and their families of low-income, that are at risk for HIV/AIDS, as well as special needs. "I truly believe if you give a child a book it will take them places they may never go, but if they can read about it, what a difference it can make in that child's life regardless of their circumstances. We have found that through reading programs their grades have improved - it takes one book at a time" Rita said proudly.

She feels more time should be spent reading and less time on playing video games, cell phone texting and watching endless TV.

Children's Books on Wheels facilitates reading project collaboration *"Out the Box"* thru Solutions for Better Living, located in an apartment complex in 3rd Ward, Texas where monthly a literacy program is provided for over 30 children and their families that are economically challenged in an effort to promote reading.

Rita Wiltz   Founder/Executive Director of Children's Books on Wheels
Email rw2619@msn.com

Rita Wiltz's

Recipe for SUCCESS!

1. Be self-motivated and stick with the mission.

2. Be culturally sensitive.

3. Strive to reach your goals.

4. Never stop learning.

5. Reward volunteers.

6. Take time for God, and your family.

7. Work hard, pray hard.

THE ACHIEVEMENT OF YOUR GOALS IS ASSURED
THE MOMENT YOU COMMIT YOURSELF...

"Until one is committed, there is hesitancy, the chance to draw back, always ineffectiveness. Concerning all acts of initiative (and creation), there is one elementary truth the ignorance of which kills countless ideas and splendid plans."

"The moment one definitely commits oneself, then providence moves too.

All sorts of things occur to help one that would never otherwise have occurred.

A whole stream of events issues from the decision, raising in one's favor all manner of unforeseen incidents and meetings and material assistance, which no man could have dreamed would have come his way.

Whatever you can do, or dream you can, begin it. Boldness has genius, power and magic in it."

Begin it now.

Johann Wolfgang Von Goethe

Commitment Agreement

Are you ready to make the necessary commitments for the growth of your business – starting today?

List your top 5 commitments below and make this agreement with yourself!

I commit to _____ by _____ (date)

I commit to _____ by _____ (date)

I commit to _____ by _____ (date)

I commit to _____ by _____ (date)

I commit to _____ by _____ (date)

OK – are you REALLY committed? Sign here: _____

Quick and Easy Recipes
for the Busy Entrepreneur

Even when we have the opportunity to work from home, the time flies by and before we know it, it's time to fix a meal.

On the following pages, you'll find an eclectic selection of recipes from those contributing to the book.

Most are quick and easy making it possible for all of us, to sit back and enjoy a good meal.

Let's Get Cookin!
Bon Appetite!

Memphis-Style Ribs

Beverly Boston

Epicurious | April 2008
by Steven Raichlen
*The Barbecue! Bible 10th Anniversary Edition
(Workman)*

Advance preparation
4 to 8 hours for marinating the ribs

1 1/2 cups wood chips or chunks (preferably hickory), soaked for 1 hour in cold water to cover and drained

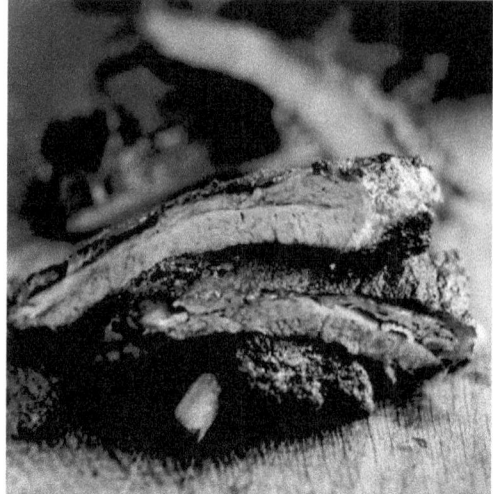

For the ribs and rub
3 racks baby back pork ribs (about 7 pounds), or 2 racks pork spareribs (6 to 8 pounds total)
1/4 cup sweet paprika
4 1/2 teaspoons freshly ground black pepper
4 1/2 teaspoons dark brown sugar
1 tablespoon salt
1 1/2 teaspoons celery salt
1 1/2 teaspoons cayenne pepper
1 1/2 teaspoons garlic powder
1 1/2 teaspoons dry mustard
1 1/2 teaspoons ground cumin

For the mop sauce (optional)
2 cups cider vinegar
1/2 cup yellow (ballpark) mustard
2 teaspoons salt

Preparation
1. Prepare the ribs and rub: Remove the thin, papery skin from the back of each rack of ribs by pulling it off in a sheet with your fingers, using the corner of a kitchen towel to gain a secure grip, or with pliers.

2. Combine the paprika, black pepper, brown sugar, salt, celery salt, cayenne, garlic powder, dry mustard, and cumin in a small bowl and whisk to mix. Rub two thirds of this mixture over the ribs on both sides, and then transfer the ribs to a roasting pan. Cover and let cure, in the refrigerator, for 4 to 8 hours.

3. Prepare the mop sauce (if using): Mix together the cider vinegar, mustard, and salt in a bowl and set aside.

4. Set up the grill for indirect grilling and place a large drip pan in the center.

If using a gas grill, place all of the wood chips in the smoker box and preheat the grill to high; when smoke appears, reduce the heat to medium.

If using a charcoal grill, preheat it to medium.

5. When ready to cook, if using a charcoal grill, toss the wood chips on the coals. Brush and oil the grill grate. Arrange the ribs on the hot grate over the drip pan. Cover the grill and smoke cook the ribs for 1 hour.

6. When the ribs have cooked for an hour, uncover the grill and brush the ribs with the mop sauce (if using). Re-cover the grill and continue cooking the ribs until tender and almost done, 1/4 to 1/2 hour longer for baby back ribs, 1/2 to 1 hour longer for spareribs. The ribs are done when the meat is very tender and has shrunk back from the ends of the bones. If using a charcoal grill, you'll need to add 10 to 12 fresh coals to each side after 1 hour. Fifteen minutes before the ribs are done, season them with the remaining rub, sprinkling it on.

7. To serve, cut the racks in half or, for a plate-burying effect, just leave them whole.

Killer Artichoke Dip

Deborah McNaughton
A yummy party treat!

Picture your friends and family enjoying themselves, exclaiming over the deliciousness of your great homemade artichoke dip. They ask you for the recipe, and you smile demurely. After all, now it's your recipe, your best artichoke dip. Don't worry: I won't tell.

This dip can be prepared a day ahead, covered and chilled. Bake just before serving and enjoy piping hot with thinly sliced toasted baguette, crackers or veggie sticks.

Ingredients
1 package (8 ounce) Neufchâtel or cream cheese
1/2 cup mayonnaise
1/2 cup sour cream
1/2 cup grated Parmesan cheese

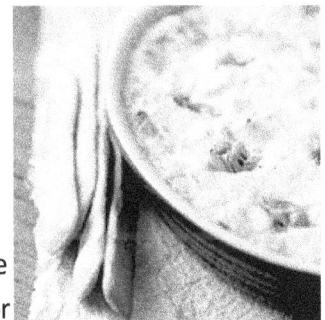

3 cloves garlic, or to taste

3 cups shredded mozzarella cheese

Freshly ground black pepper

Pinch of cayenne pepper (optional)

1 (12 ounce) jar marinated artichoke hearts, drained and

roughly chopped

1 small onion, diced

Method

Preheat oven to 350°F. In the bowl of a food processor, place the cream cheese, mayonnaise, sour cream, Parmesan cheese and garlic. Purée until all ingredients are combined. Add mozzarella cheese, black pepper and cayenne, pulsing just until combined. Add artichoke hearts and pulse again just until combined. Transfer mixture to a bowl and stir in the onion.

Bake in a 9-inch square glass baking dish for 40 to 45 minutes, until bubbly and browned. Serve immediately.

Pan-Fried Shrimp with Green Curry Cashew Sauce

Devan Tindall

1 slice (1/4 inch thick) peeled fresh ginger

3/4 cup plus 2 tablespoons roasted unsalted cashews

1/3 cup plain low-fat yogurt

1/4 cup packed cilantro leaves

1 tablespoon brown sugar

1 teaspoon curry powder

Coarse salt and fresh ground pepper

1 1/2 pounds peeled and de-veined large shrimp

2 tablespoons olive oil

In a food processor, pulse the ginger until finely chopped. Add the 3/4 cup cashews; process until smooth, 2 to 3 minutes.

Add the yogurt, cilantro, sugar, and curry powder; season with salt. Process until incorporated, 1 to 2 minutes, scraping down the sides as needed. Transfer to a serving bowl; sprinkle with the remaining cashews.

Season the shrimp with salt and pepper. Heat 1 tablespoon of the oil in a large nonstick skillet over medium-high opaque throughout, 2 to 3 minutes. Repeat with the remaining tablespoon oil and remaining shrimp. Serve the shrimp with the sauce.

Down Home Salmon Croquettes

Traci Campbell

Here is what you will need to make some very tasty salon croquettes that will leave their mouths watering and wanting more!

One 12 oz. can of pink salmon

¼ cup of flour

2 eggs

2 tablespoons of yellow corn meal

¼ cup of chopped onion

½ teaspoon of salt

½ teaspoon of ground black pepper

1 large spoon or potato masher

1 bottle of cooking oil

1 frying pan

1 spatula/pancake turner

1 serving plate

1 large bowl

1 roll of paper towels

Step 1
Combine all of the ingredients, except the flour, into one large bowl. Mix the ingredients thoroughly with the large spoon or potato masher

Step 2
Add the flour to your mixture a little at a time to get the right consistency for your taste. You may or may not need less than ¼ cup of flour

Step 3
Mold the mixture with your hands and form it into several small patties, just as you would if you were making a big home-style hamburger

Step 4
Pour enough cooking oil into your frying pan to coat it evenly and preheat it over medium heat

Step 5
Place the patties into the frying pan very gently. Put in as many as you can, but be sure to leave enough room to turn them over easily

Step 6

Cook the patties on one side until they turn a medium brown color. Now, turn them over using your spatula/pancake turner and cook them to a medium brown color on the other side as well

Step 7

Remove the patties from the frying pan and place on a plate covered with a paper towel to soak up any excess oil.

Now serve these delicious, easy to make salmon croquettes and enjoy!

Chili Cheese Eggs

Christina Scheiner

This is perfect for a fancy brunch ... or a treat for your family.

½ cup butter, melted
12 eggs, beaten
½ cup flour
1 teaspoon baking powder
Dash of salt
1 8-oz can, diced Ortega Chilies (mild)
1 8-oz. can, sliced mushrooms (optional)
1 lb. shredded Jack Cheese
{any other stuff you like, bacon crumbles, onion, etc}

Preheat oven to 400 degrees.

Beat eggs lightly, add flour, baking powder and salt to eggs.

Add melted butter, cheese and chilies.

(Add any other optional stuff). Bake in Pam sprayed, 13x8x2 pan in 400 degree oven for 15 minutes. Reduce heat to 350 degrees and continue baking for 35 to 40 minutes. Cut in squares and serve ... delicious!!! For an easy breakfast any day ... make a batch, cut in squares, wrap in plastic & freeze. Place a frozen square in the microwave for 1 minute for a great, fast breakfast anytime.

Better Than Sex? Yes!

Tuck Self

Courtesy, Paula Deen

1 18-ounce package chocolate cake mix

1 8-ounce tub of Cool Whip

1 14-ounce can sweetened condensed milk 4 Skor candy bars, crushed

1 6-ounce jar caramel or hot fudge topping

Prepare cake according to package and bake in 9x13 inch pan. Pierce warm cake all over with toothpick. Pour condensed milk over cake. Pour caramel over cake. Chill.

Before serving, top with whipped topping and sprinkle with crushed candy bars.

Zesty Rosemary Baked Chicken

Lawrence Cole – His own recipe!

Ingredients:

1 package of chicken breast, drum sticks, or thighs

Hot sauce

Pepper

Garlic Powder

Old Bay® Seasoning

Italian Dressing

Rosemary Seasoning

Non-Stick Cooking Spray

Directions:

1. Line Pyrex or other baking dish (big enough for all of the meat) with aluminum foil
2. Cover the bottom of the foil with non-stick cooking spray
3. Evenly season the bottom of the sprayed pan with pepper, garlic powder, and a light sprinkling of Old Bay® Seasoning
4. Place all of the chicken in the baking dish over the seasonings. Avoid any overlapping of the meat
5. Evenly season the top side of the meat with the pepper, garlic powder, and a light sprinkling of Old Bay® Seasoning
6. Liberally sprinkle the hot sauce over the meat

7. Liberally pour the Italian Dressing over the meat until there are no dry surfaces facing upward

8. Sprinkle the Rosemary on the top of the seasoned meat.

9. Place in oven (pre-heated to 300) and go work on your business while your food bakes. It should be ready in about 45-60 minutes (can be shorter if you increase the oven temperature – no more than 450 degrees)

* This dish should only take 5 minutes to prepare. When you're done, remove the chicken from the pan to store. After the gravy has cooled in the pan, you can simply remove and dispose of the foil for a quick-and-easy clean up as well.

Kalin's Deviled Eggs

Kalin Thomas

"When life throws you eggs – devil them!" **Ingredients:**

6 eggs (makes 12)

Mayonnaise

Spicy Mustard

Mrs. Dash seasoning

Dill

Paprika

Sliced green olives

Ziplock bag

Directions:

Boil the eggs for about 15 minutes. Remove from heat, pour out water. Put ice water or ice cubes over eggs to stop them from cooking. Shell the eggs and slice them in half (from back of egg to tip of egg). Scoop out the yolks into a mixing bowl. Crumble the yolks with a fork. Add about 3 tablespoons of mayonnaise. Add about 1 ½ tablespoons of spicy mustard. Add seasonings to taste and stir. Put the mixture into a Ziplock bag. Cut a small piece from one of the corners of the bag and squeeze out the mixture into each egg white. Top off each egg with a sliced olive and sprinkle with paprika. Makes 12 deviled eggs – great for parties!

Bean and Cheese Quesadillas

Dr. Taffy Wagner

1 pack of Spelt Tortillas

1 bag of Grated Cheese
1 can of Amy's Traditional Refried Beans

Take four quesadillas out of the packet. Place two on two different plates. Open the can of refried beans. You will use about 3 tablespoons per tortilla shell to spread the refried beans on. Then spread some grated cheese on top of the refried beans. Next, cover the shell with the fixings with a shell that has nothing on it.

In your skillet or quesadilla maker, rub with a little bit of olive oil and place the quesadilla in there. Only takes minutes to cook and be sure to flip it over so the cheese can melt. In the quesadilla maker the button actually changes color when the quesadilla is done.

Could also add your favorite meat if you want Meat, bean and cheese quesadillas.

Makes a great dish in just minutes.

Egg and Sausage Breakfast Dish

Karen Tompkins

From *River Road Recipes II, the Junior League of Baton Rouge, Louisiana.*

1 pound cooked, drained sausage
6 eggs, slightly beaten
2 cups mil
1 teaspoon mil
1 teaspoon dry mustard
2 slices crushed, day old bread
1 cup grated Cheddar cheese
3 tablespoons chopped onion
Mix ingredients and let sit overnight in a 11x 7x1 ½-inch pyrex dishBake at 350 degrees for 45 minutes.
This is a great Sunday brunch. Serves 6

Cheese Rolls

Karen Tompkins

A Family Favorite – from her sister!2 packages (4 cups) finely grated sharp cheddar cheese

1cup mayonnaise

2 finely chopped bunches green onions

1 cup finely chopped pecans

Seedless loganberry or raspberry preserves.

Serve with wheat thins.

Mix together cheese, mayonnaise, onions and pecans.

Roll into log

Refrigerate

Top with preserves

Serve with wheat thins

Chicken in Wine Sauce

Karen Tompkins

from *The Lady and Sons Savannah Country Cookbook* Paula Deen

4 large skinless boneless chicken breasts

6 ounces Swiss cheese slices

One 10 ¾ ounce can condensed cream of chicken soup

¼ cup white wine (more if desired)

Salt and pepper to taste

1 cup herb-flavored Pepperidge Farm stuffing mix, crushed

4 tablespoons (1/2 stick) butter, melted

Preheat oven to 350 degrees.

Place chicken in shallow buttered casserole.

Layer cheese on top.

Mix soup, wine, salt, and pepper, pour over cheese.

Sprinkle stuffing mix on top and drizzle with melted butter.

Bake for 45 – 60 minutes.

Chile-Garlic Shrimp

Kimberly Rhodes

From DadLuvs2Cook – AllRecipes.com

Prep Time	Cook Time	Ready In
10 Min	5 Min	15 Min

Ingredients

1 pound uncooked medium shrimp, peeled and deveined

1 (1.6 oz) package buffalo wing seasoning mix (such as McCormick® Original Buffalo Wings Seasoning Mix)

5 tablespoons unsalted butter

2 teaspoons bottled minced garlic

1/4 teaspoon crushed red pepper flakes

1/4 cup coarsely chopped fresh cilantro

2 teaspoons lime juice

4 lime wedges, for garnish (optional)

Directions

Rinse the shrimp with cold water and pat dry with paper towls. Add the shrimp and seasoning mix to a plastic bag and shake to coat.

Heat the butter, garlic, and red pepper flakes in a large skillet over medium heat until the butter has melted. Raise the heat to medium-high; when the butter begins to pop and sizzle add the shrimp to the pan. Cook and stir the shrimp until they are bright pink on the outside and the meat is no longer transparent in the center, about 4 to 5 minutes. Do not overcook.

Remove the pan from the heat and stir in the cilantro and lime juice. Garnish with lime wedges and serve hot.

Roberta's Mile High Apple Pie (Sugar Free)

Roberta Harris

Pie crust for double crust pie

Variety of apples that are available at the time.

Cinnamon

Fresh lemon

Raisins
Stevia-2 small packets
Preheat oven 400*

Core and peel enough apples to fill a large mixing bowl. Sprinkle with lemon juice and add cinnamon and stevia. Toss till coated and then add raisins. Toss again.

Make the bottom crust and place in pie pan. With the point of a knife, make some small holes in crust.   Place in oven until just slightly done. Let cool.

Fill the bottom crust with all the apples. Pile them as high as possible! (Leftover apples are good as is or cooked in the oven.)

Make top crust and place over all the apples. Attach to bottom crust and flute.

Make small slits in the crust and bake for 15 minutes. Reduce heat to 350*

Bake for one hour. Test for doneness.

Roberta's Oatmeal Breakfast Pancake

Roberta Harris

½ cup water in small pan. Add ¼ tsp. sea salt or celtic salt. Cover. Bring to boil.
Add almost ½ cup of whole grain oats. Cover. Let simmer for 30 seconds.
Turn off fire. Let sit for 30 minutes.
Into pan with oats, add 2 whole eggs, cinnamon, ¼ - ½ tsp. maple flavoring,
Walnuts (as many as you like), 1-2 packs of Stevia.

Cut parchment paper to fit glass pie pan. Place all of the oat ingredients on parchment paper. Bake in oven 350 degrees for about 15-20 minutes or till done to the touch.

Remove from parchment! Enjoy with strawberries or other fruit.   Yum!!!!!!

HERSHEY'S Double Chocolate MINI KISSES Cookies

Rita Wiltz

Hershey's Kisses brand recipes Makes about 3 ½ dozen cookies

1 cup (2) sticks butter or margarine, softened

1 ½ cups sugar

2 eggs

2 teaspoons vanilla extract

2 cups all-purpose flour

2/3 cup HERSHEY'S cocoa

¾ teaspoon baking soda

¼ teaspoon salt

1 ¾ cups (10-ounce package) HERSHEY'S MINI KISSES Brand

½ cup coarsely chopped nuts (optional)

Heat oven to 350 F.

Beat butter, sugar, eggs and vanilla with electric mixer on medium speed in large bowl until light and fluffy. Stir together flour, cocoa, baking soda and salt, add to butter mixture, beating until well blended. Stir in chocolates and nuts, if desired. Drop by teaspoons onto ungreased cookie sheet.

Bake 8 to 10 minutes or just until set. Cool slightly. Remove to wire rack and cool completely.

Stuffed Bell Pepper

Angelika Putintseva

This traditional Russian dish is easy and fast to make. Wash 6-8 big or medium size bell peppers of any color: green, red, yellow, orange, or mixed.

First prepare the stuffing. Mix 4 cups of ground beef with 1 cup of uncooked rice. Add some seasoning if you wish. Clean bell peppers from the seeds without cutting them all the way through. Fill them with prepared meat stuffing. Place them standing straight up into the pan and cover with boiling water. You can add some carrots to it if you'd like. Boil on medium fire for about 30 min. or until the meat is ready. In a middle of cooking add one cup your favorite pasta sauce for extra flavor.

It is a nutritional, delicious and easy to prepare flavorful dish.

Dr. Renee's Southern Style Mac-N-Cheese

Dr. Renee Hornbuckle

1 (12 ounce) package macaroni
1-2 Eggs
2 Cups Milk
2 Tablespoons butter, melted
2 ½ cups shredded Cheddar Cheese (or up to 4 cheeses of choice)
Salt & Pepper to taste

1. Preheat the oven to 350 degrees F. lightly grease a 2-quart glass baking dish.

2. In a large pot of salted water, lightly boil the macaroni according to directions.

3. Whisk the eggs and milk together in a large cup. Add butter and cheese to the egg and milk. Stir well.

4. Add the cooked macaroni to the mixture. Sprinkle with salt and pepper, and stir well (you need to taste to see if seasoned properly to your taste buds). Pour the mixture evenly in the baking dish. Entire mixture should be covered with the egg/milk/butter/cheese. The mixture needs to be pretty well covered. If appears not to be enough liquid, add more milk and eggs.

5. Bake uncovered, for 40 minutes to 1.5 hours, or until the bottom is brown. If top is browning too quickly, cover with aluminum foil and continue to bake.

Milk & Honey

Rev Criss Ittermann
A divine beverage from her home "Krisvilburton"

(Makes 8 half-cup servings)
4c milk (skim, part-skim or whole)
1/4 cup honey
Vanilla (1tsp, optional)
Allspice (pinch, optional)

Carefully heat milk over medium heat until warm. Slowly add honey while stirring until dissolved.

Remove from heat before it scalds. Do not allow it to boil. Add vanilla if desired. When serving sprinkle on a pinch of allspice if desired.

Notes:

* Coat measuring cup with a little milk to help the honey pour, or rinse with warmed milk to get out the remainder of the honey.

* If you reduce the recipe, place over very low heat & remove from the heat as soon as the honey is dissolved completely.

* This drink is like candy. Half-cup or small glasses are recommended. Reduce honey if you want a less candy-like drink.

*This is an easy substitute for eggnog in the holiday season.

*Drink hot or cold -- for cold Milk & Honey allow to cool to room temperature then refrigerate. Use within 3 days.

Sweet Potato Casserole

Terry Tribble

From the kitchen of her girlfriend, Lisa Tillotson McDaniel

Preheat oven to 375 degrees

3 cups boiled, mashed sweet potatoes

2 eggs (beaten)

½ cup sugar

½ stick of margarine (melted)

½ cup of milk

½ tsp salt

1 ½ tsp vanilla extract

Topping

½ cup of brown sugar

1/3 cup of flour

1 cup chopped pecans

¾ stick of margarine (melted)

Combine sugar, eggs, margarine, milk, salt and vanilla in a bowl. Add to mashed sweet potatoes Mix with a mixer until smooth. Place in a shallow 1 ½ quart baking dish

Mix toppings ingredient together in a bowl. Spread on top of sweet potato mixture

Bake at 375 for 30 minutes

Crispy Baked Catfish

Monica Hancock

From Betty Crocker's Quick & Easy Cookbook

1 pound catfish, flounder or other delicate-texture fish fillets

¼ cup yellow cornmeal

¼ cup dried bread crumbs

1 teaspoon chili powder

½ teaspoon paprika

½ teaspoon garlic salt

¼ teaspoon pepper

¼ cup French or ranch dressing

Heat oven to 450 degrees. Spray broiler pan rack with cooking spray. If fish fillets are large, cut into 4 serving pieces.

Mix cornbread, bread crumbs, chili powder, paprika, garlic salt and pepper. Lightly brush dressing on all side of fish. Coat fish with cornmeal mixture.

Place fish on rack in broiler pan. Bake uncovered 15 to 18 minutes or until fish flakes easily with fork.

NOTE: In a time crunch? Use ½ cup of a purchased seasoned fish coating mix instead of preparing the coating mixture yourself.

Macaroni & Chicken Chili

Marcia Merrill

Serves 2-3

Make macaroni as directed. (I use whole/veggie pasta)

Add cheese-I like ricotta, mozzarella or goat cheese/cheddar (as sharp or mild as you want)

Toss with canned chicken chili –already heated-you can do both at same time.

Serve with salad and/or a green veggie. 8-10 mins.

Frittata with Veggies A La Marcia

Marcia Merrill

I'm not an egg fan, but this is like the chunkiest omelet-like meal!

3-4 eggs whisk and add up to ¼ cup 2% milk. Pour in skillet, add whatever veggies you like or have on hand (I use broccoli, zucchini, spinach; potatoes...can of whole tomatoes
1/8-1/4 cup cheddar, ricotta, goat cheese, mozzarella...
Can add diced, cold chicken, Canadian bacon, ground turkey
Put all in skillet-do not flip over like an omelet
Let all set-2-4 mins.
Plate & serve w/ bagged Caesar salad

Papaya-Avacado Salad

Sheila Pearl1 lg. "red" papaya
4-6 small "persian" cucumbers
1/2 cup chopped fresh basil leaves
3-4 med. California avocados (ripe)
2 fresh lemons
season salt

Cut papaya in half and scoop out pulp and seeds; cut papaya in smaller chunks to make peeling it easier. Peel papaya and cut away any "hard" portions, leaving only the ripe, slightly soft red meat. Cut chunks about 1-1/2 inches wide and 3 inches long; then thinly slice papaya at a diagonal, creating elegant slices. Place in a bowl and squeeze the juice of one lemon over the papaya, cover and set aside.

Wash but do not peel the little cucumbers (the size of pickles, thin, crisp and seedless). Trim the ends, cut in half lengthwise then thinly slice at a diagonal, similar in thickness to the papaya slices. Place in a zip-lock baggy and set aside.

Wash the fresh basil leaves and carefully pat dry with paper towel or kitchen towel; then gently chop basil into medium pieces (not too small), filling up a measuring cup to about ½ cup, without packing the pieces down. Gently place chopped basil in a zip-lock baggy and set aside.

Cut avocados in half, peel and slice into pieces that match the size of papaya and cucumber slices. When sliced, place in a large salad bowl and squeeze the juice from the second lemon over the sliced avocados.

Add the sliced papaya, then the cucumbers and basil, sprinkle with season salt to taste (not too much; the lemon will carry the flavors very nicely!), and gentle combine the ingredients.

Voila! You have what is often the "hit" of the feast, since it is an unexpected combination, colorful, refreshing, and helps everyone digest the rest of the meal very effectively. Bon appetite!

Spring Chicken Salad

Mark Perkett

1/2 pound small red-skinned potatoes, halved
Kosher salt
2 tablespoons chopped fresh chives
2 tablespoons chopped fresh tarragon
2 tablespoons white wine vinegar
1/4 cup low-fat plain Greek yogurt
Freshly ground pepper
1/4 cup extra-virgin olive oil
4 romaine hearts, torn

1 rotisserie chicken, skin removed and meat shredded , about 2 cups
1 Kirby cucumber, peeled, halved lengthwise, seeded and sliced
4 radishes, cut into wedges
1 yellow bell pepper, thinly sliced

Directions

Place the potatoes in a small pot and cover with water. Season with salt, cover and boil until fork-tender, about 6 minutes. Drain and cool.

Meanwhile, pulse the chives, tarragon, vinegar, yogurt, 1/2 teaspoon salt, and pepper to taste in a food processor. Slowly drizzle in the olive oil and pulse to make a thick dressing.

Toss the romaine, potatoes, chicken, cucumber, radishes and bell pepper with the dressing in a large bowl. Season with salt and pepper.

Chicken Margherita

Victor Holman

Ingredients

4 fully-cooked breaded chicken cutlets*
1 (24 ounce) jar Bertolli® Tomato and Basil Sauce
1/2 cup shredded mozzarella cheese
8 ounces bow tie pasta, cooked and drained

Directions

Preheat oven to 375 degrees F.

Arrange chicken in 9x13 inch baking dish. Pour sauce over chicken, then sprinkle with cheese. Bake 15 minutes or until heated through. Serve over hot bow ties.

Chicken Soup from the Leone Kitchen

Diamond Leone

- 3 Chicken Breasts, cooked and cubed
- 1 cup frozen corn
- 2 cups chopped green beans
- 3 small potatoes cubed
- 4 carrots sliced small
- 1 small red onion, chopped
- 1 can black beans
- 1 can crushed tomatoes
- 1 can tomato sauce
- 2 cans chicken broth
- 1/2 head of cabbage
- Pinch of Oregano
- Pinch of Garlic
- Pinch of Basil
- Pinch of Italian Seasoning
- 2 cups of water

Place all ingredients in a slow cooker and cook all day on low OR Place all ingredients in a deep pot and simmer on medium heat for 2 1/2 hours until done. ENJOY!!

Cascadillo – A Chilled, Creamy Tomato Soup

Ludolph Misher, III

From the **"Moosewood Cookbook"** By Mollie Katzen 15 Minutes to prepare

Servings: 4 to 6

(It also needs to chill after preparation)

1 Chopped Cucumber	4 Cups of Tomato Juice
1 Chopped Scallion	1 Cup of Yogurt (and or sour cream)
1Clove Crushed Garlic	1 Chopped Sweet Pepper
1 Teaspoon of Honey	[Serve with several thinly sliced Mushrooms]
½ Teaspoon of Dill Weed	Salt and Pepper (To Taste)

Combine and Chill….Serve with Croutons….Garnish with Watercress… Enjoy!

Mediterranean Flat Bread Appetizers

Dawn Rickabaugh

Start with Mediterranean flat bread, and spread on a thick layer of sun-dried tomato & basil hummus (I get it from Trader Joes). Then, take sliced cucumbers and cover the bread & hummus entirely. Top with lemon pepper, and enjoy a healthy, quick and easy snack.

Quick and Delicious Pizza

Tracey Doctor

4 English Muffins split apart
1/2 Cup pizza sauce
1/2 Cup shredded mozzarella cheese
1/2 Cup shredded cheddar cheese
 Turkey Pepperoni slices

Preheat oven to 350 degrees
Place English muffin halves cut side up on a baking sheet
Spoon plenty of pizza sauce on to each English muffin
Top with cheese and pepperoni slices
Bake 10 minutes in a preheated oven or until the cheese has melted
and muffin has browned around the edges

This is great with a fresh crispy tossed salad with tomatoes, onions, croutons topped with your choice of salad dressing and a cold refreshing beverage of your choice.

Super Fast & Healthy Greek Founder Roll-Ups

Angela Gagauf

2 large tomatoes, thinly sliced
1 – 12 ounce package baby spinach (buy in pre-washed bag)
1 tablespoon olive oil
1 small onion, finely chopped
1 garlic clove, minced or put through a clove press
1 – 14 ounce can petite diced tomatoes, drained
1 teaspoon oregano
¼ teaspoon salt
¼ teaspoon black pepper
4 – 6 ounce pieces of flounder (or lemon sole)
1 – 5 ounce container crumbled feta cheese
¼ cup white wine or juice of 1 lemon

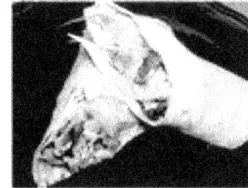

1. Spray a casserole dish with Pam and line the bottom with the tomato slices. Reserve 4 slices for later.
2. In a sauté pan, heat the olive oil over a medium-high flame. Sauté the onion until soft. Add the garlic and sauté an additional minute. Do not allow the vegetables to brown.
3. To the pan, add the diced tomatoes, the spinach, the oregano, salt and pepper. Cook over a medium-high flame until all the liquid has evaporated and the spinach has wilted. Stir frequently.
4. Place the flounder on a board, skinned side up. Divide the tomato/spinach mixture evenly between the 4 pieces. Flatten and spread the mixture on the fish, starting from the widest end. Leave about 1/3 of the fish without any mixture. Do not spread it to the end!
5. Sprinkle the mixture with the crumbled feta cheese, about 1-2 T. per piece.
6. Starting from the wide end, carefully roll the fish. Place the pieces seam side down in the prepared pan on top of the sliced tomatoes. Add 1 slice of tomato on top of each fish. Lightly sprinkle with additional oregano, salt and pepper. Drizzle the fish with the white wine or lemon juice.
7. Cover with microwavable plastic wrap and puncture the top with a knife.
8. Bake in the microwave on high for approximately 8 to 10 minutes or until done. Don't overcook!

This dish tastes delicious served with a side of rice. Drizzle the rice with the pan juices. Or, if you REALLY want to make this an authentic Greek dish, top the rice with a tablespoon or two of plain Greek yogurt (fat-free or low fat, of course). Serve with a side of salad and you're all set!

Oh So Sticky-Bun Breakfast

Leah Humphries
From the internet

Ingredients
2 tbsp butter
3 tbsp brown sugar
¼-½ tsp cinnamon
2 tbsp maple syrup
½ cup chopped pecans or walnuts
1 tube refrigerated biscuits

Directions

Heat oven to 425º or to temperature indicated on biscuit package.
In 8-inch cast iron skillet, melt butter. (or use other 8-inch baking pan.) Add brown sugar, cinnamon, syrup and nuts. Mix well
Open canned biscuits, separate and place evenly over mixture in skillet. (Can also sprinkle a little more cinnamon over the top of the biscuits, if desired.)
Bake 10-12 minutes.
Place plate on top of skillet or pan. Turn over carefully. This must be done while the sticky buns are still quite warm, as they won't come out if the topping cools.
Serve after the buns have cooled.

Creamy Dreamy Cheese Frosting

Leah Humphries

From the internet

Cheesy and pleasing is this creamy frosting. Top cookies, brownies or cakes with scrumptious cream cheese frosting.

Ingredients

9 oz. cream cheese, softened
1 tbsp. butter, softened
1 tsp. vanilla extract
1 3/4 cups confectioners' sugar, sifted

Methods/steps

Mix all the ingredients in a bowl and beat with an electric mixer. If necessary, add milk to make of spreading consistency. (lick the bowl)

Chocolate Andes' Dessert

Kellie Frazier

Ingredients:

2 packages of instant chocolate pudding mixed according to package directions
2 containers of cool whip
Milk
Andes Mints
Chocolate Graham Crackers
1 Stick of Butter

Directions:

Begin by crushing two packages of the chocolate graham crackers in a bowl until crumbly. Soften ½ stick of butter (10 secs in the microwave to soften) and mix thoroughly into the graham cracker crumbs until moist. Pour mixture into a 13 x 9 glass dish and press firmly but evenly on bottom of dish.

Next, mix 2 packages of chocolate pudding according to package instructions. Remove ½ of the chocolate pudding and combine it with 2 cups of cool whip to create a mouse. Layer the darker chocolate pudding over the graham crackers then grate 6 Andes mints over the top.

Add a layer of the mouse mixture. With the remaining cool whip add a thin layer on top of the mouse. Grate 6 Andes Mints over the top of the cool whip. For decoration you may want to add 10 pieces of whole Andes Mints to the top by sliding them into the dessert horizontally and at an angle and Viola!

Grilled Stuffed Mushrooms

Donna Baxter

Preparation Time: 10 minutes. Cooking time: 25 minutes.

4   Medium potatoes (may substitute instant)1   Cup frozen peas
2   Tbsp water
1   Large brown onion
2   Cloves garlic, crushed
1   Red Thai Chili, chopped finely
4   Medium to large portabella mushrooms
2   Tbsp Cream
¼ Cup Butter
½ Cup grated cheddar cheese
¼ Cup loosely packed, chopped parsley
½ Cup melted butter

Boil, steam or microwave potato and peas, separately, until tender, drain
Combine the water, onion, garlic and red Thai chili in a pot; cook for 5 minutes, stirring occasionally or until the onion softens.

Remove the stems of the mushrooms.

Mash potato, peas, cream and ¼ cup butter in large bowl until smooth. Add onion mixture, cheese and parsley; mix well.

Brush mushrooms with extra butter. Grill or barbeque until tender.

Divide potato mixture among mushrooms. Cook under grill for approximately five minutes or until potato is lightly browned.

Serves: 4

Chicken Pot Pie

DeBorah Madison

1 - can cream of chicken soup

1 - can cream of potato soup

1 – can of vegetables

1 – can of chicken

1 – 2 deep dish frozen ready to fill pie shell

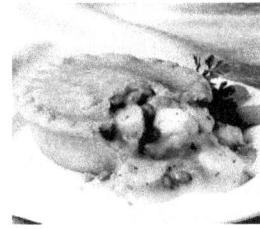

Super easy, mix all ingredients together in a bowl and pour into one of the pie shells. Place the second pie shell over the filling. Press the edge of the pie shells together, and add a few small slits in the top of the pie shell.

Place in the oven

Cook for 45 minutes or until golden brown. Cool down and enjoy

Substitutes: If you don't like canned goods like me, you can replace the can of vegetables with frozen vegetables and the can of chicken with fresh chicken.

Buy a small bag/box of mixed vegetables. For measuring purposes only, pour some of the uncooked vegetables into one of the empty soup cans. Pour vegetables into a microwaveable bowl and cook slightly. Let vegetables cool and then add to soup mixture.

Buy 1 rotisserie chicken. Cut up enough white and dark meat. For measuring purposes only, add the cut up chicken pieces into one of the empty soup cans. Add the chicken to the soup mixture and stir.

Hint: The seasoning of the rotisserie chicken will add great flavor to the potpie.

Granola

Craig Anthony Nicholas

4 cups rolled oats

1 cup crushed almonds

½ cup whole grain flour

1 tsp. cinnamon

¼ cup shredded coconut

1 cup sunflower seeds

½ wheat germ or other whole grain bran

2010 National Business Directory

¾ - 1 cup honey
1 cup pumpkin seeds

Mix all together and spread out on a non-stick cookie sheet. Bake 20 minutes in a 250 degree preheated oven. Stir and continue to bake another 20 minutes, stirring periodically to prevent burning. The granola should be lightly browned. Remove from oven and serve warm or cool thoroughly and store in tightly sealed container or plastic bags. Option: after the granola is cooled, add raisins or other organic, unsulphured, dehydrated fruit.

Homemade Chicken Pot Pie

Martha Johnson

Preheat oven to 375
Take leftover chicken or turkey, separate from bone & cut into small pieces
In a bowl add to chicken one bag of frozen peas & carrots
Add 3 large potatoes diced
Add one can of cream of celery, mushroom, or chicken soup - add water to thin
Bake one frozen pie crust (thawed) in baking dish for 10 minutes
Remove from oven and add above ingredients to baking dish
Cover with 2nd pie crust and bake for 45 minutes to one hour

Chicken Kabobs

Anne-Marie Lerch

1 lb Chicken Thighs
½ cup of Extra Virgin Olive Oil
1 Lemon
5 Cloves Garlic
Fresh Rosemary
¼ tsp Salt
1/8 tsp Pepper
Dried Oregano
2 tbl Tone's Rosemary Garlic Seasoning

Cut chicken thighs into 3 inch pieces.
Place chicken in zip lock bag.
Pour ½ cup Olive Oil in bag to fully coat the chicken (add more if needed).
Mince Garlic and put in bag.
Add salt and pepper.

334

Sprinkle with dried oregano.
Sprinkle Tone's Rosemary Garlic Seasoning.
Remove the rosemary leaves from the stem and place in bag.
Squeeze lemon juice of entire lemon into bag.
Mix well in bag.
Let sit for an hour (best if left to marinate overnight).
Put chicken on skewers and grill until cooked.

Optional
Eat with tzatziki sauce
The chicken can be eaten alone, but I just love tzatziki sauce. You can buy some at the store or here's an easy recipe.
2 cups of Greek yogurt or plain yogurt
2-6 cloves garlic
½ cup diced or pureed English cucumber
Salt
Pepper

Drain liquid from yogurt if using plain yogurt
Mince 2 cloves of garlic add more garlic to taste
Puree or dice cucumber
Mix yogurt, garlic, cucumber and salt and pepper. Let sit.

Dr. Beth Dennard's Flan Cake

Dr. Beth Dennard

A ooey-gooey version of a caramel cake!

Prep Time: 25 minutes
Cook Time: 60 minutes
Total Time: 85 minutes

Ingredients:

- 1 box of yellow cake mix, with ingredients as directed by box----substitute coconut milk instead of water, otherwise follow box cake mix directions for cake batter.
- 3 eggs
- 2 cans evaporated milk
- 1 can sweetened condensed milk

- 1 teaspoon vanilla
- Leche Quemada (Cajeta Caramel)*----WALMART HAS THIS-----I USED THE "LOW SUGAR"
- 1/2 cup toasted coconut (lightly toast coconut in either a skillet on low heat (because you can watch it carefully) or in an oven heated to 300 degrees

Preparation:

- Preheat oven to 350 degrees. Set a small bake proof container of water** inside oven also as this assists the flan to turn out perfectly. Make cake as directed on the box and set aside.
- Flan mixture: Add eggs, milk and vanilla to a blender. Blend together until well blended.
- In a Bundt pan, spray with non-stick spray and dust it with flour. Cover the bottom and the sides of the Bundt pan with the Cajeta. Sprinkle bottom of pan with toasted coconut. Add flan mixture. On top of this add the prepared cake batter. Cook for 45-60 minutes.

**The pan of water is important so that the flan doesn't overcook. Also, the pan of water needs to be preheated to ensure even temperature in the oven while baking.

In The Kitchen With....

Wow – you have to be hungry now! **While you wait for your dish to finish – why not lay back, relax and read the articles from me and my featured contributors that follow!**

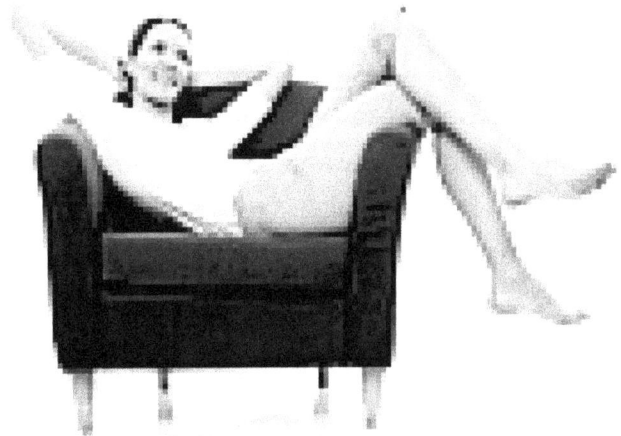

Brought to you by:

In The Kitchen with Regina Baker

Living Your Life Like It's Golden
Stop Procrastinating and Just Do It!

Small businesses come and go. That's why there's so much room available for YOU!

Being a small business consultant, I get to hear all of the stories as to why people give up on their dreams way too soon. Having a successful home based business is only as strong as your vision, commitment, belief and faith. Most people never realize the truth of that statement until they realize the passion of empowering others with their gifts and talents.

I remember when I made the decision to start my business in 1990. I was still working in Corporate America and wanted so badly to leave the 9 to 5 hustle of doing the same thing day in and day out. But what I didn't realize is that because of my job, I didn't take my business serious. I knew every week I would get my paycheck so I looked at my business more like a hobby, you know, making an extra few bucks here and there.

It wasn't imperative that I build my financial business portfolio because I didn't make my dream a priority until six years later, when I didn't have a choice!

After 10 years of dedication to my employer, I was presented with the infamous pink slip! With no notice, I was permanently laid off. There went the routine pay check and health benefits. There was no time to fumble, I had to make a decision as to how serious I would commit to either hitting the pavement for another j.o.b. or pursuing my goal as a home based business owner because unemployment checks were only temporary.

Sub-consciously, I always knew that I would have my own business, I just didn't know what to do, who to ask and then there was F.E.A.R lurking in the shadows. You know who fear is right? **F**alse **E**vidence **A**ppearing **R**eal {chuckle}

"Life Is Like a Box of Chocolates…"

It's true, you never know what you're going to get when you don't plan your work and work your plan or have a Plan B ready, I sure didn't.

Not only had I been laid off, but shortly thereafter, my husband was diagnosed with terminal cancer. Talking about a major blow! Thank God we both believed in the power of prayer, belief and faith and let me tell you, we put it to work on our behalf.

We started speaking positive affirmations, 'calling the things that be not as though they were' and aligning ourselves with what I call, 'on purpose' friends who spoke only positive words and lived the lives they spoke about.

After receiving a telephone call from one such type of friend, we decided to venture into Network Marketing. This would allow us to work from home as well as be there for my husband anytime of the day or night.

The Process

There's a process to everything in life. I say, "its how you go through the process that determines the outcome"; I still live by that quote today. Even in the midst of our challenges, we didn't give up… oh yes, there were times when I thought about it, but we continued to press through. When we make a decision to give up on something, the fact of the matter is, we give up on ourselves – that's definitely not the answer.

Because we remained steadfast in the process, it wasn't long after Ruben's passing that I was awarded a high level position as one of the top income earners – this included traveled speaking at events (and getting paid sometimes more in a weekend than most people make in a year) and empowering others with my story. Wow! I never thought 'my' story would ever amount to anything, gee I mean, who would care? I found out that I was so wrong with such limited thinking.

People all over the world are looking for validation. In other words, hearing that someone else has gone through a similar challenge as theirs, sometimes motivates them into believing they can too!

Yes You Can!

I said all of this, not to impress you about me, but to impress upon you, that you can do whatever you want to do in life when you have vision, make a commitment, believe and have faith while going through the process.

It's when we allow ourselves to go through our pre-destined journey, everything that is purposed for your life will manifest accordingly. Although I'm no longer with the company I mentioned earlier, my horizons are bigger and better. I became a Certified Business Consultant focusing on Internet Marketing and eCommerce.

If you're reading this message, this is confirmation that you have a desire to be your own boss and/or you're in the process. I encourage you to remain steadfast with your dreams and goals and to never give up because of temporary challenges. Yes, that's what they are -- temporary... because challenges are only designed to move you into a higher learning and understanding of what it takes to achieve your goals.

I'm thoroughly grateful for the opportunity to bring my purpose to life. I encourage you to do the same – YES, You Can!

"I'm holding on to my freedom, can't take it from me, I was born into it, it comes naturally, I'm strumming my own freedom, playing the god in me, representing his glory, hope He's proud of me, I'm livin' my life like it's golden -- It really matters to me" ~ *Jill Scott*

Regina Baker
Connect with Regina on www.TwitterRegina.com & www.facebook.com/reginabaker

In The Kitchen with Raven Blair Davis

Power Up Your Business with Your Own Radio Show...
Right from Your Kitchen Table

There is power in your voice! Don't believe me? Check this out.

Statistics consistently show that 20% percent of people remember what they read, and 80% remember what they hear.

eBay, Business Week, 60 Minutes, ESPN, even during the presidential campaign both Barack Obama, and John McCain, all have or have had a podcast.

Podcasting is the new era. It is what's going on, it's here, it's now, and it is not going away. In fact...... it's rapidly growing momentum all around the world.

In 2007, the market estimated that the total US total pod cast audience reached 16.5 million. In 2008, Arbitron media research released that 29 million people are listening to podcasts all over the world. The great news is the United States spending on podcast related advertising, including sponsorship, is expected to rise to four hundred thirty five million dollars by 2012.

This is just part of the reason I feel that every business, big, small, just getting started, thinking about getting started, should be podcasting. Now, you're probably wondering "What is podcasting, Raven?"

I am glad you asked! We're going to keep it real simple, we're not even going to get involved with the technology of it. Just think of podcasting as being an MP3 Audio or Video file that you can upload to different directories. You're putting your digital media files that are distributed over the Internet by syndicated download through web feed. That's all the technical stuff you need to know. It's simple, it's easy, and it's effective.

Podcasting is called the wave of the future, and as I said earlier, it is not going away. Now, if you are not part of this, if you are not using this as one of your marketing tools, I am going to share with you why you should be and how you can grow your business exponentially by simply using this simple, easy, and effective new tool, that again, is here to stay.

Yes…having a podcast/talk radio show is a great way to make that happen. It will elevate your business quickly and is very effective in creating new customers and clients as well as retaining current ones.

If you promote your business, the benefits and exposure you will achieve from your radio show will grow your business by establishing you as an expert, building a platform to market books, CDs, products and services and creating a new revenue stream.

Here are a few suggestions that will assist you in broadcasting your passion.

Discover your true passion or purpose.

Ask yourself the following questions. What makes you happy and excited so you jump out of bed in the morning? What lit you up as a child? What message or cause do you have a burning desire to share? What have you always wanted to do? Be authentic – be true to your purpose. Don't try to be an *Oprah, Larry King* or *Ellen*. Be yourself. Your audience will appreciate it and be attracted to who you are.

Identify your target audience.

Deliver one- to-one radio. Don't talk AT your listeners, talk WITH them. Picture your perfect audience and be in alignment with their needs. Your message should clearly speak to them. They should feel like your show is calling their name. Don't try to be a Wal-Mart and be everything to everybody.

Choose your format.

Your show can be 1 minute or 1 hour long. Some of the most successful shows are 20 minutes as that is the average commute time! If you are not interviewing others, 5 to 20 minutes is the perfect length, but if you are interviewing other people, your show can be 20 minutes to an hour. The combination of voices is entertaining and people will listen longer. Another option is a panel discussion, like *The View*. Pick a topic and have 2-4 people discuss it. If you're an author or speaker you may want to use the commentary format. Take a portion of your book, speech or teleseminar and deliver it in small, bite-sized pieces

Prepare for your show.

Now it's show time! For interviews, choose a topic and find the perfect guest for that particular topic. Consider experts in your field of interest that will appeal to your audience. Make it easy on yourself by requesting they send you the questions.

Another option is to do what's called an 'ask campaign' or survey. This is where you collect questions from your audience.

Choose a target date for launch! Send press releases and promote at least two weeks prior to your launch.

Now, it's your time to shine. Don't hold back and don't second guess yourself. Start broadcasting your message globally and unleash the power of your voice...Broadcast Your Passion!

Raven Blair Davis
Founder & Host of Careers from the Kitchen Table on CBS Talk 650 Radio News
www.kitchentableradio.com
www.broadcastyourpassion.com

In The Kitchen with Peggy Knudson

Virtual Assistance
The well known secret in running a home based business

There comes a time when a home based business owner or entrepreneur finds they need to make the move to using a VA. The number one priority of every business owner is to grow their business and delegating the routine administrative tasks and projects can make all the difference. Could you be a Virtual Assistant?

On many occasions I've been asked "What is a VA"? In essence it is nothing more than a person that is not onsite that assists another with a task, project, event, venture, etc. While VA's have likely been around for many years, today the field is being recognized as its own profession.

Our connected, high-tech world is the #1 reason the field and opportunities for VA's has grown. After all, the tasks and responsibilities that most VA's accomplish for their clients have been around for years. The change brought about by high technology simply allows them to be done from anywhere! Virtual Assistants have the same responsibilities and provide the same solutions as workers in traditional office settings.

As with most everything in life, there are pros and cons to being a Virtual Assistant. Here are just a few:

Pros:
- Work from the comfort of your own home
- You become an entrepreneur/independent contractor that owns your own business
- Ability to do what you LOVE

2010 National Business Directory

- No commute
- No expensive wardrobe required (I can hear some of you crying right now!)
- Set your own hours
- Choose who you work with and for
- Tax advantages (do check with a tax pro.)
- No office politics

Cons:

- One must pay their own taxes (employment and Social Security)
- Lack of social connections (face to face)
- Rarely get to meet your clients
- Expense of equipment/office supplies, etc.
- No benefits (vacation pay, sick pay, health insurance, etc.)
- Loans and other financial "needs" are more difficult being self employed

In my nearly seven years as a VA, I've used all the skills I acquired during years working in the administrative offices of a number of different types of companies. Plus I have had to learn a variety of new technology using the internet. My clients have all been entrepreneurs whose businesses are based on the internet. Their businesses range from "one man operations" to teams of VA's working together "virtually" for the common good and success of the client.

As a VA, you get to choose what you do! Imagine not having to do the things you simply don't like any longer. For the optimum control over what you do, I suggest you consider a "niche". In my circle of VA's, many have done just that.

Here are six common niches:

- E-Commerce
- Event Planning
- Customer Service
- Desktop Publishing
- Marketing
- Product Creation

E-Commerce simply means doing business online. It usually involves the selling of your client's products via the internet. E-Commerce has been the single most important advance brought about via the internet that has made conducting business virtually work. The basics of E-Commerce involve helping your client to be found (websites), a way for their customers to purchase (shopping cart, paypal), and delivery of the product (electronic or physical delivery).

Event planning is just that, assisting your client in creating an event. An event can be attended in the traditional live attendance setting or virtually via a teleclass, teleseminar or webinar. These virtual options are increasingly popular as the cost of travel rises.

Customer service takes many forms in the virtual environment. You may be answering a toll free line provided to prospects and customers. Answering emails or queries sent via electronic helpdesk or chat software. It is no different than the customer service at your corner store. Making the customer happy in any business is a key to success.

Desktop publishing involves creating brochures, flyers, catalogs, booklets and handouts to name a few. You may even be asked to format a book to submit to one of the many print on demand publishers now available. This is a particularly fun task if you are the creative type.

Marketing can involve you in a myriad of tasks and responsibilities. Do you like to write? There is no end to the people you can work with if you can write a compelling email or sales letter for a website.

Product creation also means different things depending on your clients. I've personally taken a series of articles a client has written over the years, brought them together with graphics into book form. CDs and DVDs can be created and sold from interviews, teleclasses, and live events. Packaged together or on their own they make for great products your clients can then sell via their websites and the usual outlets such as Amazon and Barnes and Noble as well as "back of the room sales" at conferences and events. Your client is the subject expert; the VA turns that output into product to sell.

Now that I've gone over some of the basics of what a VA does and how it's accomplished virtually, along with the pros and cons, let's discuss what it takes to be a VA.

Are you:

- Responsible, Reliable and Dependable? Do what you say you will, be available when you say you will?
- One who lives by the highest of ethics? It is not unusual for a client to share credit card, banking and other very personal information with their VA.
- A self starter? Are you able to get out of bed without having to "make an appearance" at the office?
- Eager to help others succeed in their endeavors? You must whole heartedly partner with your client for the success of their business which directly leads to the success of YOUR business!

So now you want to be a VA!

Great! What next? I recommend that anyone who wants to be a VA look to the internet. Search on virtual assistance, review the many (and growing) numbers of VA associations. Network!

Yes, even in the virtual world networking is as important as ever. I've personally found my referrals are often from other VA's that I've gotten to know while working with my clients. I have also received inquiries and positions as a result of my membership in VA Associations.

It is also very important that you have your own website! You can look to membership in a VA association for your website solution as many provide low cost options to getting a website created and maintained.

In addition you must expand your knowledge base to include doing business virtually and online. Following are some key areas to study and become familiar with to know how the system of E-Commerce works.

- Shopping Cart: www.1shoppingcart.com and www.wahmcart.com
- Payment Gateways/Processing: www.authorize.net and www.paypal.com
- Phone Systems: www.workeasy.com and www.virtualpbx.com
- Email Marketing/Client Contact Systems: www.constantcontact.com and www.aweber.com

I encourage you to go to these sites, understand what they do and reach out to each company for a free trail so you can actually get to know how the systems work.

The next lists of sites represent a variety of solutions commonly used in the VA world. This is just a taste and by no means represents all that are available:

- www.audiogenerator.com – used to capture and add audios to websites. Create audio postcards to be sent via email.
- www.assessmentgenerator.com – create assessments and quizzes
- www.godaddy.com and www.aitdomains.com – domain registrar and website hosting
- www.blogtalkradio.com - a wonderful way to get your client "on air" and building name recognition

- www.googleanalytics.com - to help your client get the most from their websites
- www.lightningsource.com – on demand printing
- www.voiceshot.com - web based voice broadcasting
- www.wordpress.com and www.typepad.com – blogging sites

The next area that you can't learn enough about is social networking via the internet. It seems there are more and more of these sites popping up daily! This is an incredible way for your clients to network, get known and grow their business.

Being a Virtual Assistant is not for everyone. Starting one's own business takes courage and a strong commitment to success.

Personally I absolutely love the ability and opportunity to work virtually. Working with various clients gives my day a good deal of variety. For 30 years I focused on one "client" at a time. During those years my clients were also known as employers. Now I'm my own employer. I get to do what I love! Being trusted and relied on by clients who are also small businesses is personally rewarding. If you've found what I've said to resonate with you, give being a VA a try!

Peggy Knudson
Director/Owner
Outstanding Virtual Assistance
www.outstandingvirtualassistance.com

In The Kitchen with Arika Lewis

Words...

The cornerstone of Every Business

I work closely, every day with online business owners. While some of my clients take their marketing efforts offline, the majority are strictly online businesses. Therefore, my specialty lies in online marketing.

Because of this, when Raven asked me to write an article for her book sharing my knowledge as an affiliate manager, copywriter, content expert and marketing opportunist, I had a difficult time trying to figure out how to tailor what I have to offer to an audience of both online and offline business owners. So much so that I even tried to get out of it a few times.

Thanks goes to Raven for kicking my tush to do it anyway, but even more for her faith that I COULD do it. After hee-hawing around about it for a few weeks, it finally hit me! Content and Words - That's the key to making every business (online or off) successful!

You see, in the online marketing world there is a lot (and I mean A LOT) of emphasis put on content. As much as those of us who work on the Internet may get tired of seeing it, there is absolute truth in the phrase "Content is King." The same is true for every single business out there.

How you present yourself and your business will either make or break you.

In a conventional business (although I think before long, if not already, the number of online businesses may just surpass offline ones making them the norm) content is more commonly referred to as words or conversation and nonverbal actions when you're speaking. It can also mean your advertising, but for the sake of this article we're going to stick with communication and how you present yourself and your business through the words you speak and the actions you use while doing so.

As a website owner you don't have that "look you in the eyes" ability like those who own a brick and mortar business. What you share with your prospects and current customers has to make up for that. Content is the way it's done. You have to make a personal connection with your readers just like you would do face to face. It's not always an easy task, especially with the precautions everyone takes when searching the web for the information they need.

Do you see the challenge?

That's just one of the challenges I see business owners faced with every single day. They wonder, "How do I create credibility in a sea of competition that has gone beyond just my little neck of the woods and now encompasses the entire world?"

Need an example? Here you go! If you own a car repair shop in a small town, you may have little or no direct competition in that town and business probably booms for you. But, let's say you own an online business that sells baby toys. You are immediately in direct competition *(a dirty word and when it comes to online business I don't believe there is such a thing, but that's another article for another day)* with every single website that sells the same or similar toys as you do. You have to work hard at getting people to know, like and trust you. They need to know you are who you say you are, you won't steal their cash and run, and your product and customer service is of the quality they deserve. There are many ways to do this, but the most important one starts the minute people see your website listed in a search result.

Here's the kicker…

If you don't IMMEDIATELY (within 2-3 seconds) catch their attention enough to make them want to click through to your website, you can probably forget about having them as a customer.

If they do like what they see in those few short lines at Google and click through, you still have to prove to them RIGHT away you are the one they want to do business with. You've got approximately 15 seconds (and that number is shrinking every day) to grab their attention with your_____.

Can you fill in the blank? If you said "words" you're absolutely correct!

Once you have their attention, your goal is to KEEP it and you continue to do that with the words they read. The same is true no matter where your business resides – in a building on the corner of town square, a corporate office, or your kitchen.

In an offline business, when someone walks in your door, the way they are treated and greeted will determine whether they stick around and buy from you as well as whether or not they come back again in the future.

Back Up Those Words

Now that you know just how important your words are in your business, there's one more thing I want to be sure stays in your head every single time you open your mouth to greet a customer or write a sales page or any other content for your business.

It's not just WHAT you say, but HOW you say it that matters.

I can remember as a hormone ridden teenager, my mom saying something similar to me whenever I'd get a little snippy about something. I hear her in my head quite often... *"Arika, it's not WHAT you say. It's HOW you say it."*

How you come across to your audience will make all the difference in the world. If you have children or a spouse, you'll know EXACTLY what I'm talking about here. Words said in normal conversation can be innocent and non-threatening to you, but if they say the same words in anger, the way they make you feel is completely different, right? It's the same with your potential customer.

This is where your personality has to come through. Here's a little secret:

People can see right through fake and they will run as fast as they can from it!

If you're not being honest with who you really are in your writing and speech or if you're in it for ulterior motives, (i.e. only seeing the cash and not seeing the person holding it) it will show and ultimately it will affect the outcome of your business.

With that, I'll leave you with a few tips to help you when it comes to creating content, not only business, but life too.

1. **Listen first.** – You can't possibly know what it is people want from you as a business owner if you don't listen.

2. **Be honest and sincere**. – If you don't really mean it, don't say or write it.

Be Yourself! – There's no one in the world who can be you better than you. Know who you are and let that come through in your words and your actions whether it's in person or in print.

Arika Lewis
Content & Marketing Opportunist
www.Facebook.com/arikalewis
www.Twitter.com/arikalewis

In The Kitchen with Marcia Merrill

Strategies for Starting A Business..
Getting it Right from the Beginning

The first thing you do when starting a business is to make a decision as to what kind of business you want to start. Next you'll need to figure out what structure your business will fit into for tax and legal purposes. This is known as a business entity.

Determining the Right Entity for Your Business

Go to the Small Business Center in your area or www.sba.org. Most small businesses will choose either a Sole Proprietorship or an LLC (Limited Liability Corporation). There are other types of business entities and a quick trip to Small Business Administration website will give you the best detail for each and help you decide which is best for your situation.

I wanted a set up that would allow me to develop many domains under one umbrella. What the best option for me was...I hadn't a clue. An attorney friend advised me to go with an LLC. He said it was better as it would be harder for anyone to sue me & seize my personal property. Now, that doesn't mean this particular entity is right for everyone. So, if you're lucky enough to have a lawyer friend like me, talk with them. If not, head over to Legal Aid and check it out. (www.LegalAid.com)

As you can see I believe in consulting experts and using FREE services whenever possible.

Do You Need a Business License or Insurance?
Once you've decided which kind of business model fits the best with your type of business, it's time to investigate if your state or city requires you to have a business license and/or insurance.

Again, research your area's laws and if necessary consult a Labor Attorney. Just make sure whomever you talk to is well-versed in starting a business.

Creating an Online Presence

Every business needs to have a presence on the Internet. If you're going to be a brick n' mortar business, you still need to be found! Nowadays, it's often assumed you have a website no matter what type of business you're running. Even with a physical building, the often usual method of deciding whether to buy your service or product is online reviews, customer comments and whether you are on the Internet. It adds credibility too!

Brainstorm ideas for, check availability of and then register a domain name for your business. Here are some tips for choosing a domain:

1. Make it easy to remember
2. Tie it into your business name and branding.
3. Do your best to get the .com version of your domain name.

Dotcoms tend to be the easiest to remember and the most mainstream. Most consumers assume a web site is a dotcom. Some say you should get every domain extension for your .com, which means the .net, .org. biz, .info, etc. versions. It depends on the domain name in my opinion. For instance, I have transitionchickblog.com only as I seriously doubt anyone else would buy the variations. However, with my main site, www.eCareerCorner.com ,I also own .net and .org extensions.

The domain registry I use for all of my domains is www.bulletproofwebservices.com. There's also GoDaddy.com and many more.

Hosting & Web Site Design

Once you've registered your domain, you'll need to host it. While I won't get into the nitty-gritty details of hosting, I'll say this – without it your website won't show up on the Internet. So, yes it's a necessity. You can find hosting from various places, including Host Gator, Reliable Webs, and more. Do some research and find the one that's right for your needs.

You'll also need to get your website up and running. This too could be an entire article on its own, but there are a few choices when it comes to how you get it done:

1. *Design it Yourself* – If you have the skills and knowledge to do so.
2. *Free Website Builders* – Some of these are ok but don't give you the control and flexibility to change a lot of things other options might and they may place ads on your site. Do your research.
3. *Web Designer* – This is the pricey end of the scale, but there are designers out there who will do a great job without costing you thousands of dollars. Just make sure you're clear about what it is you want and how much your budget allows before hiring someone.

Business Cards

Next, get business cards printed. There are often deals at www.vistaprint.com for 250 biz cards FREE. You can order more for $10-$40. I have used them for my various biz cards, postcards, pens & address labels. You can also try www.printsmadeeasy.com.

Business Checking Account & EIN

This is a biggie! Keep your personal finances separate from business. In order to open a business checking account, or to take payments, you need to call & request an EIN. You can also go online to the IRS and fill out the form to get your EIN (Employer Identification Number).

Business checking account minimums vary so, shop around. First, I was with a bank with a 5K minimum balance! For the pleasure of this, I got to pay 13 bucks per month!

What was I thinking?! I switched and now am with a bank with a $5 minimum balance!

These are just a few of the decisions you must make when it comes to starting your own business. Depending on the type of business, where you live, etc. there may be others.

Marcia Merrill, The Transition Chick! ™ is a Life Transitions and Marketing Coach.
www.eCareerCorner.com
http://www.examiner.com/x-1044-Career-Transition-Examiner

In The Kitchen with Taffy Wagner

Small Business Financial Plan

Your Personal Money Management Skills Carry Over to Your Business

One reason small businesses come and go is due to finances. For that reason alone, regardless of where you are in your business, you should have a sound financial plan.

As a Personal Finance Educator and Expert, as well as a small business owner, I have seen firsthand what can happen to a business if you do not know how to manage money in your personal life and then start a business. In order for your business to be financially successful, you must know how to manage money, establish realistic financial goals short term and long term and plan ahead.

I remember starting my first business in my early twenties. I was young, on my own, working for someone else and starting a business on the side. My plan at that time was to be retired by the time I was 30. Young and excited about being in business, I had not done enough research but felt that since a friend had presented this opportunity, I couldn't go wrong! Hmmm. WRONG! There was an upfront investment and purchasing products monthly that needed to be sold in order for me to make money. Sure it was good that I had a regular 9 to 5; however, that was not in my plan to pay out money every month without making a profit. This ended up being a short-lived business and taught me several lessons – do your homework prior to starting a business and have a financial plan for your business to avoid being upside down in your finances.

That experience left me with a "sour taste." However it did not destroy my desire to pursue being an entrepreneur.

Opportunities Present in Unlikely Sources

Many years later, I was presented with an opportunity to work for a friend of a friend in counseling. Initially upon hearing what he was doing, I was fascinated because it was educating juniors and seniors in high school and their parents about careers and college. He'd been doing this business for years in another state and had recently moved here. Therefore he was breaking new ground.

An interesting side to this story is the owner had a full-time day job and was attempting to build this business part-time in order to generate extra income to reduce his debt. One of the challenges he faced was dealing with the administrative side – scheduling appointments and handling follow-up calls.

There was no investment on my part but instead I worked as his administrative assistant. I thoroughly enjoyed doing this because it allowed me to establish relationships with students and parents. It wasn't my business at that time, however; within six months, the business owner and I were married. I then became the co-owner and co-counselor.

Since this business was strictly an evening position, I went back to work for a temporary service in order to get my finances in order. Whether you are working for someone else or are already a business owner, you need to have a PLAN B so you can continue with business and life. My PLAN B was to work for someone else temporarily while that business was being built.

Little did I know, three years later we would choose to close that business due to a lack of clients and schools to work with. However, when those doors closed the finances were in order and we were moving on to a new chapter in our marriage.

Dual Business Owners

As a business owner, you have to be ready for change. All of our finances were in order. We bought our first home based on one income. I was working 9 to 5 and also had a part-time business and my husband also worked 9 to 5 but later was unemployed.

A Financial Lesson

My part-time business produced income immediately because there was no overhead –there was no pressure in getting clients because they were already there!

After being in our first home approximately two years, my husband was not unemployed. We decided that he didn't need to rush out and get another job because of the skills he has with graphics. Progressive Graphics was born and my business funded his in cash except for one piece of equipment.

If your personal finances are in order, you will manage your business finances the same. We utilized one piece of equipment to establish business credit for him. This was a great move for the business and provided us with a reference if we needed it in the future.

We continue to both have our separate businesses and realized that there were other avenues our businesses could provide income for us. As a business owner, you must have a Plan B – an alternative way of getting things handled, otherwise you could end up as a statistic – a business not surviving the first five years.

As a business owner, it is important to not only stay focused, but to be don't be so stringent with your financial plan that you set your business up for failure and later become disappointed. Having a financial plan for personal and business relieves the financial stress and strain of not having one. I enjoy being a business owner, staying true to who I am and being creative. It's your turn to be the business owner you have always dreamed of.

Dr. Taffy Wagner, CEPF
Financial Expert
www.moneytalkmatters.com

About Raven, aka, The Talk Show Maven!

America's Leading Authority on Leveraging the Power of Your Voice!

The Talk Show Maven Looking to the Future

One of the things Raven Blair Davis is not, is a fly by night, one hit wonder! She's got BIG plans for the future. Keep your eye out for all the wonderful things she has planned, some of which include:

Careers from The Kitchen Table Reality TV Show - Raven's taking her increasingly popular, Careers from the Kitchen Table Radio show to the streets and teaching men and women all over how to start their own business from home. *(coming Fall 2010)*

Raven International - Raven's own broadcasting network, where she'll mentor, train and feature other podcasters and talk show hosts. It will also air replays of Raven's favorite hand-picked shows 24/7. Now you'll never miss an episode of your favorite radio show!

Careers from the Kitchen Table (www.careersfromthekitchentable.com) Airs live on CBS *(formerly CNN)* News Talk 650 Radio every Saturday at 2pm CST, CFKT targets men and women (home based businesses & enthusiasts) who are looking to spend more time at home with their children, perhaps have lost their job or have been forced into early retirement and are looking for ways to create a consistent income all from the comfort of their own home.   Be sure to stop by and sign up for your free newsletter and receive your copy of **"The Real Power of Social Networking: Profit on Facebook"** by Regina Baker

Women Power Talk Radio (www.womenpower-radio.com) - Named one of the Best Top 100 Business Podcasts by Anita Campbell's Business Trends two years in a row, Women Power was created to help women of all ages ignite the unstoppable power that lies within them. Sign up for your

free newsletter and receive the e-book **"Seven Action Steps on 'How to Ignite Your UnStoppable Power'"** http://www.womenpower-radio.com

Mentoring from MLM Divas Live (www.mentoringfrom-mlmdivaslive.com) - Secret Home-Based Business Ingredients from MLM Women Millionaires Listeners will discover three secret ingredients needed to cook up network marketing success.

Raven's Celebrity Rave (www.ravencelebrityrave.podomatic.com) - Aired on WBLQ AM Radio. Raven rolls out the red carpet and celebrates those who give back by spotlighting celebrities all around the world...from ALL walks of life...who are making a difference by paying it forward!

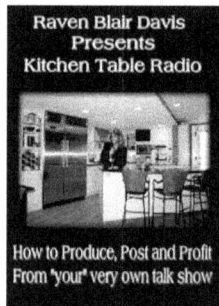

Raven's Books

Kitchen Table Radio Home Study Course (www.kitchentableradio.com) - In this course Raven shares the secrets that made her an award winning radio show host and teaches her students step-by-step how to produce and profit from their own radio show.

BONUS AUDIO: Join Raven and many celebrities as they congratulate and celebrate Graduation with the students! http://www.audioacrobat.com/play/Wfrz1xSh

---

Broadcast Your Passion to Profits (www.broadcastpassion.com) – In this book, Raven shares how you can attract more customers to your business with the power of your voice using radio, Internet radio, and podcasting as your platform.

BONUS AUDIO: Hear Raven being interviewed on the power of YOUR voice! http://www.audioacrobat.com/play/W3HLJDhZ

How to Turn Your Telephone into a Cash Cow (www.telephonecashcow.com) – An audio eWorkbook that includes 9 innovative outlets in which Raven shares once again how effective the power of your voice can be in successfully creating or growing your business. When your potential clients hear your voice chances are they will connect with you more than through email. 20% of people remember what they read versus 80% who remember what they hear.

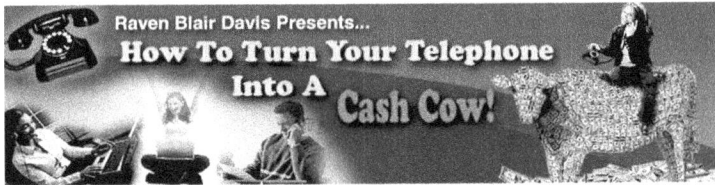

BONUS AUDIO: Join Raven as she explains the *Insider Secrets to Cold Calling!*

http://www.audioacrobat.com/play/Wn35XKnb

Raven is living proof that you CAN make your dreams a reality with a bit of hard work, dedication and desire. It's up to YOU to make it happen. Every single person, even you, has the ability within to become UNSTOPPABLE!

Raven says: *"From a seed that was placed in my heart in the hospital ICU Unit to interviewing famous thought leaders and celebrities – YES dreams do come true if you follow your passion, be committed to your purpose and NEVER EVER give up on your dream! If you can dream it….you can achieve it!"*

Following are pictures of Raven hanging out with mentors and celebrities!

Raven & Alex Mandossian

Raven & Jim Rohn

Raven & Lisa Nichols

Raven & Joan Rivers

Raven & Sherri Shepherd

Raven & Kim Kiyosaki

Raven & Ellie Drake

Raven & Marla Maples

Raven & Master P

Raven & Sheryl Lee Roth

Raven & Kim Fields

Raven & Kahliq Glover

To hear more heart to heart celebrity interviews, be sure to visit http://www.womenpower-radio.com and subscribe to the newsletter too! Sign up for your free newsletter and receive the free e-book **"Seven Action Steps on 'How to Ignite Your UnStoppable Power'"**

BONUS AUDIO: Get to know Raven as she is interviewed by Kellie Frazier. http://www.audioacrobat.com/play/Wgf6Vtm00

Interested in booking Raven to speak at your next event!
You will not have anyone falling asleep!
email: raven@womenpower-radio.com or call 800-431-0842

Raven's Recommended Resources

RAVENS TOP 10 FAVORITE BOOKS!

1. **The Secret** Rhonda Byrne
2. **Unstoppable** Cynthia Kersey
3. **Think and Grow Rich** Napoleon Hill
4. **The Game Of Life and How to Play It** Florence Scovel Shinn
5. **Change Your Attitude Change Your Life** Denise Brown
6. **Do You** Russell Simmons
7. **Success Principles** Jack Canfield
8. **Your First Year In Network Marketing** Mark Yarnell
9. **Think Like A Champion** Donald Trump
10. **The Law of Business Attraction** T Harv Eckard and Adryenn Ashley

RAVENS TOP 10 FAVORITE AUDIO BOOKS!

1. **The Strangest Secrets** Earl Nightingale
2. **It's Not Over Until You Win** Les Brown & Ona Brown
3. **The Challenge To Succeed** Jim Rhone
4. **The 4 Hour Work Week** Tim Ferris
5. **One Minute Millionaire** Mark Victor Hansen & Robert Allen
6. **The Magic of the Colors** Jerry Clark
7. **Choose To Be Rich** Robert Kiyosaki
8. **Multiple Streams of Internet Income** Robert Allen
9. **Affirmacize** Ona Brown
10. **THE Greatest Networker In The World** John Milton Fogg

RAVENS TOP 5 INSPIRING VIDEOS/MOVIES

1. **The Secret**
2. **Pursuit of Happiness**
3. **Facing The Giants**
4. **Pass It On**
5. **Pay It Forward**

Here's a great site for inspirational movie clips:
http://www.walkthetalk.com/pages/inspirational-movies.htm

Be sure to check the back of the book for Raven's Recommended Businesses

Thanks to the Incredible Team!

Without your hard work, this book would not be in our hands today!

Certified Business Consultant, Ecommerce, and Internet Marketing Consultant
http://www.ReginaBaker.com
Reginabaker@gmail.com

Regina Baker, Executive Producer and Co Host

Darnell Brown, Graphic Artist Extraordinaire
http://www.blucanvis.com
Darnell@blucanvis.com

Outstanding Virtual Assistance

Peggy@outstandingvirtualassistance.com

http://www.outstandingvirtualassistance.com

Brannon Nealy,
CKT Internet TV
Producer

The Digital Broadcasting Network
TheNeXt Generation of Broadcasting
Digital Broadcasting Network
www.thedigitalbroadcastingnetwork.com
Brannon Nealy
713.429.5600 Office | 832.668.4254 Mobile

Arika Lewis, Copywriter
arikarlewis@gmail.com

Joelle Niedecken, Personal Assistant to Raven and our very important second set of eyes!

Jaemi Nicholson, Production Manager
JBN Productions
Audio Editing – Videomercials
jaemibnicholson@yahoo.com

Dr. Taffy Wagner,
PR Coordinator

taffy@taffywagner.com
www.moneytalkmatters.com

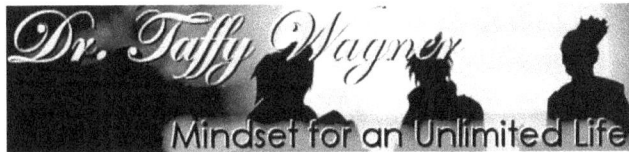

Dr. Taffy Wagner
Mindset for an Unlimited Life

Heartfelt THANKS to you all!

Thanks to our Sponsors

The fastest way to grow your business is by increasing the number of people you expose your business to. The more the better. There are plenty of Leads companies willing to exchange your dollars for their names. PM Marketing-NetworkLeads knows you deserve better.

The best way to grow your business is by increasing the numbers of people you expose your business to, as well as increase the quality of what you do, what you say, what and how you present, and how you duplicate this with your downline.

When you work with PM Marketing, you have access to Leads, Tools, Systems and Training. The owner is Peter Mingils. Peter's taught with Dr. Charles King at the University of Illinois in Chicago at the UIC Network Marketing Certification Course. He was a corporate sponsor and on the Board of Advisors for the Direct Selling Women's Alliance (DSWA). He is also the President of The Association of Network Marketing Professionals (The ANMP).

PM Marketing offers 27 Weekly Webinars and Conference Calls for Training and Support, 20 Educational Movies, Several On Line Training Courses, 400+ Archived Audio recordings, and much more for free for their customers and their down lines.

Without exception, you have never seen anything like this before.

Please go to http://www.networkleads.com/bookspecial for a glimpse.
Call and ask for a personal presentation. Mention this book for special offers.

Contact
Peter Mingils
peter@networkleads.com
(386) 445-3585

WAHMCart is perfectly suited for small business owners who need more features than the free, limited shopping carts, but can't afford the high price tag of the top-tier packages. Your time is valuable – invest in it now! To learn more about Wahmcart, download our FREE Guide: Benefits & Power of Whamcart
http://wahmcart.com/download-free-guide

Lola Scarborough
YOGA LOLA STUDIOS
A Yoga, Healing & Learning
Center

1701 Highway 3 South
League City, Texas 77573
281-684-3168
lola@yogalola.com
www.yogalola.com
www.bodybuddiesyogalola.com

Vote Today to Help our Kids
be Gang FREE!

http://www.refresheverythin
g.com/iamhappyproject

CROSSROADS
COLLECTION
CrossroadsCollection.com

www.crossroads-collection.com
rgreen@crossroads-collection.com

Great for your Health,
Great for your Bank
Account!

www.o2evolv.myevolv.com

ENJO®
CLEAN THE WORLD

Great Cleaning Products

Better Business Opportunity

www.enjoUS.com

HSW

Michael Rodriquez, President
Creating Liquidity for the Equipment Finance Industry

michelle.rodriguez@hswfinancial.com www.hswfinancial.com

Raven's Recommended Businesses

AMBIT ENERGY
Ken and Gretchen Umbdenstock
www.umby.energy526.com
www.umbyljoinambit.com
gretchenumbdenstock@yahoo.com
847-417-2229

AMERIPLAN®
Joelle Niedecken
jniedecken@ameriplan.net
http://www.deliveringonthepromise.com/dreamsrock

WALLY AMOS
www.chipandcookie.com

ANGELWAYS.COM
Kathleen Elmore C.S.C
832.233.1988   832.236.3475

ANDREW ANGLE
Master of Business Acceleration™
Phone: 800-651-9027
Email: NetGainAssociates@gmail.com
For a free outsourcing checklist and audio, visit http://www.OutsourceExperts.com/Raven

ARDYSS
Dorothy Jackson 832.275.9336

AUNT K'S PLACE
Lea Rutherford-Williams
877-257-3721
www.auntksplace.org
www.auntksplace.com
www.etenterprises.us
www.LeaSpeaks.com

AUSTIN PROPERTIES UNLIMITED MULTIPLE LISTING SERVICE
Realtor - Alvernad Austin
www.har.com/LadyAustin

REGINA BAKER
Internet Marketing Consultant
http://ReginaBaker.com
To Learn More About Wahmcart, download our FREE Guide: Benefits & Power of Wahmcart:
http://wahmcart.com/download-free-guide

BEVERLY BOSTON
Master Coach-For BIG Thinkers
www.BeverlyBoston.com
Email:info@BeverlyBoston.com
604-727-4363
For the next generation Big Thinkers get 3 FREE reports on client attraction and solid business building principles for your small businesses go here: www.BeverlyBoston.com

BETH DENNARD, ED D
Bright Futures Consulting
www.brightfuturesllc.com
Email: bdennard@brightfuturesllc.com
281-486-0023

JAYNE BLUMENTHAL
www.jayneblumethal.com
Get your copy of "The Secret Path to Health, Wealth and Sand Between Your Toes" by visiting the site and signing up.

DR. LINNE BOURGET, MA, MBA PH.D.
www.whatyousayiswhatyouget.com
Every woman must know her best to have the most success with the least stress! For help from the national leader in strengths-based business growth, visit www.whatyousayiswhatyouget.com and sign up for our free monthly positive leadership newsletter with practical tips to strengthen your success! Free articles, Dr. Bourget's full bio, and client list, testimonials PLUS 40 products to help you with more gain and less pain! Email us for small business consulting offerings.

CATHY A. HANSELL, CCSR, MS, JD
President, Breakthrough Results, LLC
Executive Producer and Host, Safety Breakthrough Talk Radio
Email: chansell@breakthroughresults.org
www.breakthroughresults.org
888-609-6723; 908-652-1366

ALI BROWN
www.alibrown.com

LES BROWN

www.lesbrown.com

PATRICIA BUNCH, P.C.

Attorney at Law
Pat@patbunchlaw.com
713-800-7750 (tel)
713-800-7751 (fax)
Patricia Bunch focuses on your legal health. She is both a lawyer with an LLM in taxation and a CPA. She focuses her practice on estate planning including wills, trusts and probate and tax controversy including audits, appeals and offers in compromise. She is admitted to practice before the Tax Court.

JACK CANFIELD

www.jackcanfield.com

CHRIS CARTER

The legal and business advice your business needs at a price you can afford. Visit today and receive the audio "Your Guide on Hiring an Attorney"
Cris@CrisCarterLaw.com
www.CrisCarterLaw.com
www.CrisCarterMVP.com

TRACI CAMPBELL

Go to the contact page on www.traciscampbell.com and send us your email address and enter in code RAVEN10 in the subject line to receive a FREE audio and transcript as well as 20% discount on The C.H.A.M.P Within program!! (book and workbook)

MARY ANNE CASEY

EPT Practioner /Life Coach
Physical-Emotional-Spiritual
www.EFTHappyLife.com
281-221-2436

JANET CAROLL, RN

713.439.0352 cell 832.216.3713

CHANJO, INC.

"For Cultural and Spiritual Empowerment"
Kathryn Perry, CHT
702.341.6735

LAWRENCE COLE,
The Xtreme Marketing Guy
Winning at Life International, LLC
http://www.xtrememarketingguy.com
email: lcole@xtrememarketingguy.com
phone: 888.474.2161
facebook: http://www.facebook.com/xtrememarketingguy
To get your FREE report on "The 7 Deadly Sins of Small Business Marketing", Visit
http://www.xtrememarketingdoneforyou.com

KATHLEEN B SCHULWEIS, CPCC, PCC
Confidence Connections
Strategic Coaching for Success
323-935-6477 Office
http://www.linkedin.com/in/confidenceconnections
Need a Confidence Boost?
Visit http://www.confidenceconnections.com for help and support!

MARIANA COOPER
www.trustyourahamoments.com
www.ahamoments.tv
www.facebook.com/ahamomentsinc
To get your free gifts to include the full audio of my sold out Teleseminar "God Won't Deliver a
Million Dollars Into Chaos" , including a powerful guided meditation and the free transcript plus
a subscription to the Aha! Moments Ezine with free tips, articles and info for Enlightened
Entrepreneurs go to: www.trustyourahamoments.com

CURVES
Jeanine Savvas
713.41.02186

DR. SARAH DAVID, PH.D.
sdavid@consultant.com
Visit www.empoweredwomensinstitute.com for a free report on the 7 Characteristics of
Successful Entrepreneurs and an opportunity to take a free personal brand assessment,
subscribe to the Empowered Women's Institute Newsletter for exciting upcoming
announcements on pre-launch activities, training, networking and an opportunity to be a
Charter Member as we launch our new online community to help you lead, learn and connect
with other empowered women!

BILL DAVIS
Lifestyle Coach
www.mydailydirector.com

KELLY DAVIS
Business & Leadership Developer
www.ecobusiness.com/kbdavis

DEE'S BODY FITNESS
713.825.2013
hardbodydee@sbcglobal.net

DISTINCTIVE PUBLICATIONS FOR THE WORLD
Rob Macomber
802.484.5581

TRACEY DOCTOR
Holistic coach and strategist
Executive producer and host of
amazingwoman-talkradio.com
Email for a free 15 minute private phone-consultation
Traceydoctor@aol.com

THE ENCHANTED SELF
Dr. Barbara Becker Holstein, Founder
 732.571.1200
www.enchantedself.com

FRANKLIN QUEST EDUCATION AND LEADERSHIP FOUNDATION, INC.
Tyra Franklin, MBA/PA
"Your destiny is hiden among your fears"
 http://franklinquest.pbworks.com

KELLIE FRAZIER
http://www.kelliefrazier.com
http://www.leaderscafe.co.uk

ELLEN GAVER
http://www.EcoMomTeam.com
EcoMomTeam@charter.net
805.474.822

CHUCK GAW
www.theattractionteam.com

LOU GILES
Independent Associate
832-513-5916
www.smartchoicelegal.com

GREAT SMALL BUSINESS ADVICE
Allison Babb
Small Business Coach
www.GreatSmallBusinessAdvice.com
Email: info@greatsmallbusinessadvice.com
Phone: 678-401-7948
For a 1-hr audio on How to Attract More Clients, you can go to
www.greatsmallbusinessadvice.com/audio

MONICA HANCOCK
Window Fashions Designer
www.creationsbymonica.net
Email: mhancock@creationsbymonica.net
Phone: (281) 820-1977
For ideas on window treatment designs, you can go to www.creationsbymonica.net

ROBERTA HARRIS
Motivational Life Coaching
Motivational Speaking
www.robertaharris.com
rdhartist@att.net
713-256-9037

VICTOR HOLMAN
Business Performance Coach
www.Lifecycle-Performance-Pros.com
Email: victor.holman@lifecycle-performance-pros.com
Phone: 202-415-5363
To get a FREE BUSINESS MANAGEMENT KIT and jumpstart your business, go to
www.Lifecycle-Performance-Pros.com

HOME TEAM REALTY
Nancy L.B. Chen, GRI
281.496.7500
cell 832.818.6688

DR. RENEE HORNBUCKLE
www.reneehornbuckle.com
reneehornbuckle@sbcglobal.net
If you're already a Coach or you would like to become a client, you can learn more about the benefits of being a Compass Client/Coach. Visit www.mylifecompass.com/womenofinfluence to find out more and join my team as a client or become a Certified Compass Coach!

IMPACT COACHING LLC
Susan Brown, Ed.S.
Certified Leadership and Success Coach
www.impactcoach.wordpress.com
susanbrown.impactcoaching@gmail.com
Internet Radio Show: http://thewinonline.com/shows/awaken-the-leader
Take the first step in getting your personal leadership development plan by Contacting Susan for a free consultation at 678-787-2406 or log on to her website at www.impactcoach.wordpress.com.
Listen to Susan on *Awaken the Leader Within* found at:
http://thewinonline.com/shows/awaken-the-leader
678-787-2406

INTERNATIONAL GIFT EXPRESS
A Gift of Excellence
Carol Newman www.vernoncompany.com/newman.htm
415-381-5252

CRISS ITTERMANN
Life & Small Business Coach
LiberatedLifeCoaching.com
email: info@liberatedlifecoaching.com
Phone: 866-993-8932
For an exclusive 60 minute free audio called "SURRENDER™ to Passion" please visit
www.revx.me/table

MARTHA JOHNSON
www.Help2GrowLifeCoaching.com
Help2GrowTalkRadio: www.help2grow.podomatic.com
678-949-9195

JENKINSON ENTERPRISES
Glenn M. Jenkinson   281.309.2050

CYNTHIA KERSEY
www.unstoppable.net www.unstoppablechallenge.com

KIMBER KING
Kimber_king@msn.com
801-923-8744
Kimber King is an expert in Social Networking and what it takes to make money from home using the internet. Visit www.kimberking.com for a FREE 30 minute recording that you will learn 4 simple steps you can start using right now to turn your "play-time" on Social Networking sites like FaceBook and Twitter into profits!
http://search.barnesandnoble.com/Making-Money-from-Home/Donna-Partow/e/9781589976085

CHRISTINE KONOPKO
Licensed MassageTherapist
cakonopko@hotmail.com

DIANE LAMPE
Entrepreneur and mentor, best-selling author
www.lampeteam.com
diane@lampeteam.com
972-670-7691
For how to create a business helping protect families
Or to view our services, you can go to www.lampeteam.com
1ZX580110317925854

LEARNING RX
Clara M. Samuelson
832.886.5878 www.learningrx.com/sugerland

DIAMOND LEONE
Creative Coach
www.DiamondLeone.com
Email: diamondleone@gmail.com
Phone: 703-209-9012
To get a free guide to help you discover what you're passionate about, go to
www.diamondleone.com/passion

ANNE-MARIE LERCH
Business Strategist & Mindset Coach
www.CoachMeNow.com
Email: info@CoachMeNow.com
Phone: 1-877-83-SMILE (76453)
For a free Audio Summary of "Think and Grow Rich" go to
www.CoachMeNow.com

HONEY LEVEEN, LUTCF, CLTC
Your LTC Insurance Specialist LLC
www.honeyleveen.com
Phone: 713-988-4671

TERRI LEVINE
www.terrilevine.com

LAURA LOPEZ
www.Laura-Lopez.com
www.LauraLopezBlog.com
www.twitter.com/connectedleader
http://womenspeakerswhorock.com/
Laura@Laura-Lopez.com
713.828.8829
Become a better leader and achieve stronger results through others! Download your free e-workbook by Laura Lopez to help you assess and plan your approach to becoming a connected and committed leader. http://www.laura-lopez.com/Assets/Free_CCL_Eworkbook.pdf
Award-winning Author, The Connected and Committed Leader
Motivational Speaker, Certified Birkman Method Business and Life Coach
Expertise in Leadership and Branding

DEBORAH MADISON
www.prepaidlegal.com/hub/dmadison and www.greatworkplan.com
713.208.9622
888.298.1888

BERWICK MAHDI
Relationship coach
berwick@relatuinsgipfitnesscenter.com

ALEX MANDOSSIAN
www.productivetoday.com www.alexmandossian.com

MARKET TRENDS CONSULTANTS
Hermeka Bibbins
713.640.2949 832.9696374
 markettrendsconsultants.com
"Providing marketing for the latest trends"

MARCIA MERRILL,
AKA, The Transition Chick- www.eCareerCorner.com
Marketing Coach-Guerrilla Marketing, Career/ Life Transitions Coach
Please visit my web site & sign up for your FREE Transition Triumph Toolkit! And get my newsletter as a Bonus! Contains valuable information, resources & special discounts!

PAUL McCORMICK
"The Millioniare Mentor"
866.333.0852
theauthenticmillionaire.com

MONA-VIE
Ruth Van Buren mymonavie.com/ruth
702.437.4900 cell 702.354.4900
"Drink it! Feel it! Share it!"

MS Lisa
Floral Designer & Event Planner
dimensionsflorals@hotmail.com
281-948-7123

MY SUCCESS BOX
Tina Downey
698. 574.8740
Dream, Believe and Achieve, Inc

MYANDA SOLUTIONS
Shaun Stephenson
Community Wealth Building
Speaking Engagements
Special Events & Programs
Inspiration and Collaboration
Life/Self Empowerment Coaching
The Circle of Ten Movement
609-560-8370
Shaun6@comcast.net
www.shaunstephenson.com
http://thecircleoften.com

MY HEART TIES & APPLE CREATIVE GROUP
Leah Humphries
Entrepreneur & President
www.myheartties.com
www.applecreativegroup.com
Email: leah@applecreativegroup.com
Phone: 814-833-1950 / 814-746-6325

LISA NICHOLS
www.lisa-nichols.com

NJ HOME STAGING AND REDESIGN
Angela Gagauf
Email: a@njhomestagingandredesign.com
201-317-9072
To learn more about NJ Home Staging and Redesign and to receive our free report, "The Top 10 Mistakes to Avoid When Showing Your Home", visit our website at
www.njhomestagingandredesign.com

NUMIS NETWORK
Mark Perkett
marekperk@cox.net
http://www.perksprofits.com
949-212-2682

SHEILA PEARL
Life Coach & Speaker
www.SheilaPearl.com
Email: info@LifeCoachSheila.com
Phone: 201-303-5990
For "3 Magic Tips for Feeling Good NOW", go to
www.LifeCoachSheila.com/3tipsFor a 30-min. Discovery Conversation, call Sheila

PEOPLESMART ENTERPRISE
Founder -Master Director
Carol Dysart
www.peoplesmartenterprise.com
 858-524-6300

ELIZABETH GILMOUR
Master Pilates Practitioner
www.PilatesofChampions.com
email: lissa@pilatesofchampions.com
Phone: 281-890-3777
Call or write today for an appointment to discuss how the *Pilates of Champions Experience* can work for you.

DEBORA MCNAUGHTON
www.azuliskye.com
LUDOLPH L. MISHER, III
http://facebook.com/ludolphmisher
http://www.MatureCougarWomen.com
Ludolph@maturecougarwomen.com

JOELLE NIEDECKEN
http://www.dreamsrock.com
jniedecken@ameriplan.com
877-303-4065
432-689-9447
Visit http://www.deliveringonthepromise.com/dreamsrock TODAY to receive your FREE prescription card valued at $100

OUTSTANDING VIRTUAL ASSISTANCE
Peggy Knudson
http://www.outstandingvirtualassistance.com
907-731-5758 – Isn't it time you take your business to the next level?
Call for your free, no obligation consultation today!

POWERFUL YOU! INC
Sue Urda
media@powerfullimitationseveryday.com
973.248.1262

PRACTICAL ASSISTIVE TECHNOLOGY SOLUTIONS
Phyl T. Macomber {and Rob}
www.practicalatsolutions.com
802.484.3537

CATERINA RANDO, MA, MCC
Business strategist, master coach, speaker & publisher
Author of *Learn to Power Think*
http://www.attractclientswithease.com
http://www.powerdynamicspub.com
http://www.caterinaspeaks.com
Phone: 415 668-4535
Email: cat@attractclientswithease.com
Call or email Caterina and mention this book to receive a $200.00 discount on any coaching course or book publication project.

HELEN RACZ
Teacher of Vibrational Law, Speaker, Energy Healer and CieAura Founding Master Retailer.
www.HelenRacz.com
helenracz@comcast.net
281-578-7949
For free resources to support entrepreneurs with releasing limiting beliefs and energetic blocks to prosperity, go to www.HelenRacz.com/cieaura

RAPID BUSINESS BUILDING
Christina Scheiner, the Massive Income Mentor
Email: info@rapidbusinessbuilding.com
Phone: (415) 897-7001
For the free Ebook, Rapid Building Building NOW !!!, go to:
www.RapidBusinessBuildingNOW.com

RE-MAX
Jilian Wilson "Realtor for life is priceless"
281.265.5533 ext1132
direct @ 281.642.9004

DAWN RICKABAUGH, Broker
Owner Financing Coach
Note Queen / Rickabaugh Realty
P: 626.292.1875
F: 626.451.0454 Download your free copy of my book, "Seller Financing on Steroids"
www.NoteQueen.com

MARY RIVES
Energetics of Health and Wellness
www.energeticsofhealthandwellness.com

RM CREATIONS
Renee and Major Jones
www.rmcreations.com
713.443.3748 281.880.8668

KIMBERLY RHODES
Kimberly@MLMSecretsForWomen.com or
Kimberly@MyIncomeInsurance.com
Email for a free E-book
Focusing: The Key to Success

ROBERT "ROSIE" AND VIKKI "TAYLOR" ROSENKRANZ
Vikki Cummings-Rosenkranz, Internationally Certified Energy Wellness Consultant
www.EarthPatriot.Net
www.EarthPatriot.Info (catalog and income opportunity page)
Rosenkranz@EarthPatriot.net
713.298.5808 281.770.7092

SC HEALTH SOLUTIONS
Sharon Cadle, CEO/Founder
www.LeSharonbeautiboutique.com

TUCK SELF, THE REBEL BELLE
A Southern Voice for Bold Self-Expression
(803)736-9240
www.therebelbelle.com
Tuck@TheRebelBelle.com
Grab a copy of my free e-guide!
If you are ready to liberate yourself from past conditioning, contact Tuck at (803) 736-9240 or Tuck@therebelbelle.com

SIMPLE FOCUS HYPNOSIS CENTER
Devan Tindall
Hypnosis/Life Coach
www.simplefocushypnosis.com
devan132@hotmail.com
713-439-0454
For a free 30 minute consultation call 713-439-0454
Or Email Devan devan132@hotmail.com

LORI SNYDER
www.coachlorisnyder.com
516-708-9261
Would you like to get a fresh start towards empowering yourself? During this six week e-course, you will discover, explore and create a whole new outlook to start building your best life. You will also learn powerful new tools that you can use to make the best decisions and choices to become truly happy and successful in every area of your life.
GO to www.Coachlorisnyder.com and go to the products page and sign -up for free e-course.

SUCCESS CIRCLE COACHING
"Women helping women thrive"
Mary McHenry
303.258.3803
www.successcirclecoaching.com

TAXMAMA®
 Eva Rosenberg, MBA, EA
www.TaxMama.com Where taxes are fun!
www.TaxMama.com/TaxQuips   And Answers are free
www.IRSExams.com Become an Enrolled Agent
www.MarketWatch.com   the TaxWatch column
800-594-9829   818-993-1565
www.twitter.com/taxmama

THE VISION BOARD TRAINING

Bonnie Bruderer

VisionBoardParties.com

www.facebook.com/VisionBoards

Will you be the next business to have a Vision Board Kit? We make the product, you make $$$! $500 of the private label fee www.TheVisionBoardTraining.com

DR. JOE VITALE

www.mrfire.com

THE VOICE OF THERMOGRAPHY

Dr. Robert L. Kane

650.868.0353

www.thermographyexpert.com

KALIN THOMAS

www.seetheworldproductions.com

Email: kalinthomas@yahoo.com

Phone: 404-863-8182

For more on how Kalin got into the TV industry and travel writing, listen to
Her 1-hour interview with Raven at http://www.womenpower-radio.com/archives.html.

KAREN TOMPKINS

Classical Feng Shui Consultant

www.FengShuiBeyondtheMyth.com

Email: karen@fengshuibeyondthemyth.com

Phone: 214-774-9019

For *The 8 Myths of Feng Shui* and *From Hitler to Haiti, 56 Years of Feng Shui Influences on Global Events,* go to www.FengShuiBeyondtheMyth.com

TOXIC FREE CONSULTANTS

Craig and Jackie Grigsby

Email: cgrigsby002@comcast.net

Phone: 713-301-0772

Free consultation on how to make your home toxic free!

V.A. 2 Go

Virtual On Site Assistance

Maury Williams

800-409-6250

VISIONARY HOLDINGS, LLC

Michael Flint

678.427.7602

DR. TAFFY WAGNER, D.MIN
Certified Educator in Personal Finances and Consultant www.WifeCFO.com
Email: drtaffy@wifecfo.com
Phone: 303-576-0670
For a no-cost report on how to settle debt, you can go to www.wifecfo.com/products

WESTERN & SOUTHERN LIFE
Craig Anthony Nicholas
Sales Representative
www.wslife.com
800-289-0849

WOMAN'S WELLNESS CENTER
Terry Tribble, MBA, CMF
www.HoustonLaceBrows.com
Email: info@houstonlacebrow.com
Phone: 713.522.PINK (7465)

CHILDREN'S BOOKS ON WHEELS
Rita Wiltz
Executive Director
330 Rayford Road #201
Spring, Texas 77386
281-844-7596

WORLDSPEAK LANGUAGE PRESCHOOLS AND IN-HOME CHILD CARE SYSTEM
Angelika Putintseva
Director and Founder
www.WorldSpeakSchool.com
info@WorldSpeakSchool.com
310-441-5222

Next – Raven's final thought

Dream Big and be Committed to Your Dream…. Make it more than a dream, make it a…reality!

I would like to thank the World's Greatest Mirror Illusionist, Elvis C. Walker, President and Founder of the Angle of Hope Foundation http://www.angleofhopee.com for creating this beautiful glass mural (shown below) and my **Big Dream which I INTEND to make happen – interviewing President Barack & Michelle Obama while they are in office**. Elvis not only had this beautiful mural of MY Big Dream delivered to me but he also had it delivered to the White House…. *How cool is that!*

Remember, your dream belongs to you and you're responsible for making it happen. Never give up and take the action steps to manifest it, after all, it's your dream and Yes – *YOU DESERVE IT!*

This is my Big Business Dream and I'm going after it…. What's yours?

Email me at raven@careersfromthekitchentable.com and tell me your Biggest Dream that you have for your business and how you intend to manifest it and you'll receive a personal word of encouragement from me (feel free to include your telephone number if you would prefer me to call you with my words of encouragement!) You can view the full color version at http://www.careersfromthekitchentable.com/audios/

You will also receive a "free" professionally produced commercial on your new product, service teleseminar, event or book launch. Your commercial will air on my popular www.careersfromthekitchentable.com show (a $197 value – yours free)